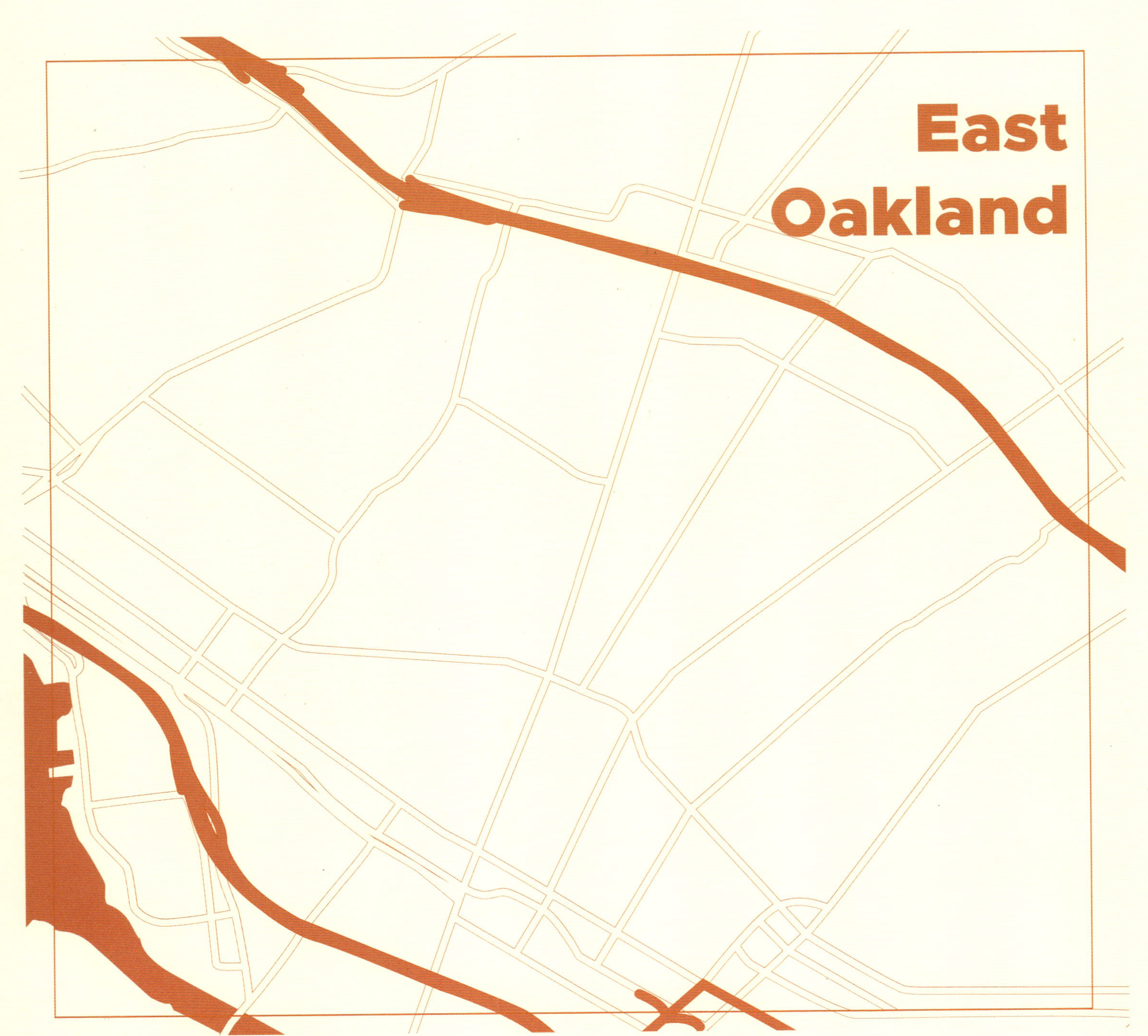

East
Oakland

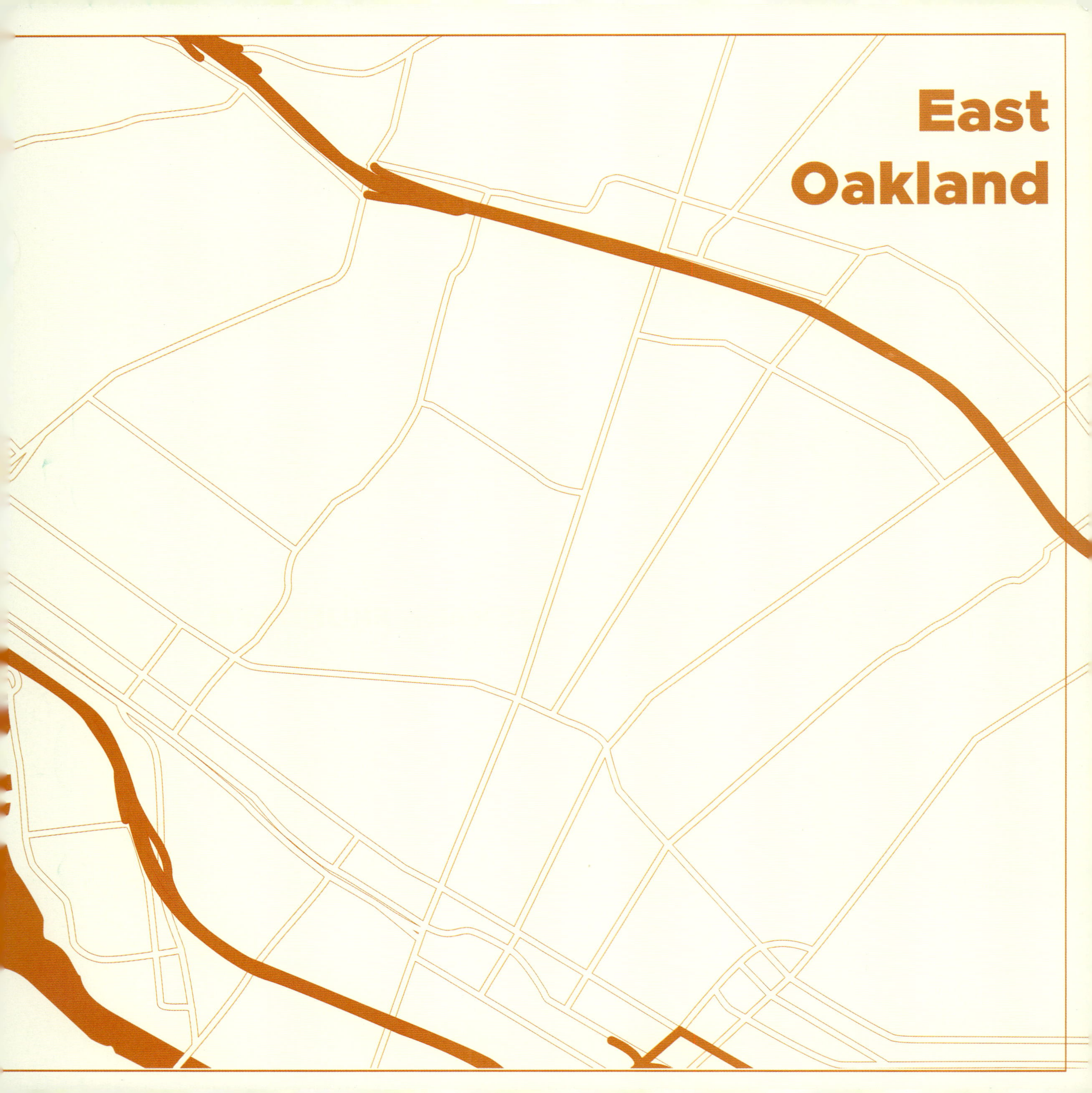

East
Oakland

"**T**hrough these politically-fueled and site-specific visual art works, essays, and incantations *Painting the Streets* timestamps the rage-and-joy-informed creative practices of this generation and models the Black radical tradition of simultaneously codifying the moment and archiving the movement."

**ASHARA EKUNDAYO**
curator, arts organizer, and cultural theologian
at Artist As First Responder

"*Painting the Streets: Oakland Uprising in the Time of Rebellion* provides vital documentation of and perspective on the murals and artworks created in Oakland in the summer of 2020 as a form of protest and activism directed toward systemic police brutality and racism and the outright murders of Black men and women. A coalition of Oakland organizations known as "Art for the Movement" led by the Black Cultural Zone and including the Oakland Museum of California, Oakland Art Murmur, RBA Creative, Spearitwurx, and other Oakland artists and arts leaders, has been committed to this documentation since its inception in June 2020 and our alliance is honored to endorse this groundbreaking publication. We believe the artworks included in this publication are artifacts of a social justice movement and carry with them important stories and context. The book helps convey that the commitment to document, preserve, and present this protest art is not simply an art initiative; it is part of the movement of the truth, reconciliation, reparation, and reimagining necessary to addressing injustice and racism."

**CAROLYN JOHNSON**
Chief Executive Officer, Black Cultural Zone

*dedicated to*
*all of the Black and Brown people*
*who have been murdered by repressive systems of state violence*

*dedicated to the artists who remember,*
*paint our names on walls, rail with words—*
*the weavers, the ancestral griots*

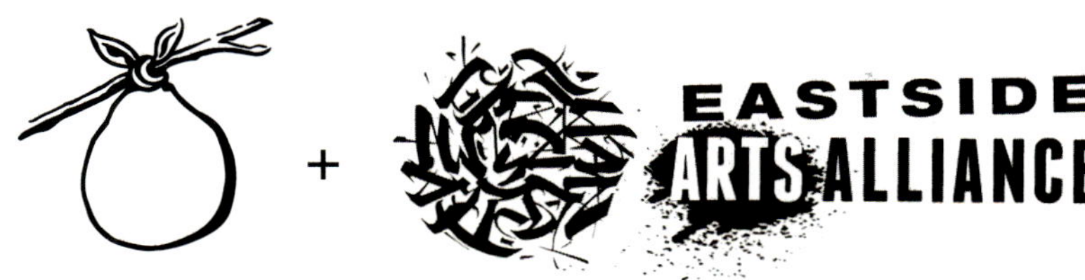

# NOMADIC PRESS

**OAKLAND**

111 FAIRMONT AVENUE
OAKLAND, CA 94611

**BROOKLYN**

475 KENT AVENUE #302
BROOKLYN, NY 11249

WWW.NOMADICPRESS.ORG

**MASTHEAD**

FOUNDING PUBLISHER
J. K. FOWLER

ASSOCIATE EDITOR
MICHAELA MULLIN

DESIGN
JEVOHN TYLER NEWSOME

## MISSION STATEMENT

Through publications, events, and active community participation, Nomadic Press collectively weaves together platforms for intentionally marginalized voices to take their rightful place within the world of the written and spoken word. Through our limited means, we are simply attempting to help right the centuries' old violence and silencing that should never have occurred in the first place and build alliances and community partnerships with others who share a collective vision for a future far better than today.

## INVITATIONS

Nomadic Press wholeheartedly accepts invitations to read your work during our open reading period every year. To learn more or to extend an invitation, please visit: www.nomadicpress.org/invitations

## DISTRIBUTION

Orders by teachers, libraries, trade bookstores, or wholesalers:

Nomadic Press Distribution
orders@nomadicpress.org
(510) 500-5162

Small Press Distribution
spd@spdbooks.org
(510) 524-1668 / (800) 869-7553

## NOTE ON FINANCIAL TRANSPARENCY

All net proceeds from this book will go into visual arts programs in the flatlands schools of Oakland. All net proceeds from this book will go into the Nomadic Press Painting the Streets Fund, a separate bank account at Beneficial State Bank with an oversight committee composed of 5 people, including J. K. Fowler (Nomadic Press), Elena Serrano (ESAA), Leslie Lopez (ESAA), Andre Jones (BAMP), and Rachel Wolfe-Goldsmith (BAMP).

This oversight committee will decide where these funds are sent. We will share the project's impact annually on project partner websites. Here are a few schools that we have already earmarked to receive funds: Ile Omode, Madison High School, McClymonds High School, Roosevelt Middle School, Elmhurst Middle School, Castlemont High School, Urban Promise Academy, West Oakland Middle School, and POC Homeschoolers of Oakland.

## FUNDING SUPPORT

This project was in part made possible by funding support from the following organizations:

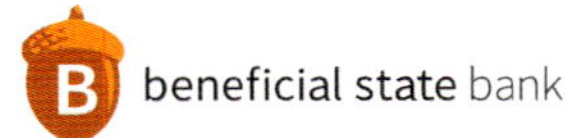 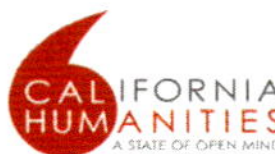 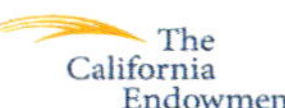

*Painting the Streets: Oakland Uprising in the Time of Rebellion*
© 2022

All rights reserved. No part of this book may be reproduced or transmitted in any form or by any means, electronic or mechanical, without written permission from the publisher.

Requests for permission to make copies of any part of the work should be sent to: info@nomadicpress.org.

A book like this is only made possible through the dance of a village. Much love to our collaborators and fam at EastSide Arts Alliance, without whom this journey would not have been possible. Elena, Leslie, Greg: much, much love.

Innumerable thanks to funders who made the intensive production of this book possible: Beneficial State Bank Foundation, Kelson Foundation, The California Endowment, and others who wished to remain anonymous. This project was also made possible with support from California Humanities, a non-profit partner of the National Endowment for the Humanities. Visit www.calhum.org.

For author questions or to book a reading at your bookstore, university/school, or alternative establishment, please send an email to info@nomadicpress.org.

Cover art: "Our Movement" by Rachel Wolfe-Goldsmith (rachelwolfegoldsmith.com), photographed by JJ Harris (techboogie.com)

Published by Nomadic Press, 111 Fairmount Avenue, Oakland, California 94611

First printing, 2022

Library of Congress Cataloging-in-Publication Data

Title: *Painting the Streets: Oakland Uprising in the Time of Rebellion*
p. cm.
Summary: *Painting the Streets: Oakland Uprising in the Time of Rebellion* features a selection of Oakland murals that emerged in tandem with the inter/national protests against the police brutality/murder of Black people and systemic-institutional racism in the US. The book also includes an introduction, interview, poetry, and essays by writers in solidarity with the Black liberation struggle.

[1. ART / Graffiti & Street Art. 2. ART / Individual Artists / General. 3. LITERARY COLLECTIONS / American / African American & Black. 4. LITERARY COLLECTIONS / Essays. 5. POETRY / Subjects & Themes / General. 6. LITERARY COLLECTIONS / Interviews. 7. LITERARY COLLECTIONS / Women Authors.] I. III. Title.

LIBRARY OF CONGRESS CONTROL NUMBER: 2021949441

ISBN: 9781955239240

# PAINTING THE STREETS

### Oakland Uprising in the Time of Rebellion

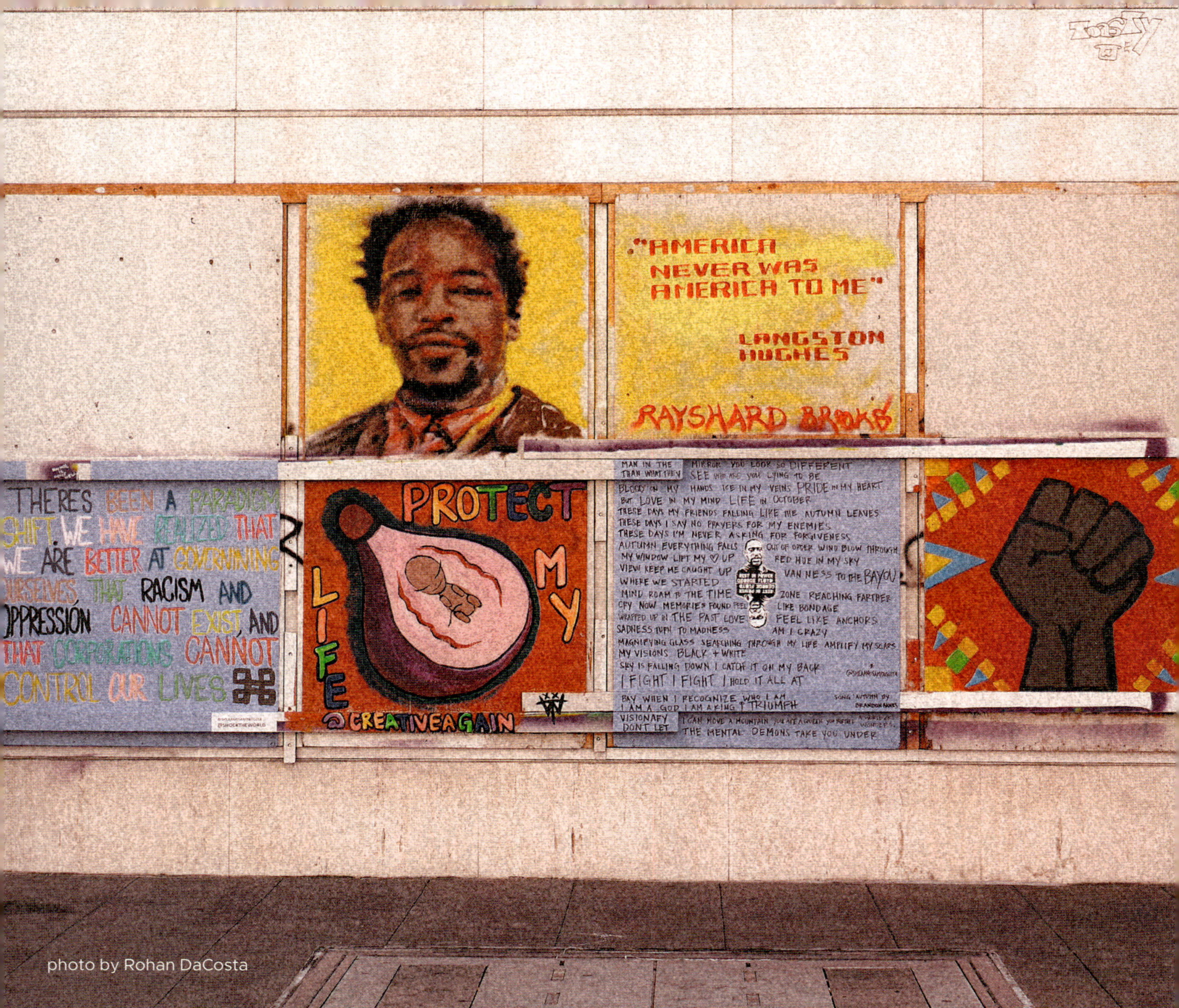


photo by Rohan DaCosta

# PAINTING THE STREETS

## Oakland Uprising in the Time of Rebellion

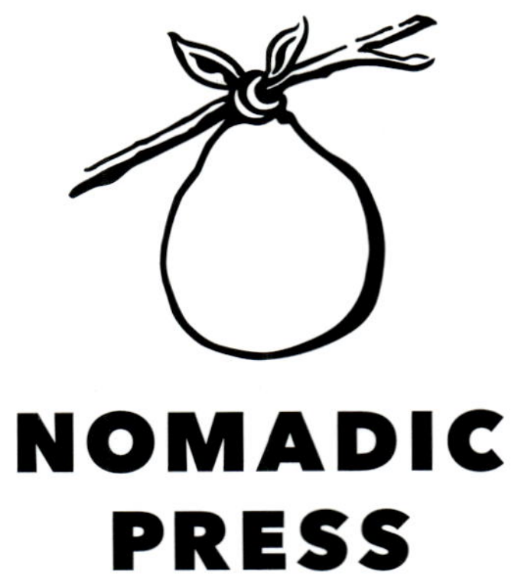

NOMADIC
PRESS

# Contents

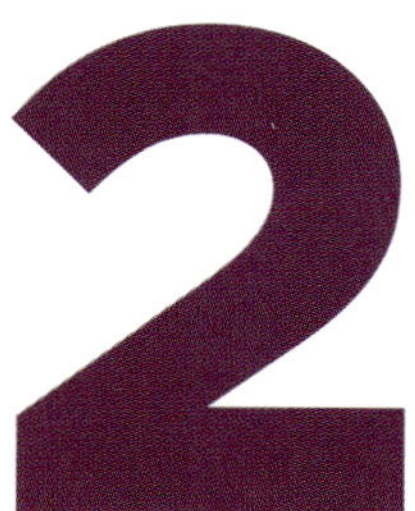

# 2

## Featured Artists



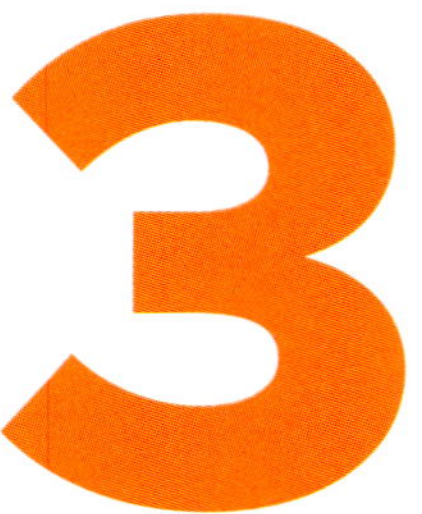

# 3

## In Spirit With Revolution



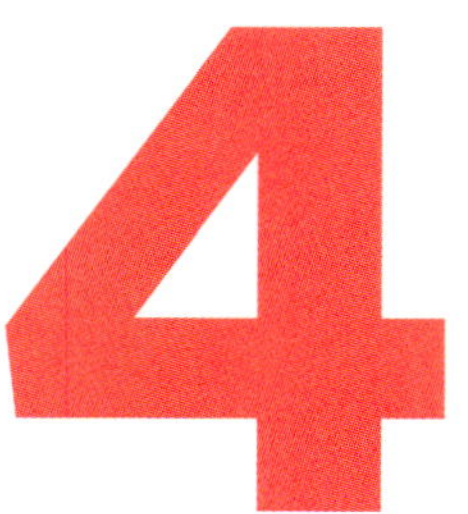

# 4

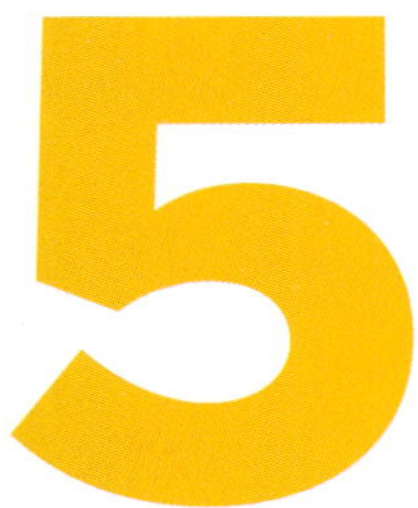

# 5

## Essays

# 6

## Poetry



**(poetry cont'd)**



## Bios

# Notes from Organizers

Poets, painters, writers, photographers, publishers—cultural workers. Workers.

"Truth and Beauty"—these are the words poet, activist, scholar, revolutionary Amiri Baraka would almost chant to us as we were grappling with the injustices of the world. What we must do as cultural workers is strive for truth and beauty. This is indeed a very beautiful book and inside is the truth of this particular moment, in this particular city. The pandemic perhaps made folks more empathetic, so this time when another Black man, another Black woman was murdered by the police it bothered more than just us. Protests erupted all over the world when George Floyd and Breonna Taylor were murdered. In Oakland, painters took to the walls, showing us all the pain, knowledge, heart, and soul that we were all holding inside. Writers and poets did the same, singing and dancing the pain, getting stronger and more sure of what must change. We've tried to include pieces here that give us all of that.

Our focus is on Black artists—it is Black people who were murdered and who have been being murdered since white folks made Black the different one, the one easily identified and exploited.

EastSide Arts Alliance moves in the spirit of the Black Arts Movement and the Xicano Arts Movement. Our mentors understood and embraced their role as artists who sought to understand and change when necessary the worlds they lived in. We now work to create an abundance of jazz, theater, visual art, dance and poetry—keeping people connected to upending systems of oppression and reimagining the way things should be.

We now want to see what artists are up to. To show their responses to this moment of movement.

We are all beautifully here and determined to do the right thing.

We trust this inspires.

**ELENA SERRANO**
**EastSide Arts Alliance Collective**

> "I have no choice but to read the city walls for signs of my life"

**TONGO EISEN-MARTIN**
**"I Do Not Know the Spelling of Money"**

**T**ransitory states abound. Yet so much remains as the recognizable reminder of what the U.S. has never adequately admitted to, or addressed. *Painting the Streets* is tribute to Black lives lost as well as a window, a glimpse into a period of time where so many of us had reached our limit, yet again. Millions took to the streets, thousands of artists across the nation and worldwide made visual the terror, anger, inherent resilience, exhaustion, and unbounded possibility. This project is not meant to "capture" or documentarily freeze the period of time between May and October of 2020, nor does it represent everything that occurred within that time period. How could it? Tear gas, militarized police, nightly gatherings at the intersection of 14th and Broadway in Downtown Oakland, sounds of choppers overhead and the bullhorn voices of community organizers on the streets. And all the while, the backdrop of a raging pandemic dancing with the troupe of murderous clowns in and around the White House.

To freeze a transitory body of street art written in response to a particular period of time with a patrilineage of a homicidal state apparatuses built to quell and destroy. Yet we are here, constituent, collective arbiters of what constitutes this state. And we are busy. The question of what's next lingers, some denying its existence, some casting their own visions for what may be.

All books take a village, and this book took the Town. With endless thanks and gratitude to all of the workers who joined us on this journey, we hope that this book (perhaps one of a few to come), serves as tribute and remembrance for lives lost at the hands of state systems while offering another platform to the future-casting brilliance and love that runs rampant through these streets.

Amidst, and within, interlocking outdated, white supremacist systems built to engender manufactured competition and scarcity, it is a revolutionary act to rest, root, and radiate the world that we desire. Abundance. Ancestral griots have been showing us the way since time immemorial. As sister Fannie Lou Hamer once said in a speech by the same name, "Nobody's free until everybody's free." Freedom over fear. Let us be free.

### J. K. FOWLER
**Nomadic Press**

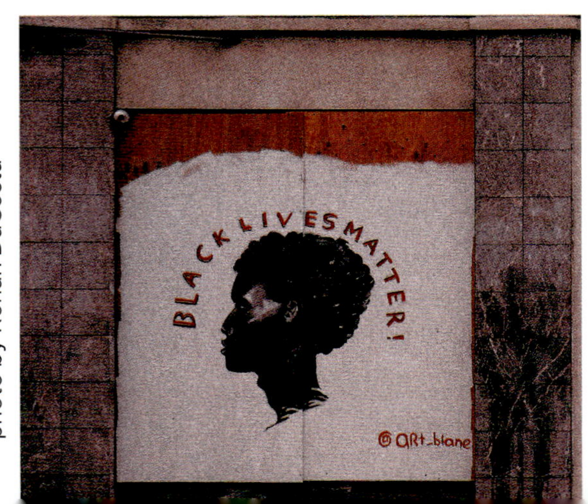


photo by Rohan DaCosta

# Introduction

Alicia Garza

The last decade has been marked by protests and unrest not seen at this scale in the modern history of the United States, and perhaps the world. This most recent wave is new only in name Black Lives Matter—though not in content. And the movement that accompanies it is yet another tributary of the movement for Black freedom, dignity, and lives. It is but one piece of a larger movement fighting back against austerity, climate destruction, racism, and fascism.

In 2020, the mainstream news media dubbed the Black Lives Matter movement as the largest protest movement in history. Yet too often, a relentless focus on the most visible forms of resistance—protest—obscure the very engine of the movement itself. This can lead us to be more enamored with the throngs of people, from every age, background, and demographic than we are with the reason that people take to the streets in the first place, and what it means for the state of civil society, government, and the economy.

An obsession with the how, and not the why, is dangerous; it allows for these movements to be viewed as brands, rather than as defining facets of our social and material life which must be addressed immediately, if we are to survive. The economic doctrine of the United States and its allies has left a trail of unbelievable misery and despair, laid bare by a global pandemic that has thrown millions of people, already living precariously, out of work and even further into harm's way. A government led by an egotistical authoritarian is the result of heightened anxiety, racism, and fear of what the future may hold under such precarious circumstances, and demographic change has made the suppressed and oppressed minority the majority with immeasurable potential.

The United States is just one in a long line of nations that has already bent, and in some cases broken, under the weight of such unsustainable circumstances—the latest victim of another powerful movement that has taken hold of governments around the world. At the core of this devastation is an insatiable drive to accumulate more and more wealth at any cost, even if that cost is the destruction of the planet and human life.

Our fight to live has been boiled down to the barest bones—the deaths, the videos, the protests, whose lives matter, are the police good or bad, is it just about Black people or is it about all of us? These are the unfortunately-obtuse questions that stand in the way of a clear path forward. At the same time it is often about these things, it is most often not about any of these things.

The most simple answer to what we are fighting for, what we are protesting about, and what is wrong, is that we are fighting to live. That we want to live in a world where no life is more precious than another, where no life is disposable. That we must intervene forcefully and decisively against that which is killing us slowly and quickly, and that time is running out.

These are the things that we already know, the warnings that so many have been heralding for decades now, as the drive for progress makes life more and more difficult, more and more uncertain. We see the effects each day in our communities—boarded up windows, shuttered businesses, growing tent cities, fires that cause destruction at levels we have not seen before, piles of belongings on sidewalks, discarded from a place where someone once belonged.

Ever adept at naming the problem, we know the impacts of being thrown away. We are now being called to drive the solutions that may very well save our lives.

To be hopeful in these times may seem foolish to some. Optimism that we can change our circumstances may be viewed as a fool's errand, and yet, it is hope that lies at the foundation of our ability to resist unjust and unequal circumstances. It is hope that drives us to innovate, to create, to conspire. This is not the type of hope that ignores our present circumstances, that is deluded by the subversive nature of false solutions and individualistic assessments of good people and bad people, rather than systemic achievements that have been honed and tested over time. It is hope that reminds us that our desire to live freely is stronger than our resignation to die.

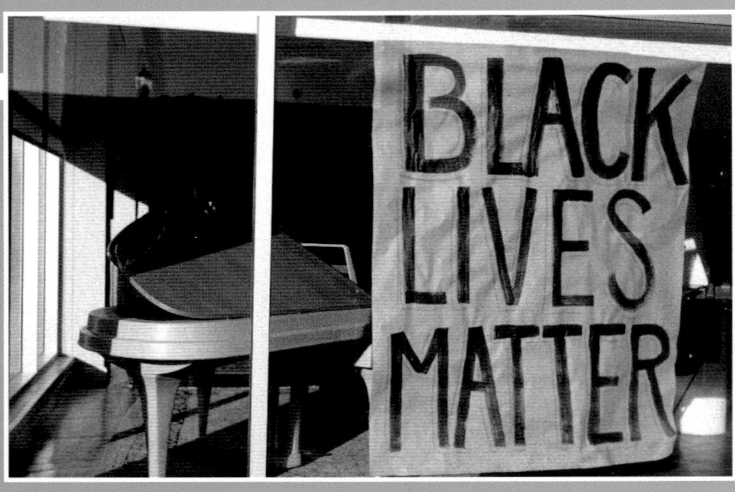


photo by Rohan DaCosta

Hope is why we can organize for truth when a life is stolen from our communities. It is why beautiful political murals can line the streets of boarded up businesses after weeks of protests. It is where poetry and theater emerge on a quest to tell the truth that has been buried or obscured, knowing that someone will hear it. Yes, it is hope that change is indeed possible which springs forward after every protest, after tent cities are torn down and herded away in city dump trucks, after the wail of a mother who sees her child's body lying in the street under a tarp. The story of what changes the world is not only a correct assessment of the scale and depth of the problem, it is also a gathering of those who remain, to keep fighting, to keep loving, and to keep building. To restart the clock is to tell the time, but it is also to know that time was not created for us to follow—it was created for us to keep starting over again, in the hope that soon, we will get it right.

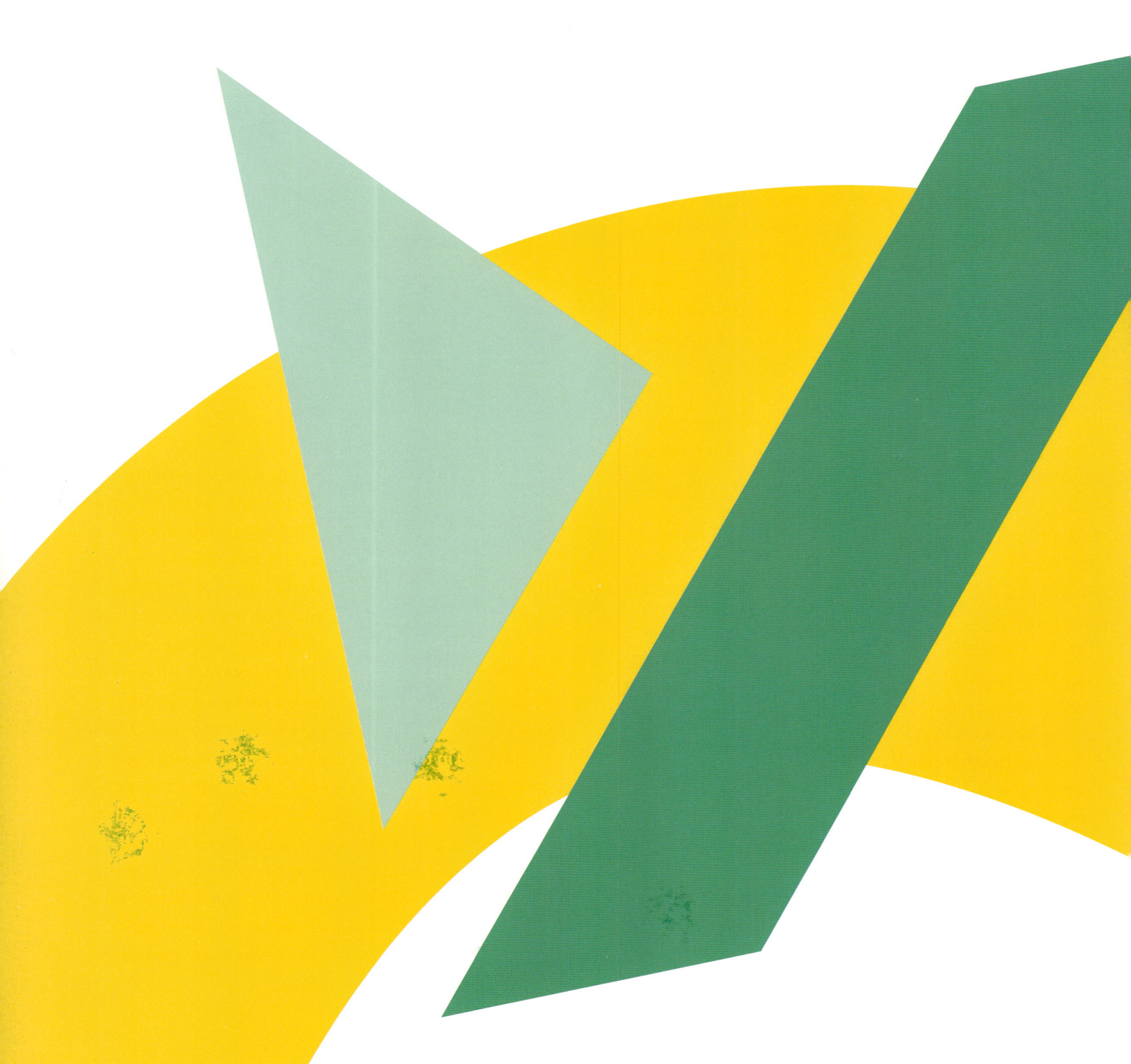

# ESSAYS

1

# Guiding Principles That Honor, Preserve & Protect Protest Art In Oakland

## Black Cultural Zone's Art for the Movement Team:
## Carolyn Johnson, Mizan Alkebulan-Abakah, MPH, and Randolph Belle

**L**and is liberation! Since 2014, despite the forces of displacement and gentrification, **The East Oakland Black Cultural Zone Collaborative** has worked with a coalition of residents, government agencies, churches, and grassroots organizing groups to help keep Black folks, Black Businesses, Black Families, and Black Beauty in East Oakland. Through a strategy of building power, securing land, and directing more dollars to community-driven projects, we can secure a foothold in East Oakland that finally allows our neighborhoods to thrive.

In late May 2020, we witnessed a beautiful explosion of protest in the aftermath of the murders of George Floyd, Ahmaud Arbery, Breonna Taylor, David McAtee, Tony McDade, Robert Fuller, Dominique "Rem'mie" Fells, Maurice Gordon, Riah Milton, Malcolm Harsch, Elijah McClain, Rayshard Brooks, Oluwatoyin Salau; as well as other ongoing and unchecked extrajudicial actions against Black people and people of color. The murals and artworks in Downtown Oakland and in other locations throughout the city were created as a form of protest and activism directed toward systemic police brutality, racism, and the outright murders of Black men and women.

These artworks are artifacts of a social justice movement and carry with them important stories and context. The work to document, preserve, and present this protest art is not simply an art initiative; it is part of the movement and represents an effort to seek solutions to injustice and racism.

The East Oakland Black Cultural Zone Collaborative, along with other Black-led organizations and Black artists, is leading this effort to hold the conversation and frame a path forward, which will include working with artists to re-mount ongoing exhibitions. The Oakland Museum of California, Oakland Art Murmur, Spearitwurx, RBA Creative, and a host of allies have committed to support the Black Cultural Zone's goal of lifting Black voices in the pursuit of justice and equality.

# OUR *STANCE*

This group shares the belief that we are not owners or arbiters of these artworks. The artworks are part of a moment that is intertwined with the loss of Black lives and the movement for the preservation and upliftment of Black lives. As symbols of the movement and part of a larger story, every effort will be made to identify and contact the artist in order to secure their support for the preservation, documentation, and presentation efforts. The documentation and preservation of the artwork includes uplifting the work of the artists, and a compilation of protest stories, which are critical to documenting this movement, its meaning, and the historical pain suffered by Black people.

This effort provides an opportunity to create a sustained, multi-dimensional collaboration across the city, and a platform for conversation and dialogue in a safe space. Our goal for documenting this art and these seminal times is to elevate the work as the backdrop of a movement toward truth, justice, equity, and transformation, as this moment calls for.


# OUR *WORK*

As of this writing, we have cataloged over 423 artworks and preserved 55 that have been removed from downtown buildings, encouraging businesses to keep the art up for the world to see. We have hosted four artists' calls, both with Black Artists and Allies (white and POC folks). We are hosting a three-part series of virtual Conversations for Change, focused on "Honoring the Artists," exploring "Art as Tool for Social Transformation" and "Claiming Space—the Way Forward." Additionally, we are planning for a series of free community-based public exhibitions of the artworks throughout Oakland, as well as a companion curriculum to sustain the movement with art and culture as critical components.

This protest art is not an aesthetic addition to social change—it is the vibrant vein that runs through the movement, which inspires transformation, ignites our resilience, and channels our healing from the trauma of state-sponsored violence and racism. The work to honor, preserve, and protect this art is akin to the need to honor, preserve, and protect Black lives, Black families, and Black land. We are on the path!

# The State of Culture in the United States

G. Jung Morozumi and Leslie Lopez

**G. Jung Morozumi**

When I moved to New York City in 1979, my welcome party was a gang of crazy mad white pigs chasing me with clubs in the middle of a lightning storm. (It became a recurring nightmare). I was at an anti-police rally in Bed-Stuy and got clubbed by the cops. Their plan was to provoke a riot, but instead they rioted, beating protesters Rodney King-style, sending many to local hospitals, and afterwards, visiting them with threats. Luckily, I only got bruised (by sizzling a fence), but I was supposed to be doing security for the venerable poet Amiri Baraka, who spoke at the rally. (Lucky too, he got away). This Brooklyn precinct was notorious for shooting Black & Brown residents, and they had just killed Luis Baez, a mentally-disturbed 29-year-old man, by shooting him 21 times. Baez was unarmed, and the five cops involved weren't indicted. His mother mistakenly called the police, worrying he would hurt himself, climbing on a fire escape with cuticle scissors.

NYC in the '80s was insane with what seemed like weekly police killings of citizens. Of course, there was gang rivalry too, with crack and coke flowing—it was hard times...But the state repression was brutal and viral against Black and Brown people. Like now...

At first, I tried my hand at organizing in Chinatown for a couple of years (that was crazy too, but that's another story) and afterwards, went to Harlem and the South Bronx to organize against police brutality. There, I was the only Asian activist, unless I went to events with Yuri Kochiyama, my revolutionary 'partner-in-crime"; everybody seemed to know her in every borough. I went to more rallies and meetings protesting the murders of Michael Stewart (a graffiti artist), Michael Griffith (killed in Howard Beach), Edmund Perry (a high school student from Harlem), and several others—mostly Blacks killed by white cops...In all these cases, the charges against the police were dropped by the District Attorney's office.

And then there was Eleanor Bumpurs, a 66-year-old grand-mother who was shot and killed during an eviction in the projects of the South Bronx. She reminded me of my own Black grandmother who lived in similar projects in Harlem (my Chinese mother was adopted), and I joined the Eleanor Bumpurs Justice Committee looking for justice.

I got attorney William Kunstler (Attica, Wounded Knee, NY 21, Chicago 8...) on the case, pro-bono! But the resistance by police forces against indictment and prosecution was fierce, organized and financed with corrupt collusion between the NYPD, the DA's office, the city coroner, the police union,

and the courts. We didn't have a chance. Police forces had organized counter rallies and tried to infiltrate our Eleanor Bumpurs Justice Committee with undercover cops. They even went so far as to dissolve our resolve by removing children from custody of one of our members, cutting off power in another's home, and kidnapping and tying up an elder in the committee!

The EBJC co-sponsored a rally in Howard Beach (an Italian enclave near JFK airport), where Michael Griffith had been looking for a used car (as advertised) and was met by racist white youths with baseball bats who chased him onto the highway to be killed. When we arrived late (by subway) for the rally, we erroneously ran into a counter-rally with an armed white mob screaming, "Niggers Go Home"...we hightailed it to our colored rally...

Clearly we've been living with a white supremacist and patriarchal culture (the very foundation of U.S. capitalism), and it's a sickness, a disease that has been spread over every aspect of our lives.

Like Amiri Baraka (who spearheaded the Black Arts Movement in the '60s) said, we've been colonized by white culture, white laws, and white revisionist history. So, de-colonization became the mission of our generation.

When I moved back to Oakland in '89, I was determined to be a Cultural Activist to help heal our communities, our Third World communities, from this physical and ideological disease. I contacted my former teacher and mentor, Malaquias Montoya, and joined his art collective, Taller Sin Fronteras (Workshop Without Borders).

After 25 years punching a clock, I tried briefly to be a visual artist and teacher of sorts, but wasn't satisfied. I started organizing political art exhibits in neighborhoods without galleries. I met a crew of graffiti writers (artists), who were bombing on the tracks when I was a mailman and talked them into showing their art in a gallery. They were wary and distrustful at first, but this brother named Dream held sway and eventually we got permission to bomb a gallery in downtown Oakland from floor to ceiling. We called it No Justice—No Peace! It came on the tails of the L.A. uprising, after the Rodney King verdict. The theme that every graf crew experienced was Police Brutality. Dream knew all the crews in the Bay Area, and I spoke to them about the campaigns against police killings in NYC.

Taller Sin Fronteras became the foundation of EastSide Arts Alliance (ESSA). We aimed for a grassroots, self-owned, Third World arts institution that became EastSide Cultural Center in East Oakland. We believe in self-determination for all communities of color. We support Black Lives Matter, but we also say: "Black Power Matters!" because racism is systemic, and the path for democracy for all people has to uphold the concept to redress America's flawed history.

photo by Eric Norberg

We follow Malcolm X's edict: "Culture is an indispensable weapon in the freedom struggle." We stand by our elders' contributions to the cause and the regeneration of new leadership from the neighborhoods, especially the potential of young sisters, to develop culture for community empowerment. ESAA defines its cultural priorities to address immigrant rights, deportations, mass incarceration, stolen lands and slavery (all of which continue!)...the very roots of this country.

This book is about fighting white supremacy in our culture, as it is inherent and endemic in our society. It's appalling, the level of ignorance and lack of moral consciousness in this country! Witness the recent national election results and the vile racist language spewing from the White House. But the populace, and our communities, need a New Reconstruction of our collective historical memory and cultural consciousness, too. First, we have to imagine what we need to be liberated, what we need for survival, and what we need for a better and sustainable future. This is the basis of culture and activism: making our dreams a reality—not just imagination—but a reality. It's a process we have to begin right now, to take advantage of every new awakening ... We have to begin right now.



**U**nlike the Mexican Muralists we learned about growing up—Rivera, Siqueiros or Orozco—not using the paint brush, but using aerosol to paint murals or any public art, has become one of the most revolutionary and popular mediums for artists today. Taking the getting up quick and with style from the graffiti culture has pushed artists to create more in short amounts of time, making it a favored tool for Muralists. Especially during these times of civil uprising, we see how quickly

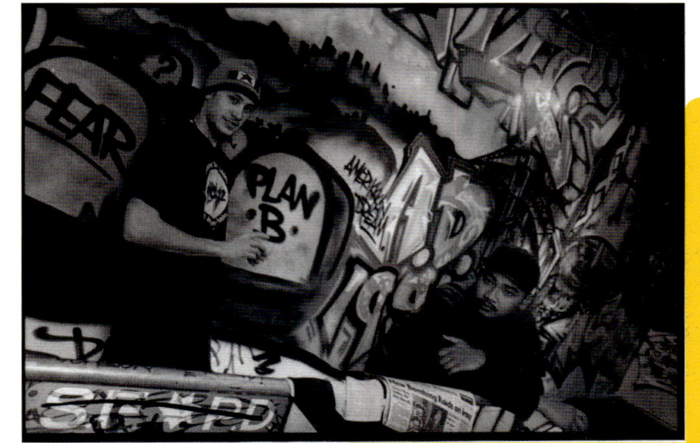

many blocks in our city bloomed into neighborhood museums overnight. Screams for justice and songs of resistance manifested in layers of paint across boarded up windows—unity and solidarity seen at the intersection of a paintbrush and a spray can. Although the mediums change, the power in the messages remains the same. For decades, from the smallest corner store mural to the largest high prime spot, walls have been used to make statements, to share political and cultural messages to the neighborhood and to those driving by. In this particular case, these walls make a really clear statement that our entire city stands for Black Lives and Third World Solidarity.

Since the birth of hip hop in the early '70s, youth of color in the barrios and the ghettos got creative and resourceful. They even became chemists, mixing inks, and experimenting with items from the local hardware store, using these to scribe

their names across city surfaces: some writing messages and public statements, reclaiming spaces, and without knowing it, sparking movements. But throughout the years and the powerful sparks, the spotlight on the role and work of women in this movement has been very dim.

As a young grafitera, my experience and existence in this field, on many levels, was a dangerous lifestyle (being pushed off the ring by male peers is just one example). My path and passion for graffiti started at a really young age. Standing in a very outnumbered scene, I set high ranks and values for myself in hopes of staying true, alive, in the game for the long run, and ultimately helping set safe roads for future grafiteras. The love I had for painting the streets grew by the minute, teaching me many lessons, unfortunate experiences, and giving me thicker skin to navigate the patriarchy, macho, and misogyny that came with the culture. I always did my own stunts, learned to code switch, and called for respect as male taggers made almost every session uncomfortable. You see, the cold streets gave us game, and taught us when and how to speak up; Reading about pioneer grafiteras, like Lady Pink (a NY grafitera from Ecuador), we knew an inclusive and respected scene was in our near future.

I grew up in the Fruitvale District but have stretched my roots throughout many parts of this city. My parents came to Oakland in the '70s with big full hearts, and even bigger dreams. My mother, like many, worked very hard to learn a new language, but most importantly, to educate herself as much as she could in order to navigate her new life in a foreign country. My father worked tirelessly, and my mother tapped

into many resources that would give her the courage and determination to advocate for herself and her family; most of those resources were in Fruitvale. She led by example, took empowering courses, and passed this down to my siblings and myself by signing us up for many free community programs. These felt safe and were available to us to stay busy, alive, healthy, and keep learning.

Many of these programs—such as R.Y.C.O, out of Spanish Speaking Citizens Foundations (Raza Youth Committee of Oakland—my mom called it the "Rrrrico thing"), followed by OLIN, Raza Youth Leadership and the Xicana Moratorium Coalition—would open up this creative and conscious path I ride on today. Engaging with Raza Studies at the age of 13 sparked a fire in me that could never be put out. And learning about injustices worldwide forced me and other young people to the streets, to man-made borders to fight for justice, and to Third World solidarity.

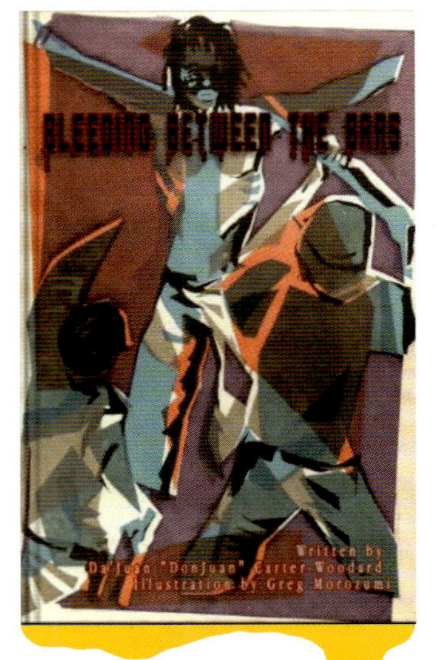


My mentors fueled me with knowledge that gave my young artist mind not only content, but purpose, to create. It gave me a path to follow in my new artist journey and voice.

Many of the programs in the neighborhood intersected during that time: I joined the EastSide Arts Alliance by volunteering for the first time at the Malcolm X Jazz Festival. I was 13 and fascinated by learning of the power of art and a Mural class… that used spray paint! Since then, I've joined in every mural project I could (and would sneak to class when my parents wouldn't let me go…I was an artist mistaken for a misunderstood child- ha!). I started to community build with ESAA—I

was so young and felt so empowered, learning how our craft uplifted Black & brown communities. It was something I could only feel and not describe. I was dedicated, passionate, and committed to continuing this work. I became one of the instructors of the class, and down the line, I wore many other other visual arts hats as a collective core member.

Many of these classes I taught while still attending high school started as after-school programs, and I recruited youth to make art in the streets and get involved with EastSide Arts Alliance, with hopes to engage and amplify the voices of young artists making radical/political art for the people. Graffiti brought dozens of students, became more accepted on campus and was the super popular class that many kids wanted to join. All of the schools I ran programming out of were historically under-served schools, in neighborhoods with high violence and crime, and where most Black & brown students attended. My role went far beyond the classroom, and making connections was necessary—stretching a web of opportunities and murals with purpose from the Dubbs to the Deep, while bringing this medium and content to these blocks, was powerful and healing.

As I got older, I focused on building bonds with the super dope younger grafiteras from the town. I created a curriculum focused on art and young women, called She'Rose. Teaching this across many schools brought to light something that was empowering and unstoppable—Sisterhood! In 2005, I made connections with other female graffiteras and began painting the yards and streets with them, and as the years passed, I focused on building safe spaces for young women to paint.

After building relationships with artists and grafiteras worldwide from Few & Far Women (one of the five international all-women graffiti crews), my crew kept me inspired, held, but most importantly, they gave me courage and empowered me. After many years of being left out of spaces, projects and productions, there was now a lane only we could claim and build on.

I took this motivation and ran with it, curating all-women yards during our ESAA traditions, and leading all-women murals that not only called out for sisterhood, but was also raising awareness of the violence against women. Using the streets as classrooms, and making each mural a healing circle on the wall, was a powerful manifestation of this new age sisterhood! Making moves like that only inspired us to keep going. It was revolutionary! Urging women to create a path of our own, and to sustain a powerful community of artists, is now the way we survive, smash patriarchy, and collectively build—this work is essential! Mujeres Muralistas from San Francisco, and Xochitl Nevel Guerrero from Oakland, are among the bad-ass muralistas that have been paving the way in the bay for many years, and now we follow, in bold and fearless ways, to reclaim the powerful work they and our great grandmother artistas have left for us.

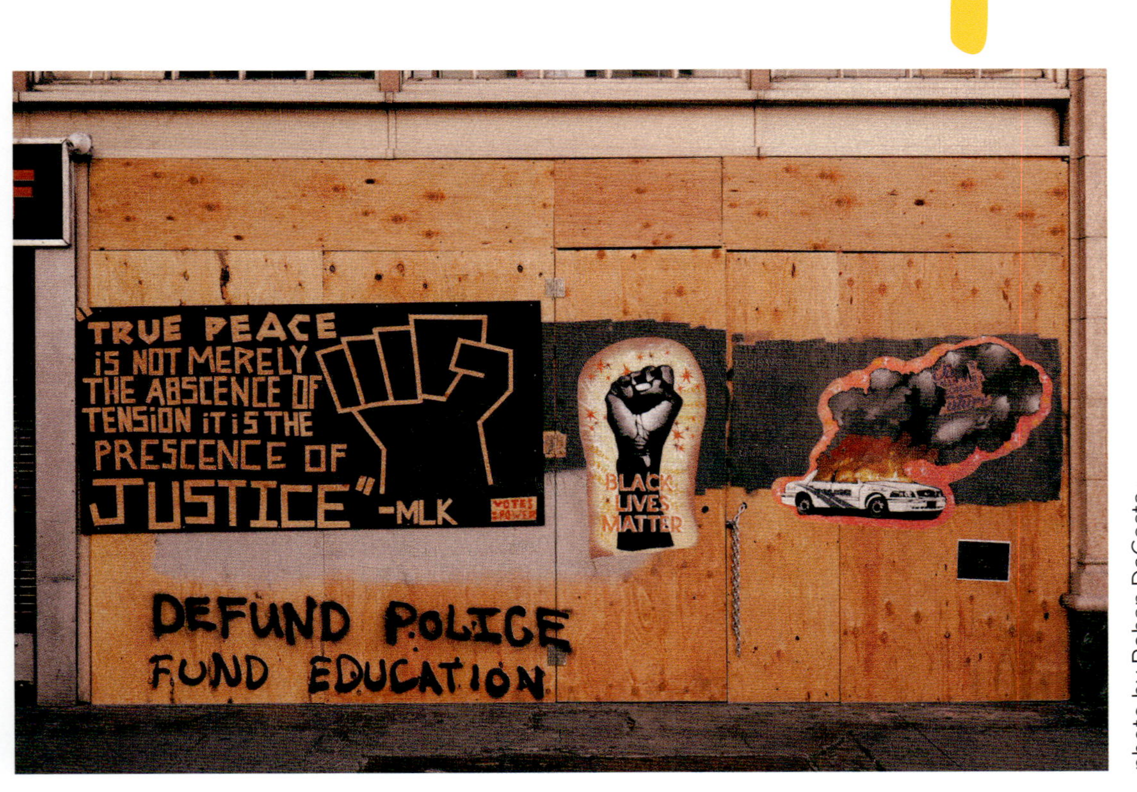


photo by Rohan DaCosta

# The New Abolitionists

Robin D. G. Kelley



For Black, Brown, and Indigenous communities—especially the poor, women, and LGBTQ folx—the police and the criminal "justice" system—along with inadequate income, housing, healthcare, and schools, as well as neighborhoods divested of services and overrun with toxins and unchecked violence—threaten our safety and security. Abolition is about dismantling systems that have caused harm—namely police, prisons, and the military—and reallocating funds to invest in education, universal healthcare, housing, living wage jobs, restorative justice, food justice, and green energy.

Abolition is neither new nor hopelessly utopian. Nor is it "reform." None of the police reforms currently proposed are new: civilian review boards, better training, altering use of force policy, more tasers, more transparency, more Black cops, better data to flag patterns of misconduct, body cams, banning choke holds, ad infinitum. These reforms have not stopped the wanton killing and beating of civilians or made communities that are consistently overpoliced any safer. Before George Floyd's execution, the Minneapolis Police Department was a poster child of reform: its diverse force was well-trained in mental health crisis intervention, implicit bias, de-escalation, and praised for being exceptionally compassionate.

A decade of unremitting police violence followed by non-indictments has inspired new movements to embrace abolitionist principles, including the Movement for Black Lives (M4BL), Dream Defenders, Black Youth Project 100, We Charge Genocide, BOLD (Black Organizing for Leadership and Dignity), Million Hoodies Movement for Justice, Dignity and Power Now, Ella's Daughters, Assata's Daughters, Black Feminist Futures Project, Leaders of a Beautiful Struggle, Let Us Breathe Collective, Hands Up United, Lost Voices, and Millennial Activists United, to name just a few. Before Black Lives Matter became a hashtag, Oakland's Black Organizing Project and the Community Rights Campaign in Los Angeles were fighting to demilitarize schools, decriminalize tardiness and truancy, and abolish school police.

We have been told that Richard Nixon's stance against rising crime and urban rebellions won him the presidency in 1968—a strategy Trump tried to replicate. But the wave of urban rebellions were responses to police violence, exacerbated by the violence of disinvestment, segregation, and poverty. The Black Panther Party was formed precisely to monitor police

violence, to create community-based models of public safety, and to provide for the social needs of Black communities where the state failed. The Panthers patrolled the streets, held know-your-rights workshops, exposed the names of brutal cops, and in various places provided free medical care, free clothing and groceries, ran free breakfast and lunch programs for children, food banks, community gardens, drug rehab centers, ambulance services, and housing cooperatives. BPP members, along with other liberation movement activists, sought to reimagine criminal justice at the Revolutionary People's Constitutional Convention held in Philadelphia in 1970. They proposed reorganizing the police as "a rotating volunteer non-professional body coordinated by the Police Control Board from a (weekly) list of volunteers from each community section." Board members would be elected and its policies approved by popular vote, and "community rehabilitation programs" would replace jails and prisons. However, through systematic raids on Panther headquarters, surveillance, agent provocateurs, targeted assassinations, and harassment, the police and FBI actually created a dangerous and insecure environment.

Today's vision of abolition, rooted in anti-prison movements, can be traced to the long 1990s, to opposition to Bush and Clinton-era neoliberalism, the war on drugs, the war on terror, prison expansion, police brutality, anti-Black and anti-immigrant racism, Islamophobia, and violence against women of color and the LGBTQ community. These movements include Mothers ROC (Reclaiming Our Children), the Malcolm X Grassroots Movement, Prison Activist Resource Center, the Jericho Movement, the Prison Moratorium Project, Critical Resistance, Labor/Community Strategy Center, Project South, Southerners on New Ground (SONG), INCITE! Women of Color Against Violence, Sista II Sista, the Los Angeles Community Action Network, the Praxis Project, Safe OUTside the System (SOS)—the Audre Lorde Project, Project NIA, FIERCE (Fabulous Independent Educated Radicals for Community Empowerment), Queers for Economic Justice, the Sylvia Rivera Law Project (SRLP), UBUNTU!, among many others. The founders and forces behind many of these movements were either key theorists of abolition or scholar-activists whose writings— even if not promoting an abolitionist agenda—profoundly shaped the current generation of activists. The current movement is unimaginable without the writings of Angela Davis, Ruth Wilson Gilmore, Mariame Kaba, Assata Shakur, Mumia Abu-Jamal, Michelle Alexander, Joy James, Beth Richie, Andrea J. Ritchie, Alexis Pauline Gumbs, Andrea Smith, Julia Chinyere Oparah (Sudbury), Erica Meiners, Dean Spade, Dylan Rodriguez, and Kristian Williams, among others.

It is not an accident that gendered violence emerged as a key abolitionist issue. It is not enough to say the names of those killed by police. We must acknowledge the tens of thousands whose deaths, disappearances, and abuse go unresolved. In other words, police not only enact harm through direct violence but by the criminal justice system's inability to address gender-based and intimate violence. In 2001, INCITE! Women of Color Against Violence and Critical Resistance issued a statement calling for "strategies and analyses that address both state and interpersonal violence, particularly violence against women," as well as the development of safe, community-based responses to violence independent of the criminal justice system and accountability to survivors of sexual and domestic violence. In 2000, following the police killing of two teenaged women of color, the Brooklyn-

based collective, Sista II Sista, created "Sistas Liberated
Ground" as an alternative to calling the police to deal with
gendered violence (at the time, the NYPD had a backlog of
over 100,000 domestic violence cases). To protect these
spaces, women were trained in self-defense and conflict
resolution. Through street performances, video screen-
ings, discussions, and direct interventions, they dealt with
violence as a community issue. As a result,
they succeeded in making their community safer
without police.

The abolition of police and prisons is not only possible, it
is necessary if we are serious about preserving Black life,
reducing trauma, creating safer communities, and investing
municipal funds in social needs rather than settling
wrongful death and excessive force cases. But it will not
happen without a political struggle. Because, truth be told,
the role of police in the U.S. was never to keep our commu-
nities safe, but to protect property and its owners, to
function as an occupying force in America's impoverished
ghettoes, barrios, and reservations, and to use coercive
force to oversee "criminalized" populations. As protesters
know firsthand, police are the first line of defense against
strikes, demonstrations, and dissident social movements.
Abolitionists know it's not enough just to win the argument,
and that abolition is not an event but a process, a struggle.
Abolitionists expose the system's oppressive character
while also fighting to ultimately end state and interpersonal
violence; end policing; create structures of accountability;
demilitarize law enforcement; end solitary confinement,
the death penalty, and cash bail; resist police and prison
expansion; roll back punitive measures; and find ways to
interrupt violence to create safety, so police wouldn't need
to be called.

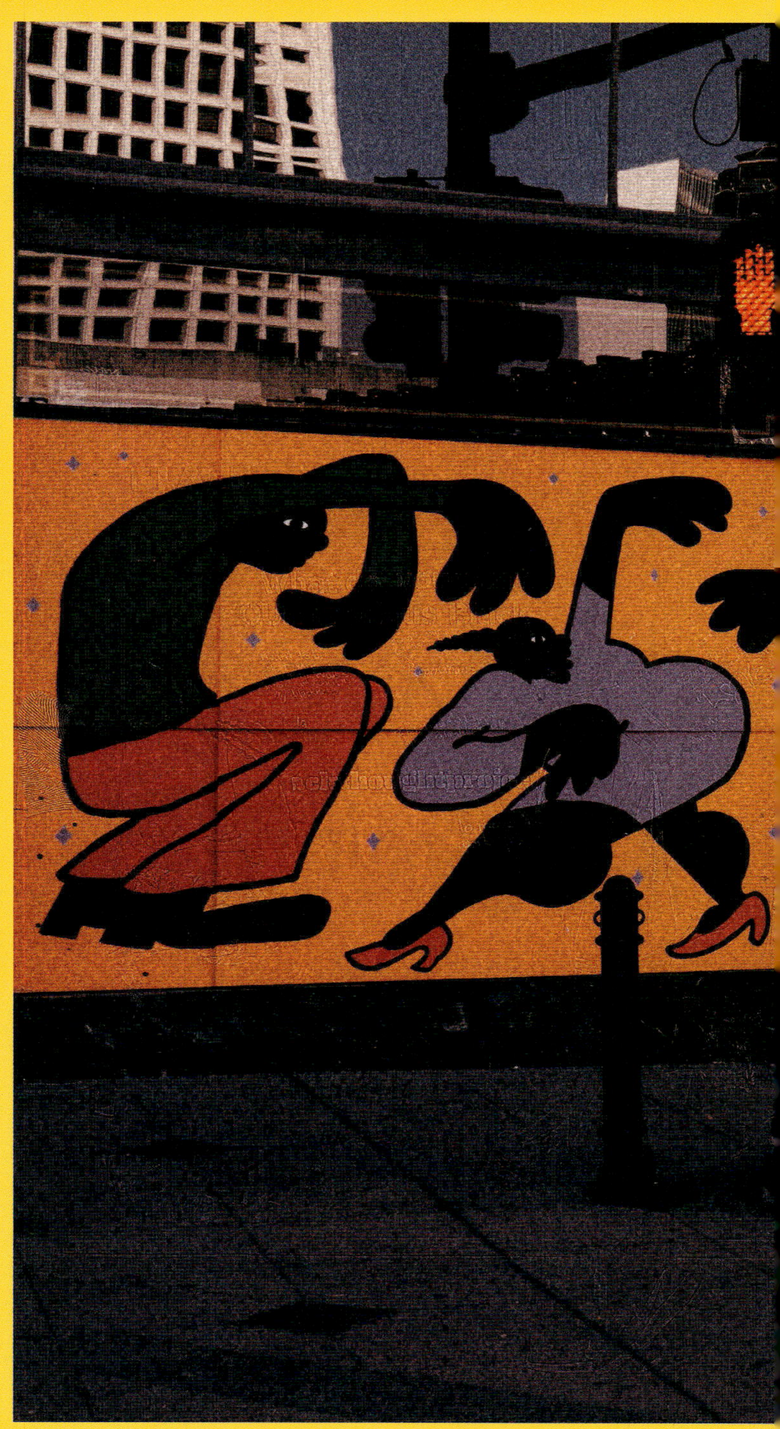

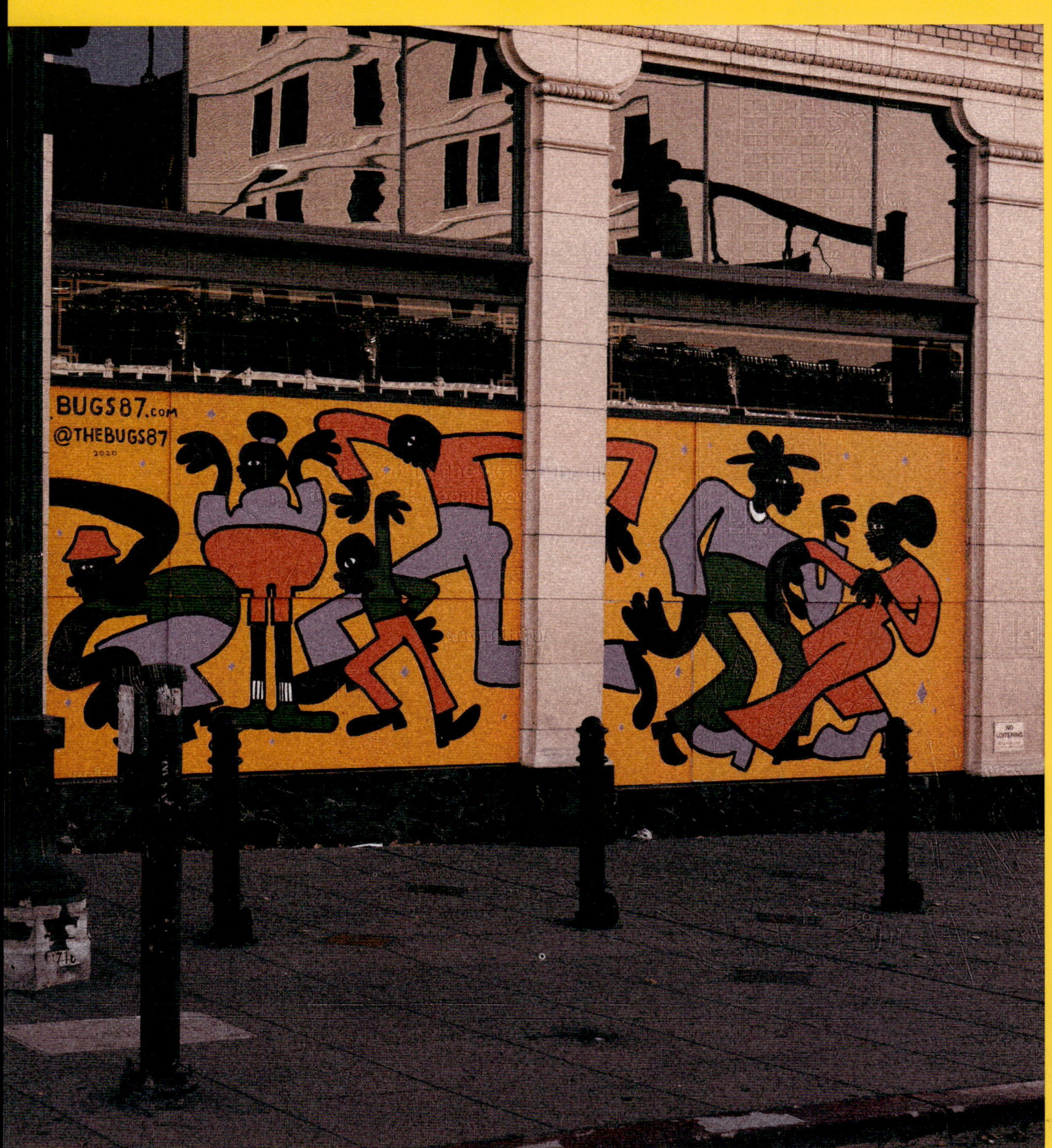


photo by Rohan DaCosta

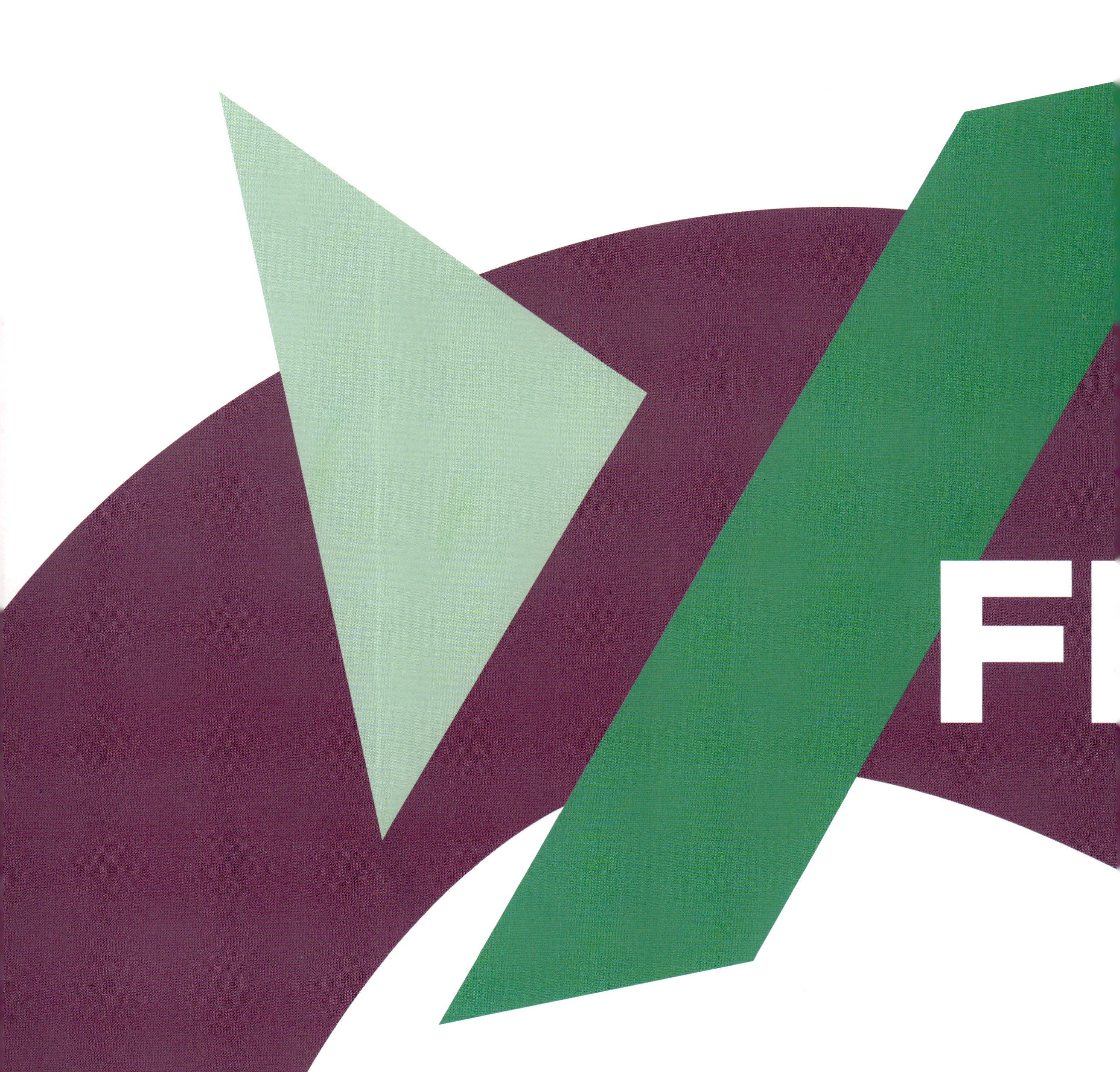

# EATURED ARTISTS 2

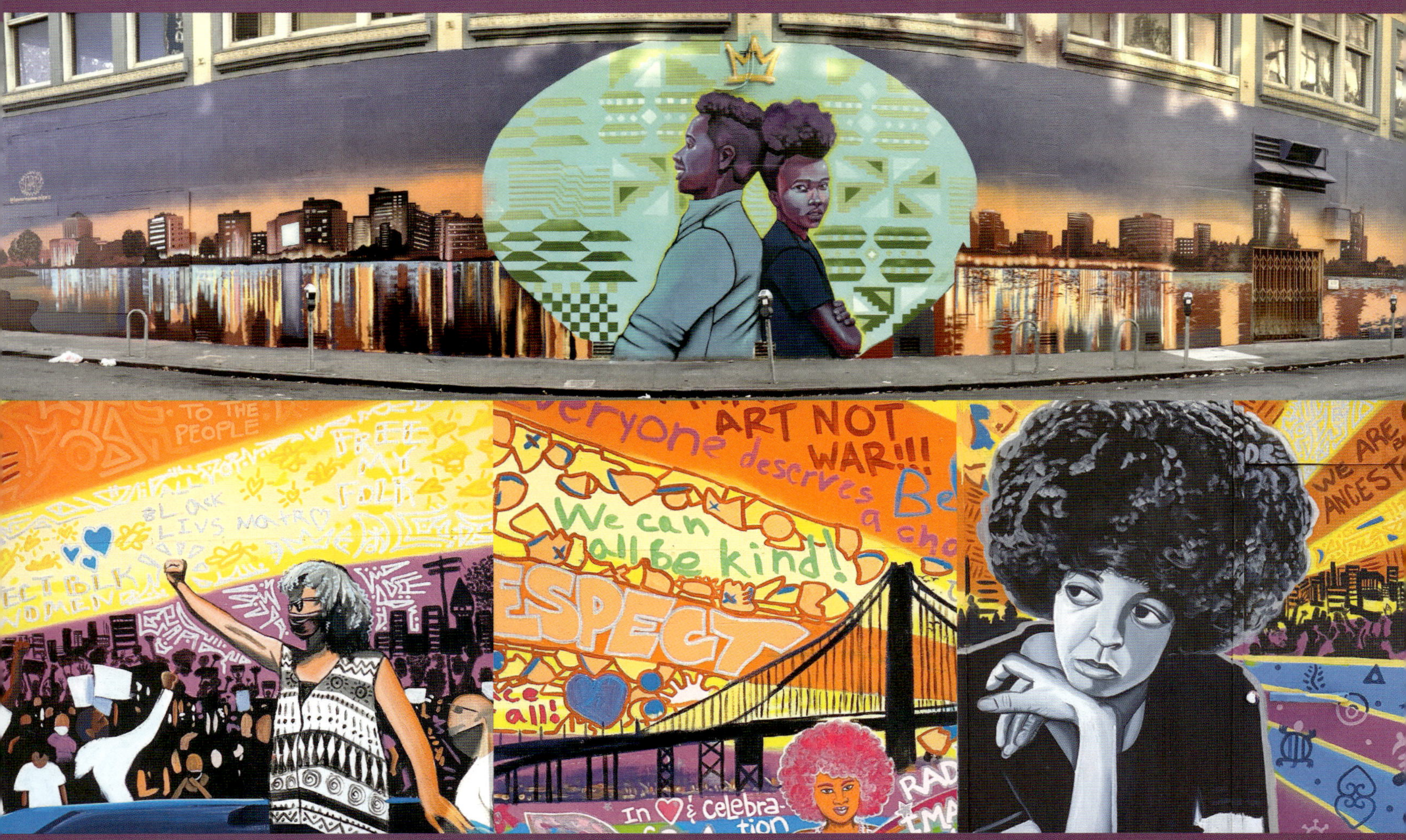

The Bay Area Mural Program better known by its acronym B.A.M.P is an Oakland-based non-profit organization established in 2015. Founder and Executive Director Andre Jones understood the need for Black and Brown representation in Public Art and assembled a team of BIPOC Artists to take action. BAMP is dedicated to fostering community involvement as an integral part of creating public art. After the murder of George Flloyd, BAMP artists created work in direct response to the continued police killings of Black people. BAMP led the charge in these efforts by organizing the Oakland Black Lives Matter street mural and pulling from it's extensive roster of BIPOC artists to paint the plywood murals on Downtown Oakland's boarded businesses.

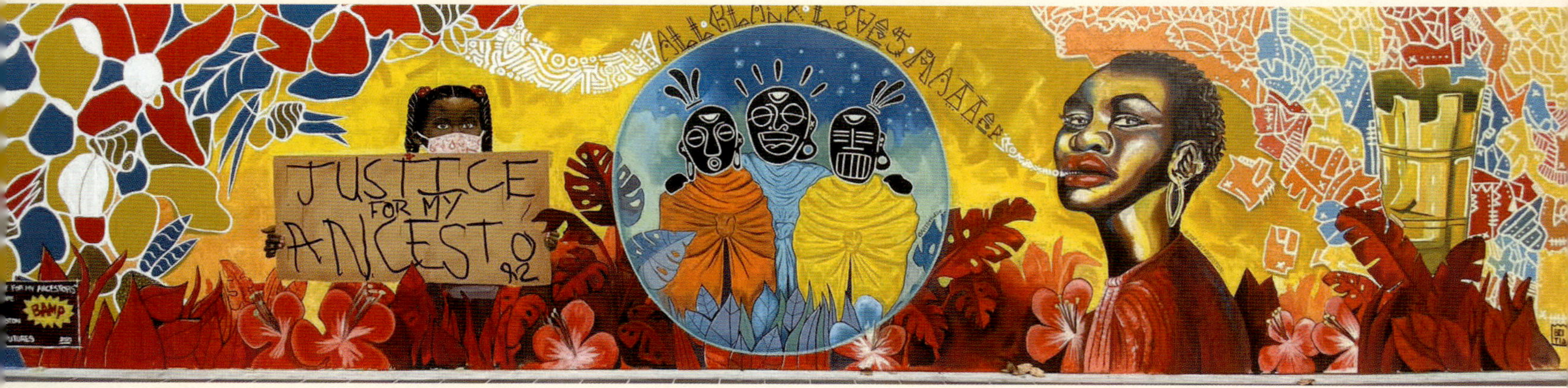



# Bay Area Mural Program

@bayareamuralpro

"**W**e believe that social justice public art is a powerful way to inform and remind underrepresented communities that they still have a voice! We use these murals to illustrate the voice of the people."

**ANDRE JONES**
BAMP Executive Director

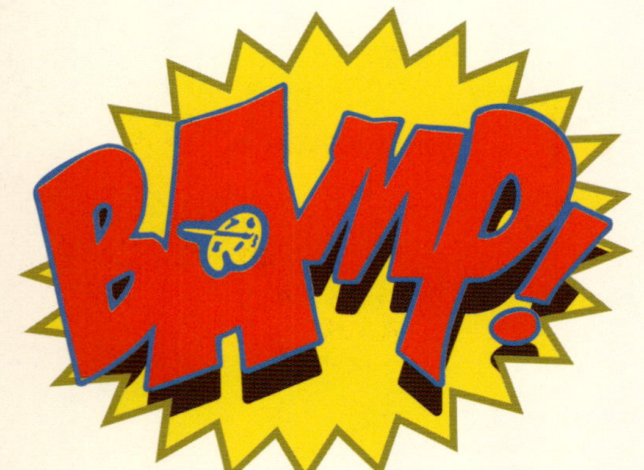



The plywood mural at the Kapor Center "Justice for Our Ancestors" is a powerful piece created by multiple BAMP team members. BAMP's Creative Director Rachel Wolfe worked with Terrion "Shido" Smith, Zoe Boston, Kalani Ware, Aaron Beitia, Corbrae Smith and Ignacia to express the lack of justice from the past to the present. Each lead artist worked on a specific section and created a fluid style that flowed from one artist to the other. The bright yellow backdrop gave narrative power and representation to the wealth and royalty of our ancestors. The mural is depicted through animation as well as photo realistic images of the primary characters. The mural was titled after lead artist Kiara Hardy a.k.a. Ignacia who illustrated a young African-American girl holding a sign with the slogan "Justice For mY ANCESTO Rs" written in children's handwriting.

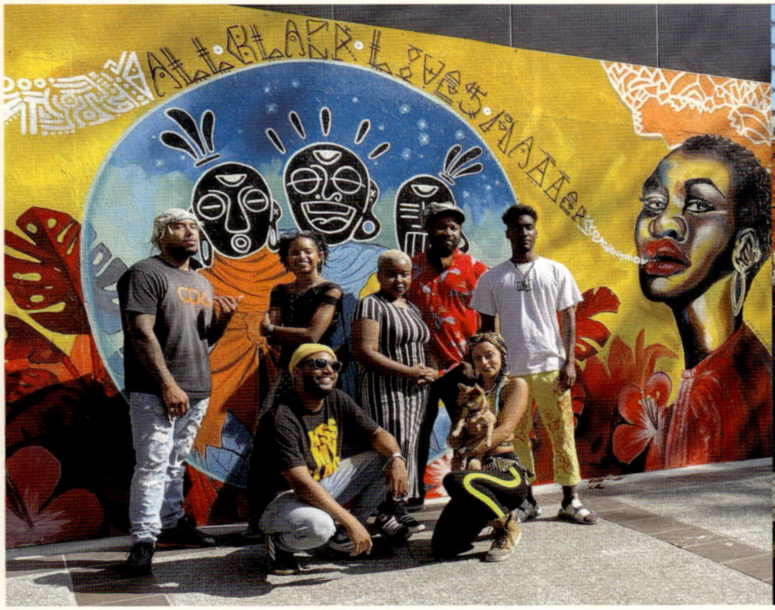

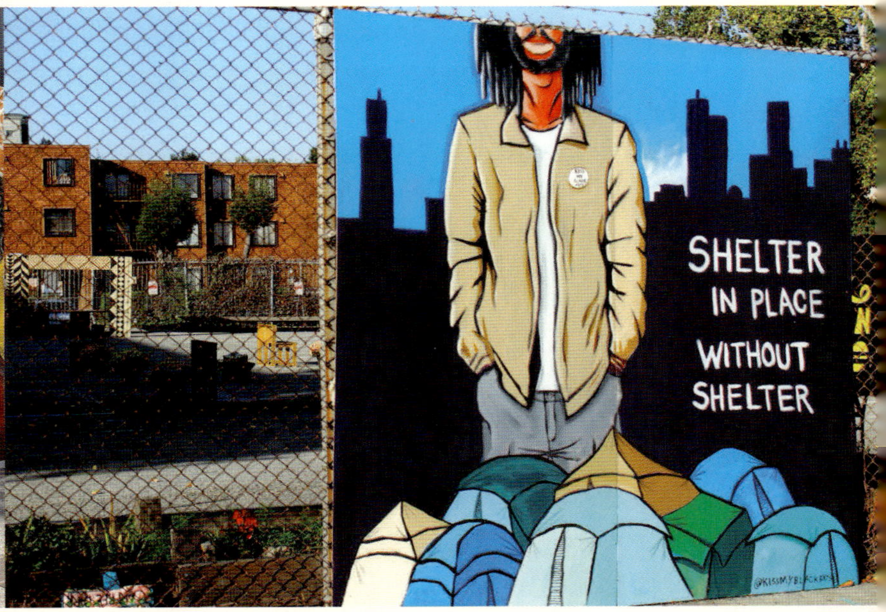

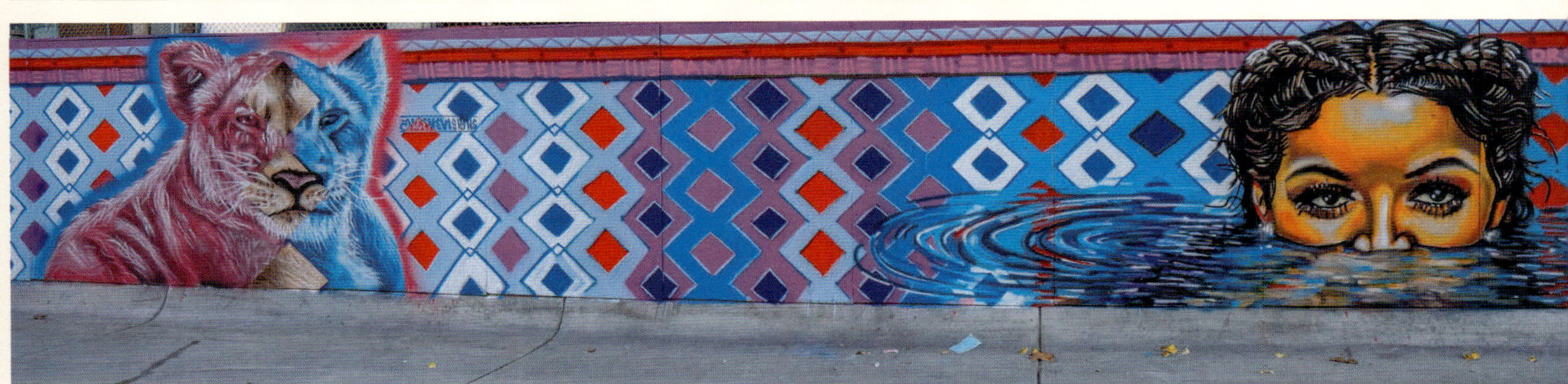

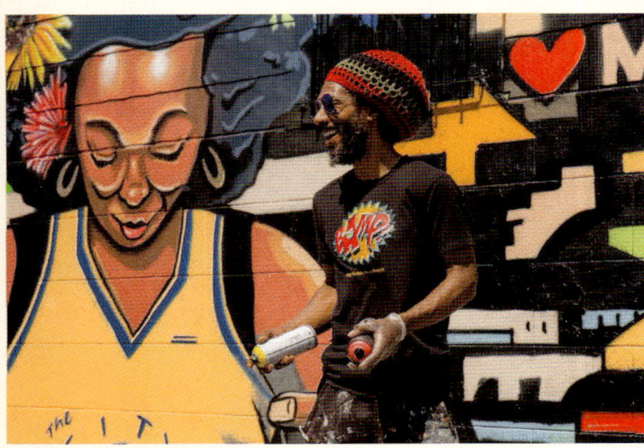


**BAMP TEAM:**

**Andre Jones**
Executive Director

**Kalani Ware**
Lead Artist

**Kiara "Ignacia" Hardy**
Lead Artist

**Rachel Wolfe**
Creative Director

**Rtystk**
Field Operations Director

**Terrion "Shido" Smith**
Lead Artist

**Timothy B**
Lead Artist

**Zoe Boston**
Lead Artist

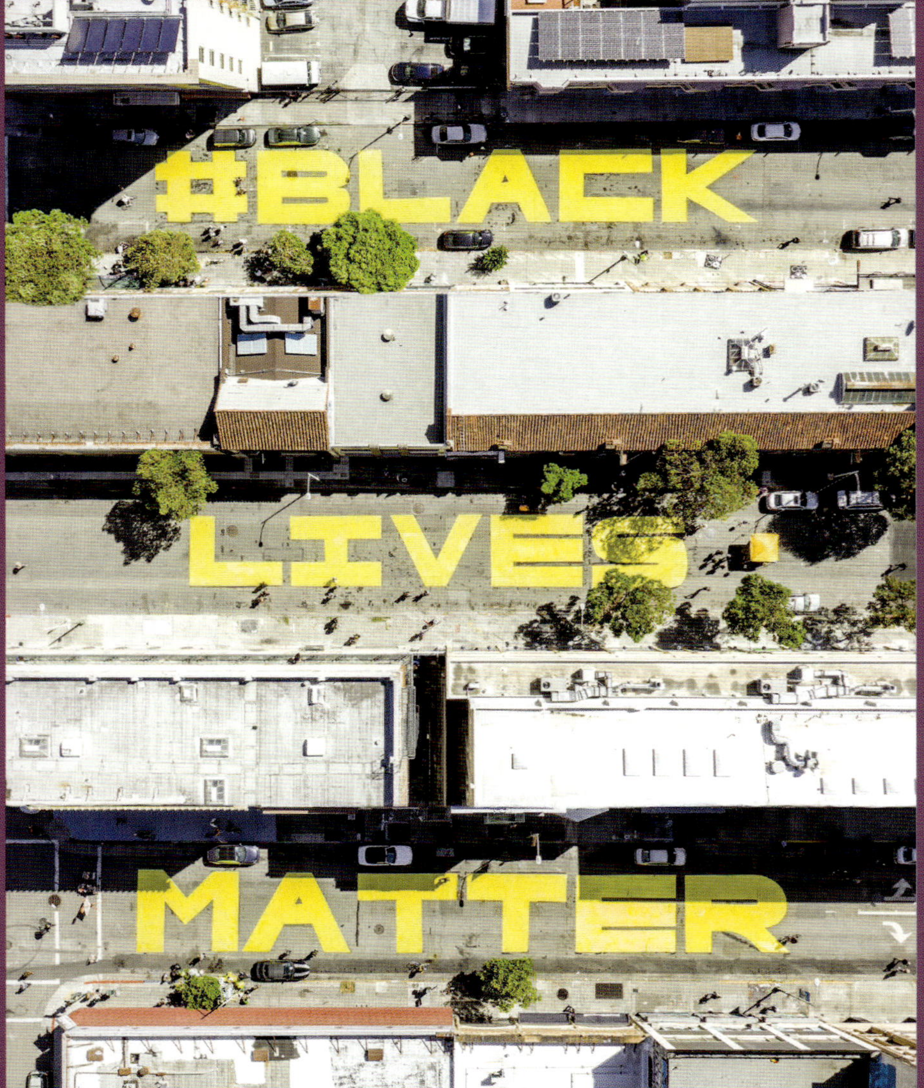



photo by JJ Harris
@techboogie

BAMP came together with Endeavors Oakland and local community artists to paint a massive yellow Black Lives Matter mural in solidarity with Washington D.C. as the second city to broadcast the message. The street painting stretches the height of two traffic lanes and the length of three blocks down 15th street in Downtown Oakland. Over 100 volunteers banded together with BAMP to create a replica mural going down San Francisco's Fulton street. Much like the BLM movement itself, the giant yellow lettering sprawled down several street blocks, and across multiple major cities, which is impossible to ignore.

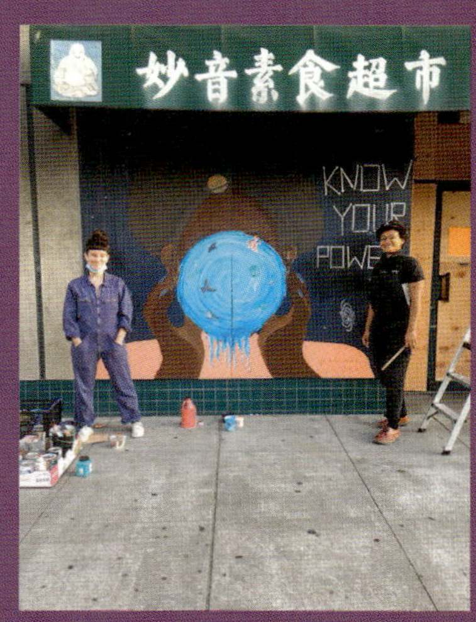
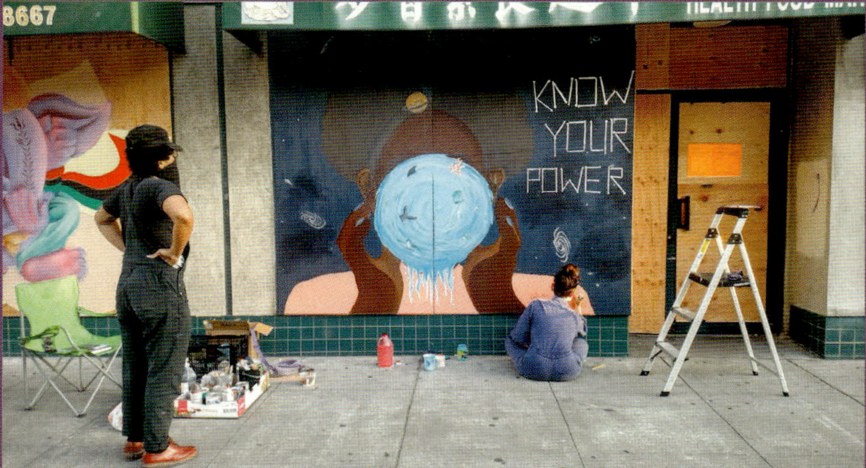



# Anya Riddell-Kaufman

@_anya_mind_

in collaboration with:
**Milan Outlaw**
@falselybukowski

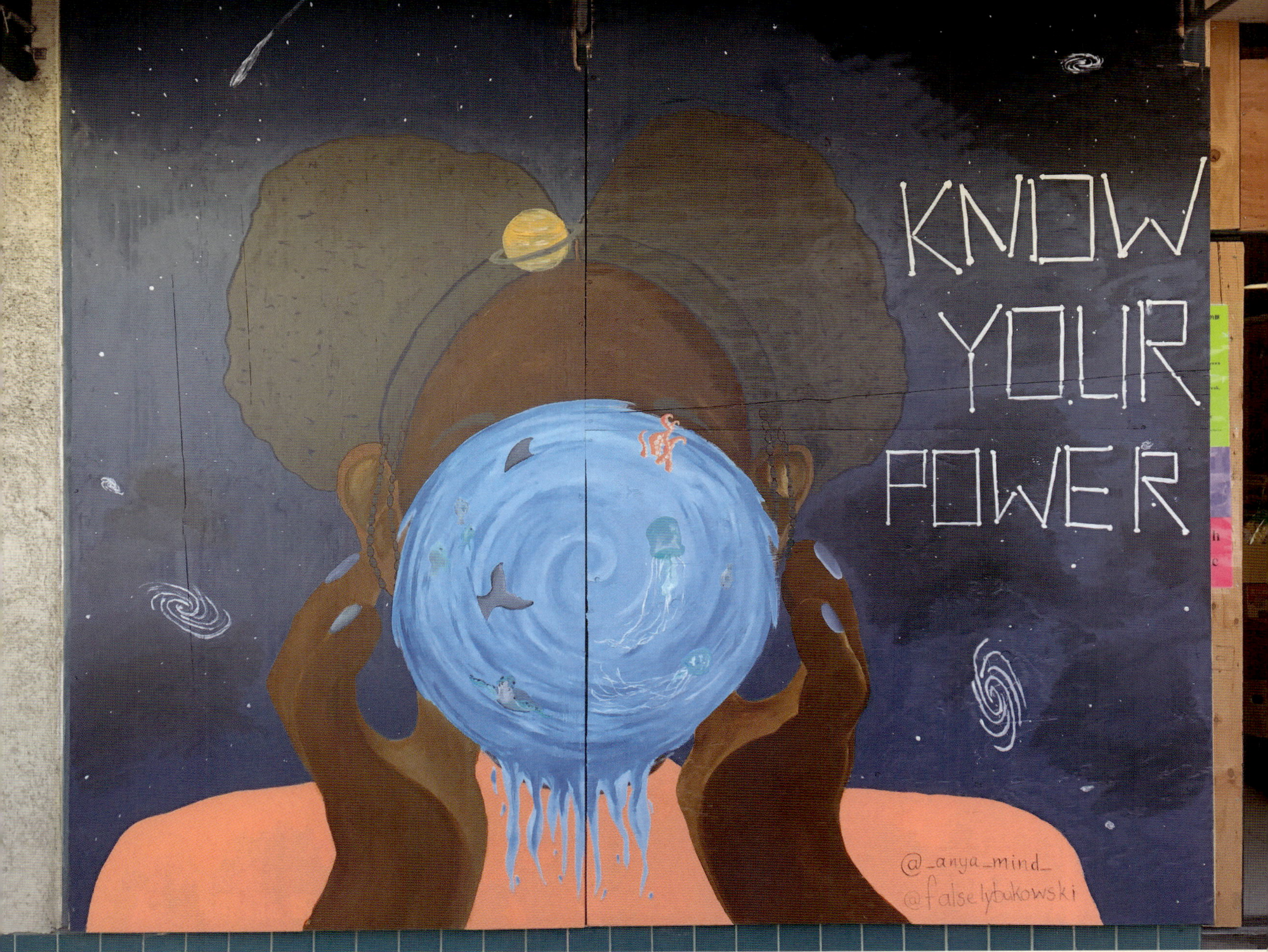


**Chinatown (Oakland)**
Layonna Vegetarian
Health Food Market ;
8th and Broadway

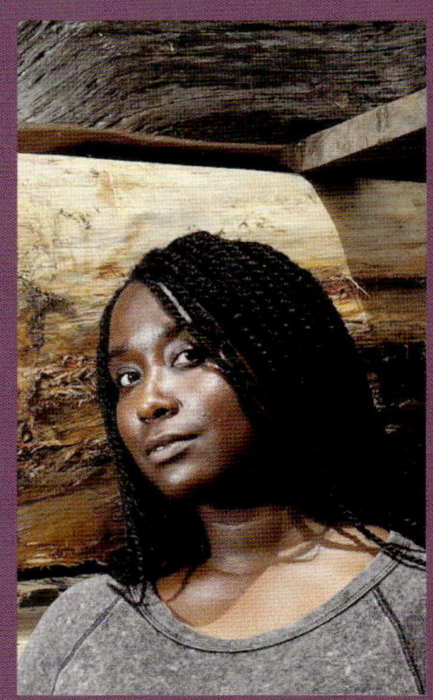

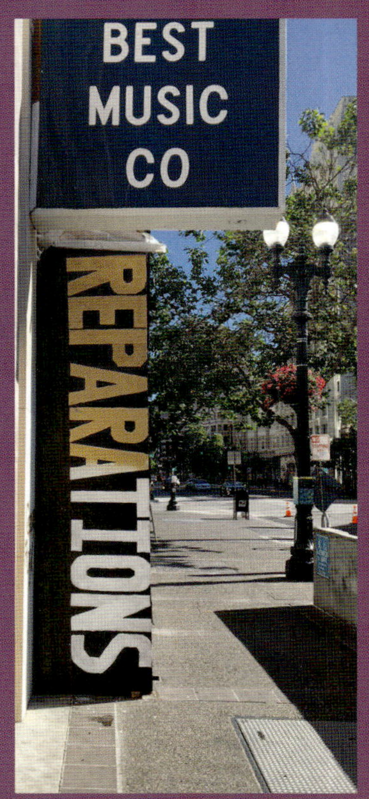


# Binta Oyafemi

@bintaoyafemi

**in collaboration with:**
**Robert Liu-Trujillo**
@robert_tres

**"A**s a Black artist, I was already renovating a storefront to create a building as artwork, a gathering space for music and community. My Black Lives Mural became a way to offer the full storefront, transforming the construction barricade as a dialogue with the street.**

*The mural became an affirmation of Black presence and power, on a corner at the heart of the demonstrations at 17th and Broadway. On either side of Black Lives, the words Reparations and Transformations as a sign of hope and resilience. The final version of the mural included a collaboration with the amazing Robert Liu-Trujillo.*

*My murals continued as a series of affirmations, from a Black Is Beautiful mural further down Broadway, to a Seize The Time, Black News, Black Love Is Power mural, abstracting a fragment from the Black Panther Newspapers in conversation with Emory Douglas, supported beautifully by the team of Aerosoul/Refa One and the team of Joseph Rivas.*

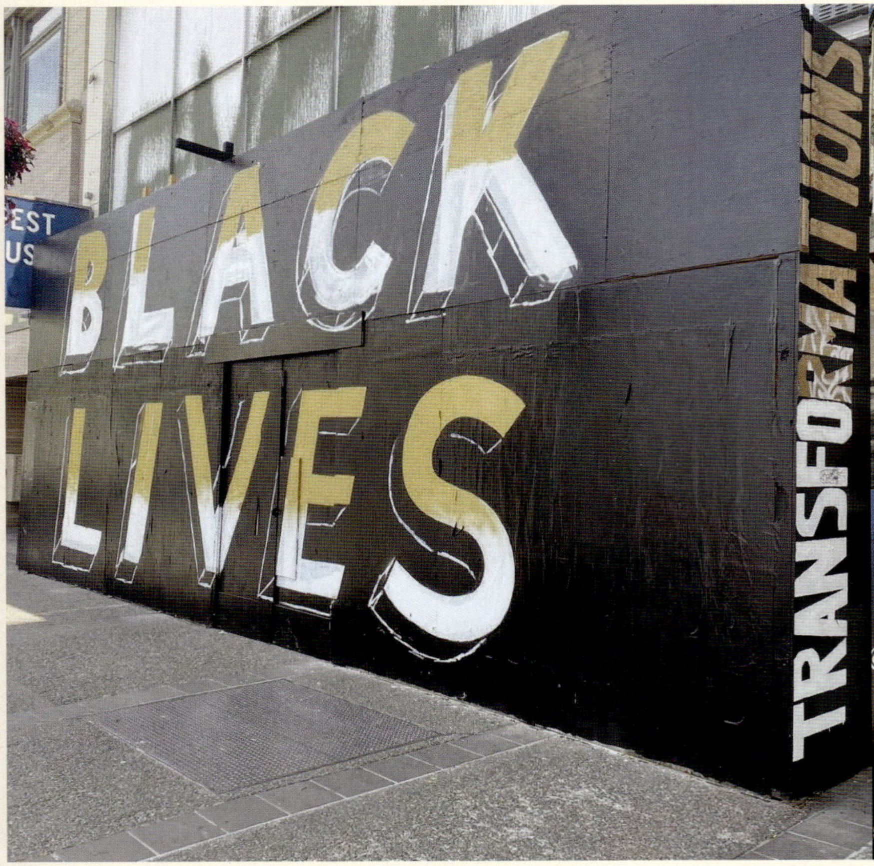

BLACK LIVES
TRANSFORMATIONS
BLACK LIVES 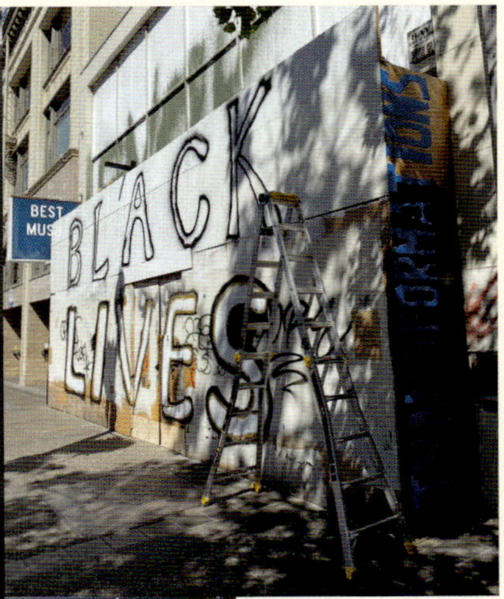
Black Owned
@BintaAyofemi
/Murals.Black
~ & ~
@Robert_Tres
Trust Your Struggle Collective


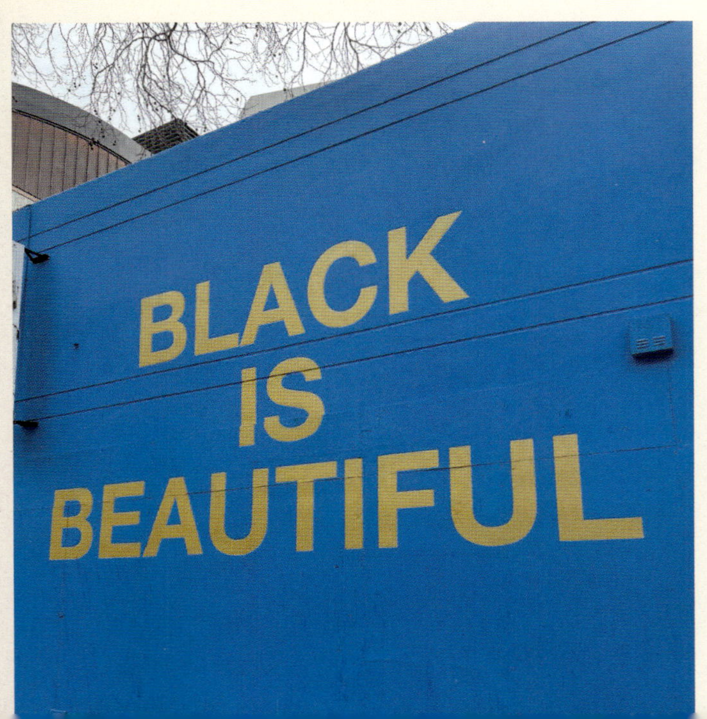

BLACK
IS
BEAUTIFUL


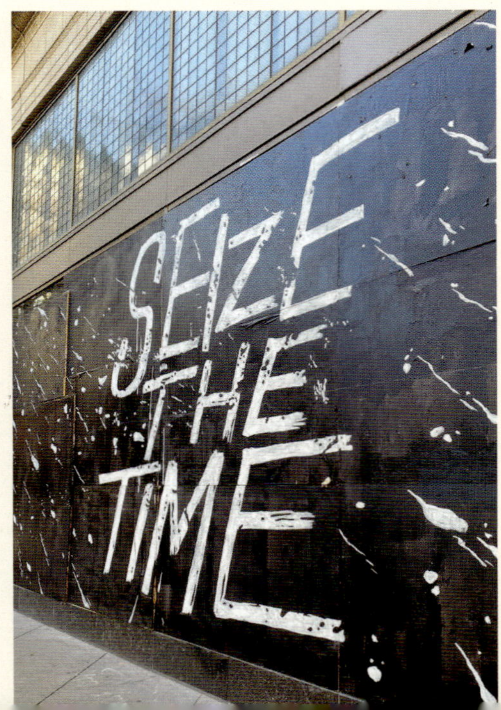

SEIZE
THE
TIME

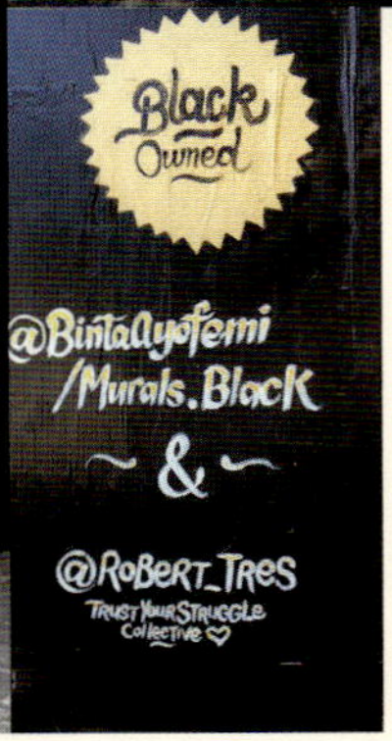

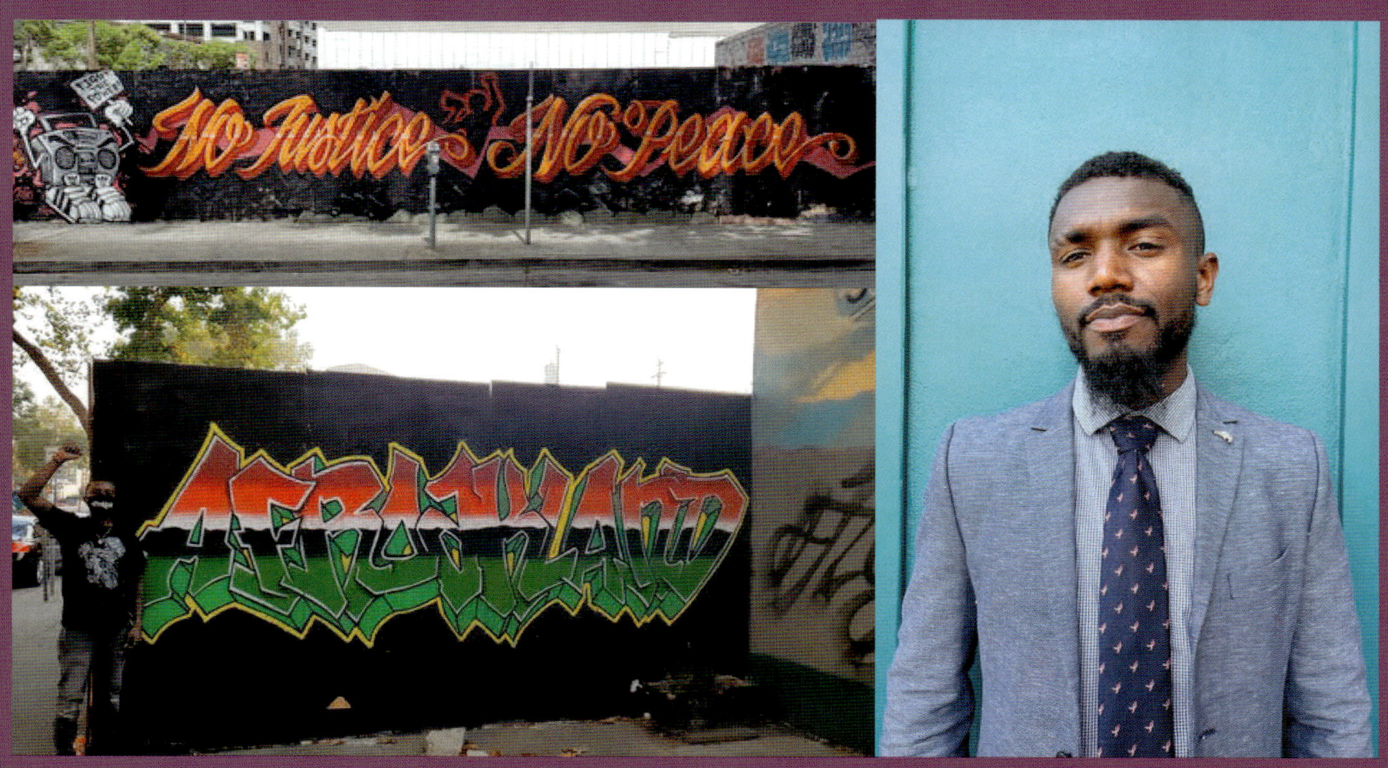

# DeVante Brooks

@aeosone

*Also known as Aeos One (pronounced A-Yos), DeVante Brooks is a calligrapher, sign painter, and muralist. Aeos has a background in street art and graffiti that spans over a decade and is a proud member of the international art collective, Aerosoul. His affinity for psychology and philosophy are utilized in the visual arts as a means to empower and serve his community of West Oakland.*

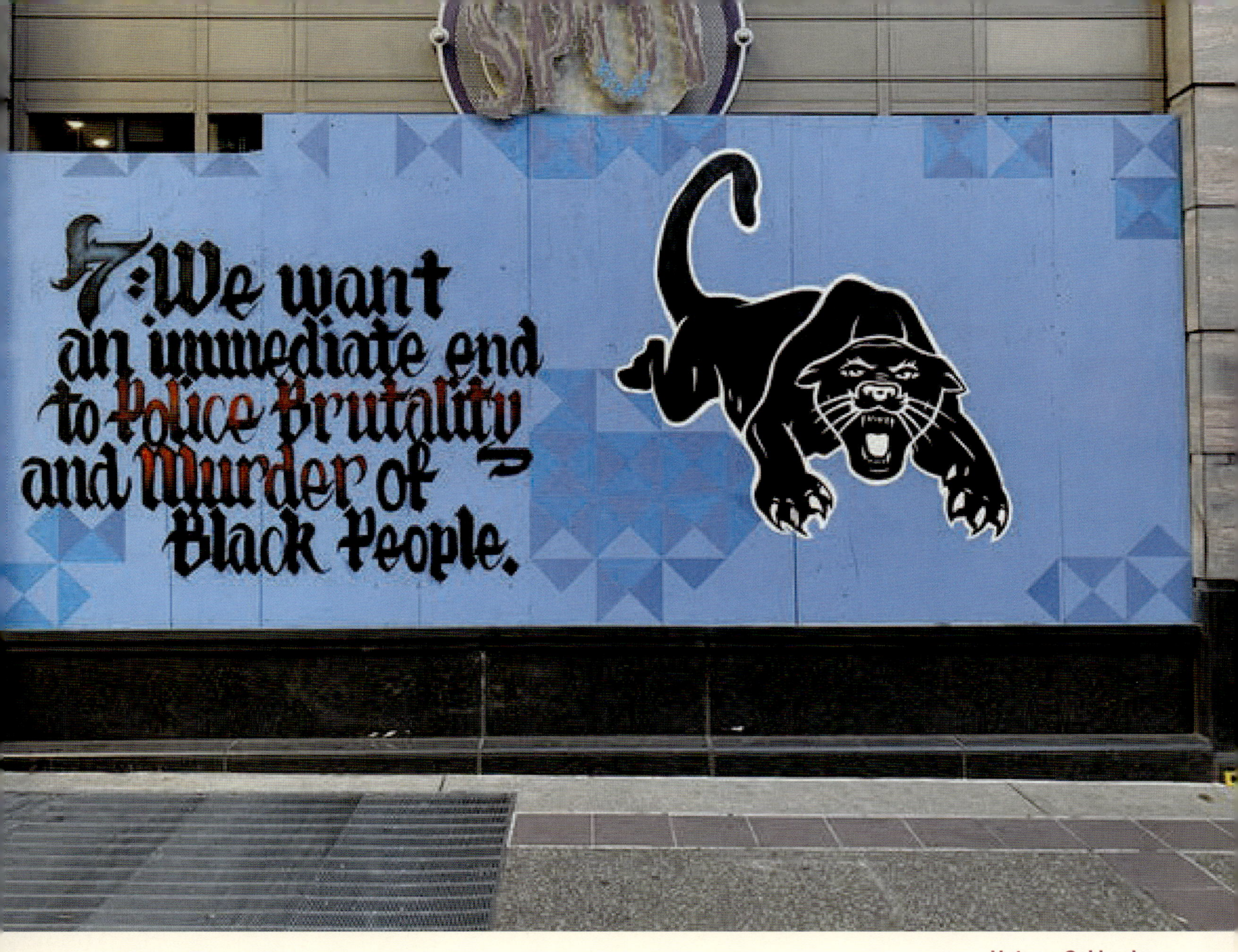


**Uptown Oakland**
Greyhound Bus Station
(Castro Street and San
Pablo Ave)

# Kufue

## @kemest510

For over two decades, Kufue has been providing Hip Hop culture to young people from California to the East Coast. He moved from the east coast in junior high and grew up painting in Oakland and the larger Bay Area. Since graduating from San Francisco State University with a degree in Behavioral Sciences in 2000, Kufue's professional trajectory has been consistently focused on inner city youth, from the ages of 12–21 years of age—providing youth development services and facilitating Hip Hop workshops and Ethnic Studies and Africana Studies classes in community and school settings, reaching the most disengaged youth. Kufue's straight-forward youth development approach, meeting the young people and their families where they are, and his engaging educational strategies, make him an effective practitioner, with many examples of transformation among the students he touches—reengaging them in the class room and redirecting their life journeys toward positive and healthy choices. All of this done through using spray can art and culture to create visual discourse for voices that have been silenced by systemic oppression.

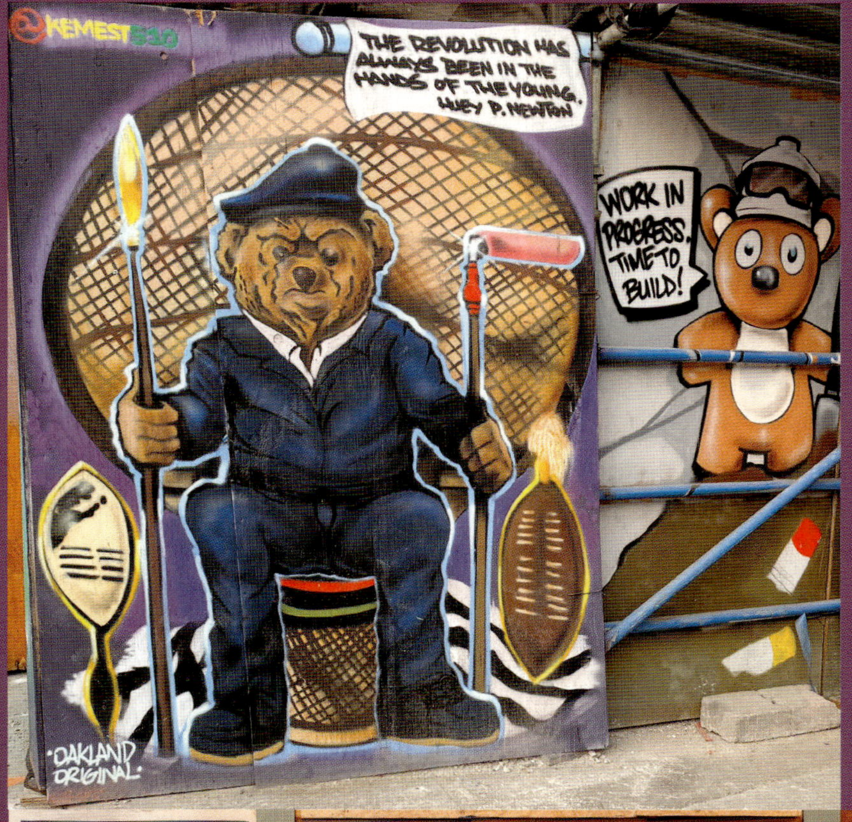


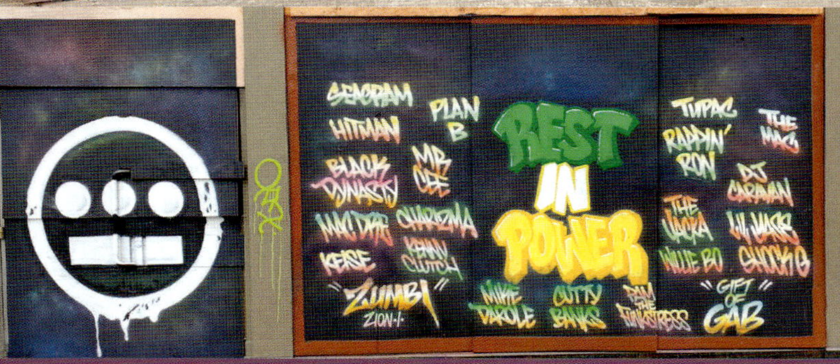

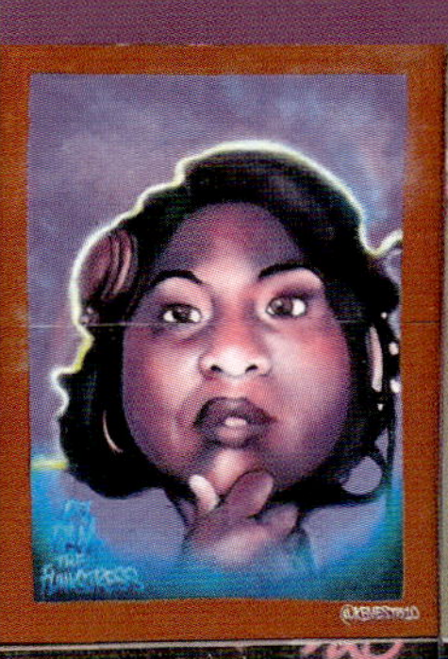

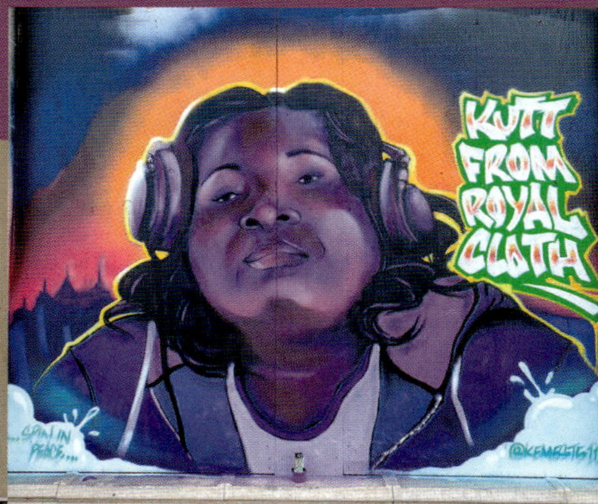

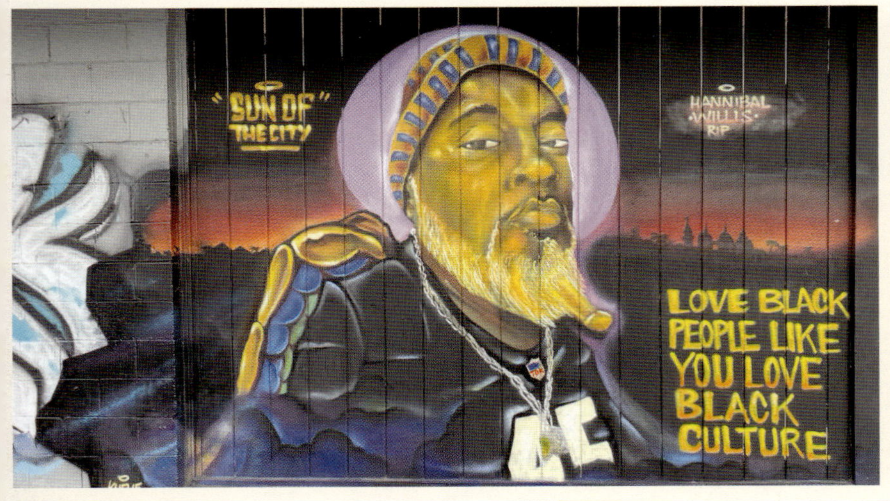


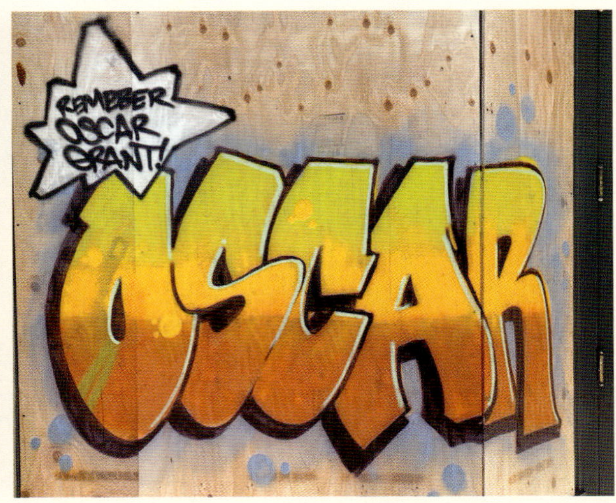


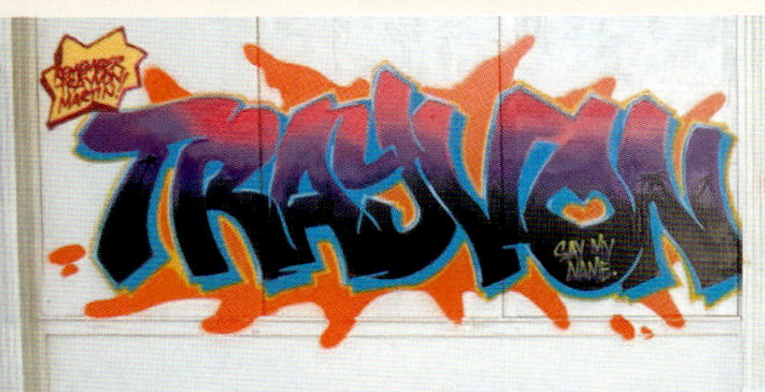


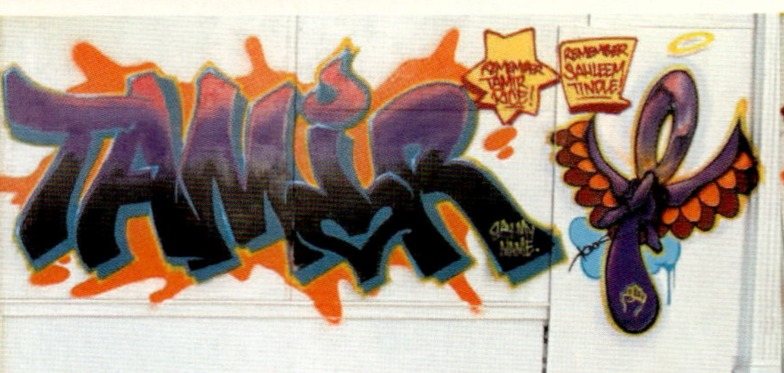


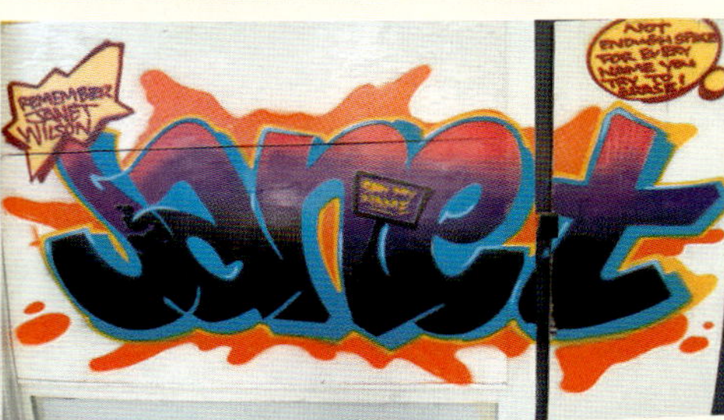


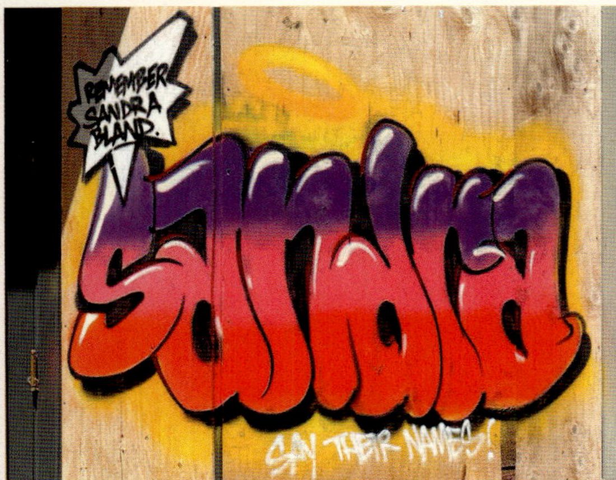


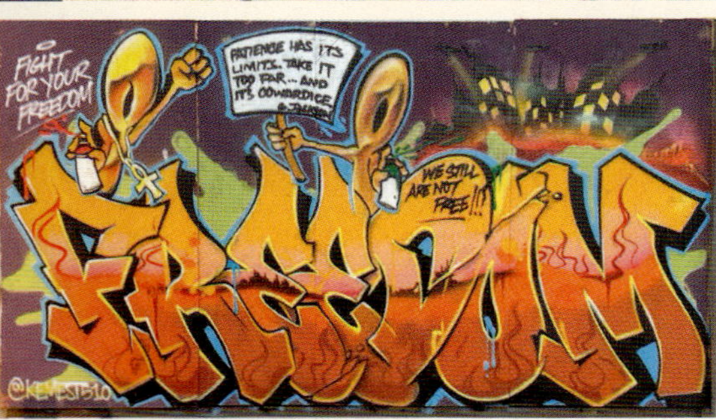


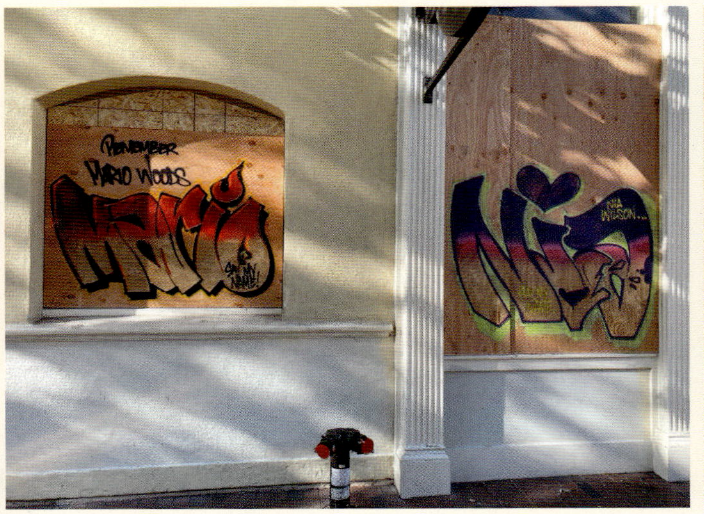


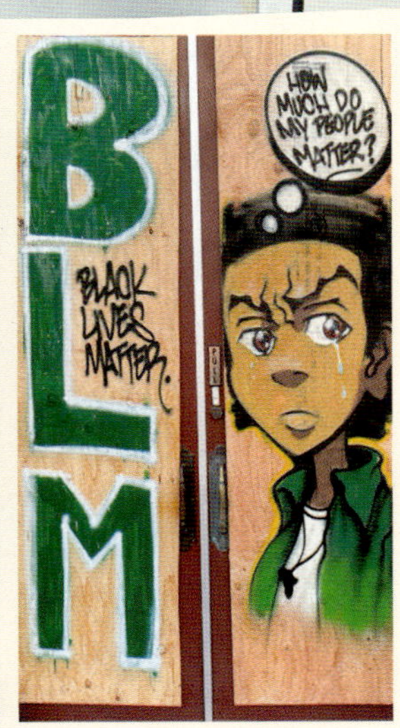


**Downtown Oakland**

# Shogun Shido

## @shogun-shido

*Shogun Shido is a mixed media creator currently residing in Oakland, California, with a primary focus in visual arts. Terrion's vision lies within their passion for ancestral arts, abstract expressionism, and storytelling. Throughout their life experience, they've faced a series of trials relating to fear, worry, and doubt. After having spent a period of time focusing on knowledge of self and projections of experience, they've realized they can use their creative platform to transmute that energy to promote love, power, wisdom. In doing so, they hope to create a spark of inspiration, promote positive living, and influence those who visually digest their creations to reflect these qualities onto themselves and others.*

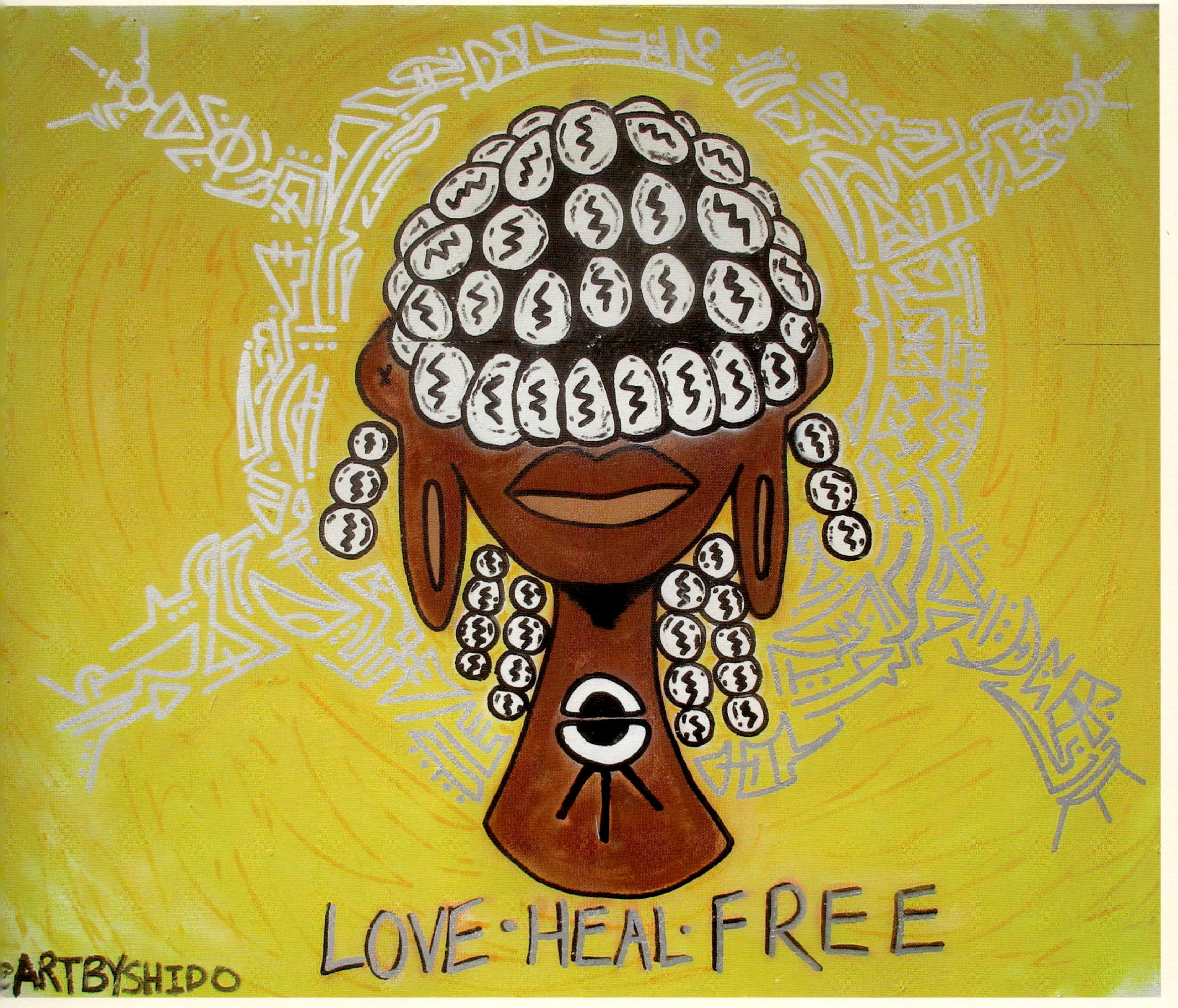

LOVE·HEAL·FREE
@ARTBYSHIDO

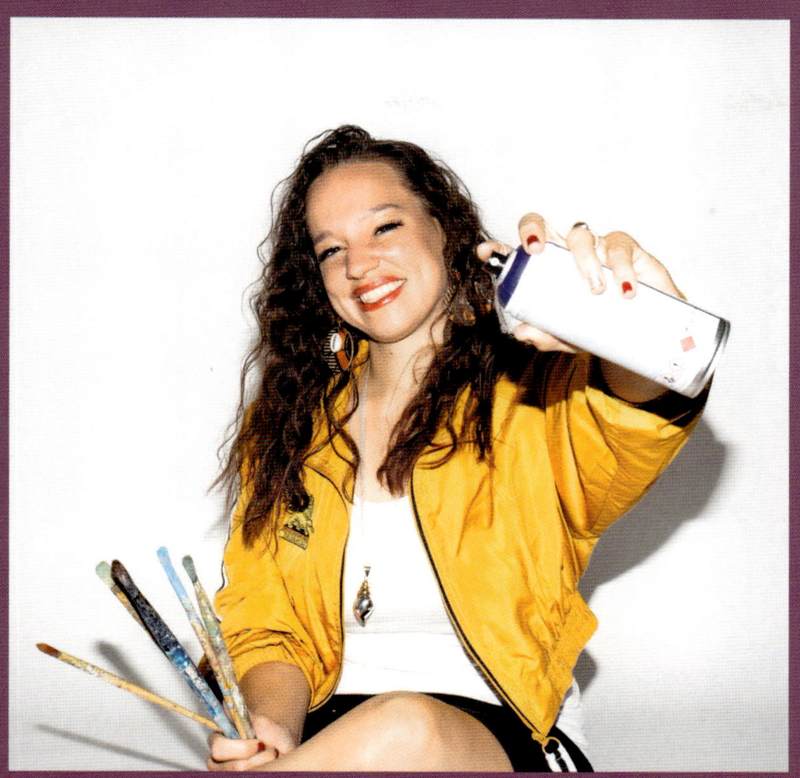

Keena Azania Romano exercises her creative mind through the exploration of diverse artistic mediums as a way to engage and understand individual and collective purpose. Romano received her BFA from Pomona College and then returned to her native Bay Area to pursue a career in the arts. Her murals can be spotted from Sacramento, California, to Oaxaca, Mexico. Inspired by cultural rituals and practices, Romano combines spirituality with urban experience to produce work that draws upon the quest for a greater understanding of intersectional beauty in this world. She fuses traditional native arts with contemporary inner-city techniques to reflect a new language that encourages the healing and empowerment process between community members and their environments. Her style is described as "vibrant and insightful." She aspires to travel and create a colorful trail of art by exploring the modern Diaspora based on her multi-ethnic experience.

# Keena Azania Romano

@lamakina510

**in collaboration with:**

## Leslie "Dime" Lopez

@ladimeuna

**and** @towand

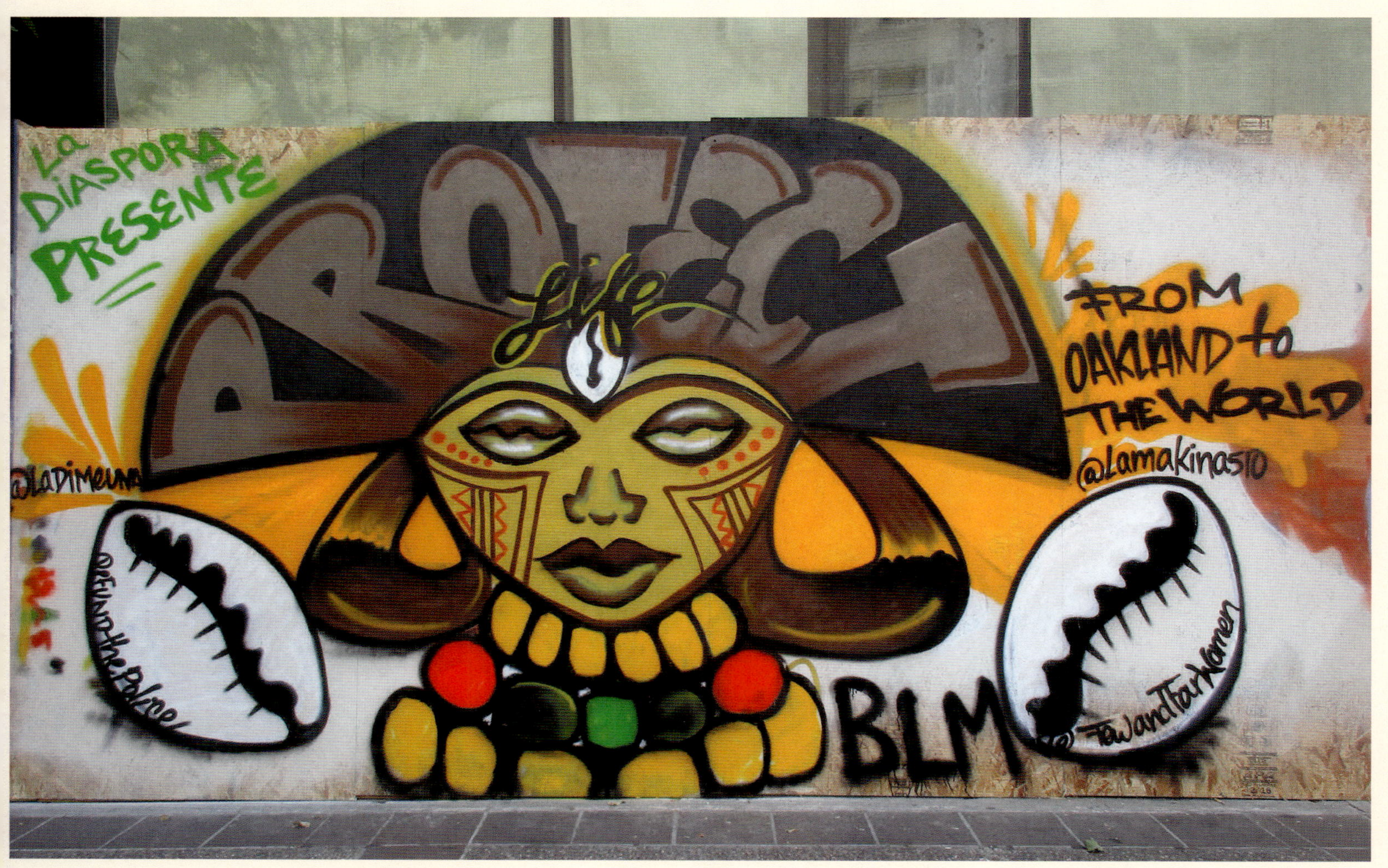


**Downtown Oakland**
19th and Broadway

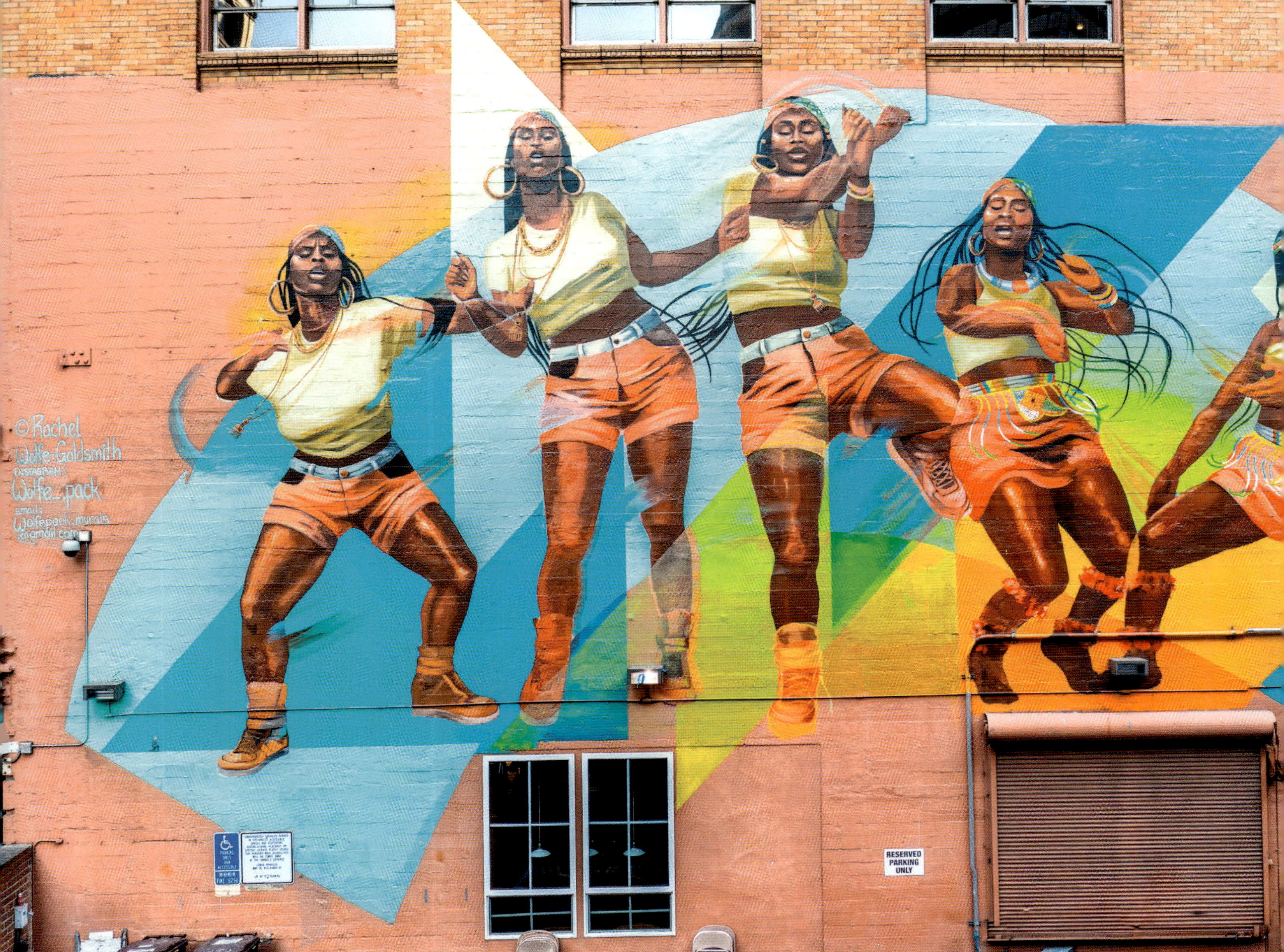


# Rachel Wolfe-Goldsmith

## @Wolfe_.pack

*Born January 13, 1991, Rachel is a fine art painter and muralist based in Oakland, California. Her education came from being immersed in life. She spent her early twenties traveling the United States and the world, building relationships with artists and mentors while painting*

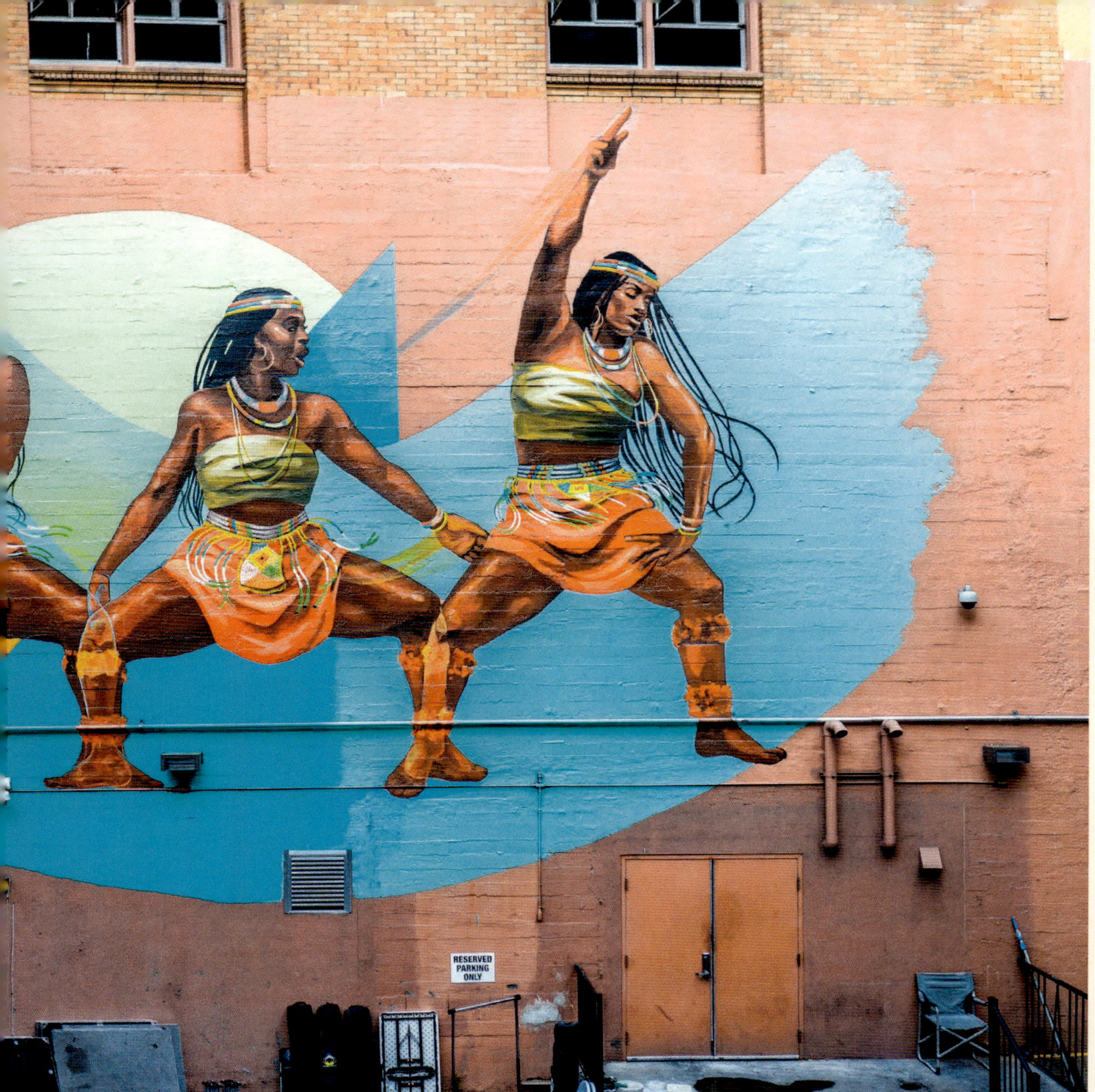



"Our Movement" was created in the wake of George Floyd's murder, and is meant to invoke joy, empowerment, and cultural celebration. Standing at 20 feet tall, a woman dances her way from being a modern woman into her ancestral roots. Located on one of the most historic buildings in the Oakland skyline, The Tribune Tower, this mural can't be missed.

*everywhere along the way. Rachel is a mixed-race, Jewish, queer woman who perceives the world through a broad range, her work reflects her diverse heritage. She is always rooting for the underdog and is interested in communicating a sense of freedom and empowerment through her work,*

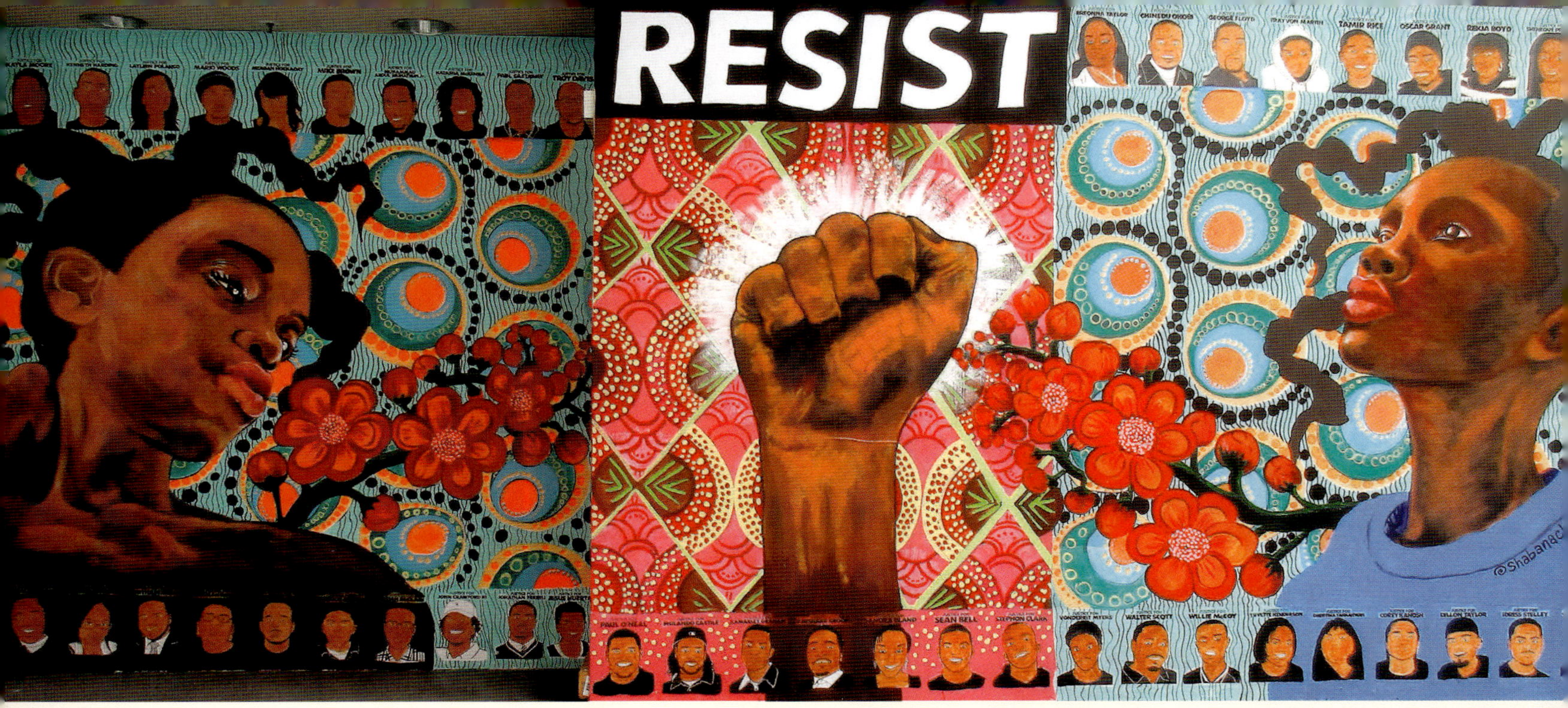

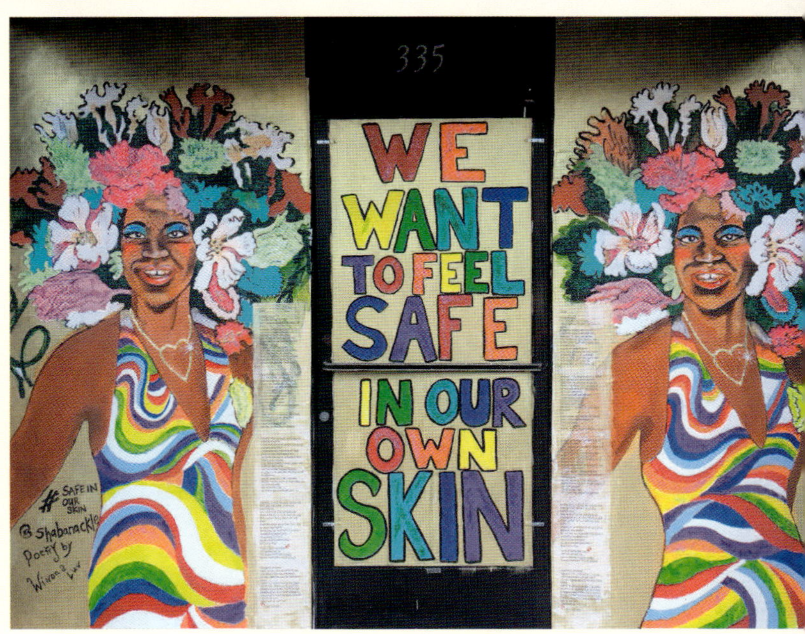


**Downtown Oakland**
Tribune Tower 411 13th street

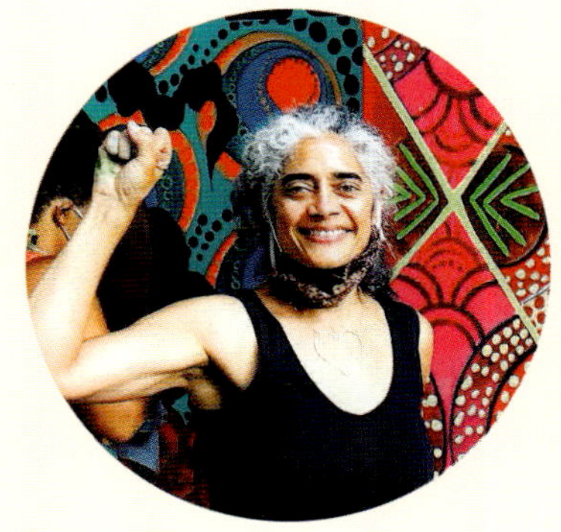

# Sharon Virtue

@shabanackle

**in collaboration with:**
**Winona Lewis**

@lewiswinonawinonaluv

**Downtown Oakland**
335 14th street

the mural "Safe in Our Own Skin," is
collaboration and features a poem b
Winona Lewis (see next page)

# dear Flower Child

hope of the future....us brown babies
swirl of bi-racial, mixed, whatever
freedom child through the passage of love and hope
free from the baggage of the story lines of separateness and disfunction
let us believe in the light passage of love that devours walls of division
why keep this funky old ignorant story alive of separation—better than, not enough?
are we so desperate to continue to lick our wounds, touch the sores, the trauma of separation and not belonging?
let's just drop it, the storyline and choose transformation
NOW!
ahhhh freedom.....
oh yeah, that's right!
we have to clear our ancestors bullshit
how I want to stream the divine spirit through my bones of togetherness...

then the chores—
picking up the quilt threads

keep our family's fortunes or choose poverty?
dive into—ANGER, INJUSTICE, SADNESS
then yes...unimaginable pure beauty and pride of the most beautiful kingdom on earth, our birth spot where it all began-
     our unimaginable divine right and purpose and home
the puppet strings gently pulling us to and fro off of our root foundation
we want to be seen and belong, to have a place at the table to lay our dreams
the seas are rough...
let's find the discipline and the courage to cut the sad ties of the past and live now, love now, create now!
heal our cellular memories by embracing all of our freckles and truly living in all parts of our spirit!
embodied deep, radiating self love!
because you know...
we do feel all of our parts so deeply!
Rainbow Flower Child
I'm talking to you—all of your magnificently beautiful YOU!
so deep and so rich
you inspire me so!
full blossom Flower Child
please continue to pop full of colorful surprise
smile as you look back to thank our ancestors for the heavy lifting and carrying of water
thank you for walking the road...
love, inspiration, activism, strength and long vision dream
sparkle some "gold dust" on us
all for equality and freedom because this is the way
together we got this
love you so...

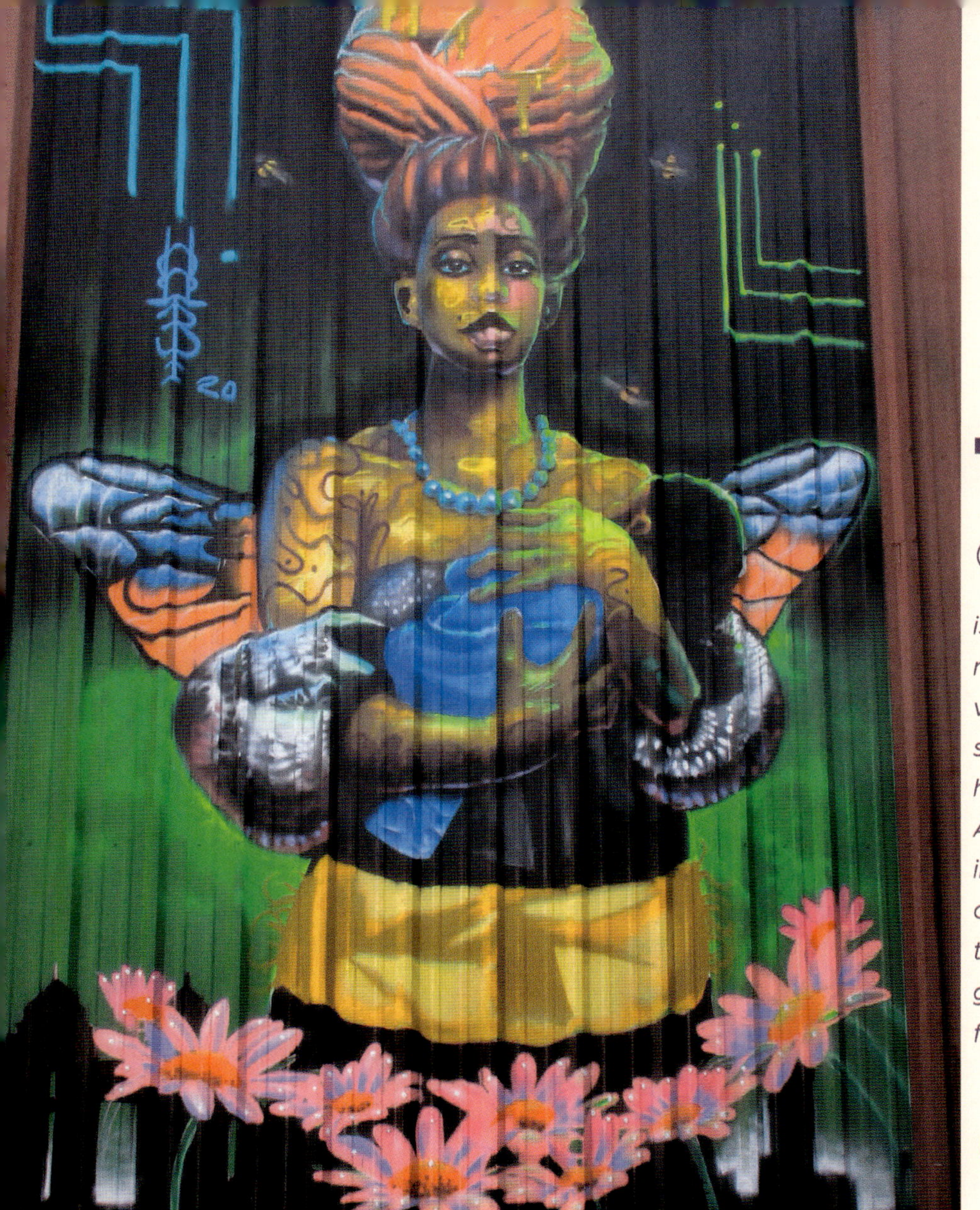

# Timothy B
## @ timothyb_art

*is a groundbreaking multimedia artist who is recognized internationally for pushing boundaries with vibrant murals and afro-indigenous illustrations. He's shaping the future of Oakland with work inspired by his afro-futuristic perception of reality along with his African ancestral background. His work creates an immersive experience empowering communities of color to embrace messages of peace and positivity that inspire change. The motivational words that guide him are that "anything is possible when love, faith, focus, and urgency are the foundation."*

**"Anything is possible when love, faith, focus, and urgency are the foundation."**

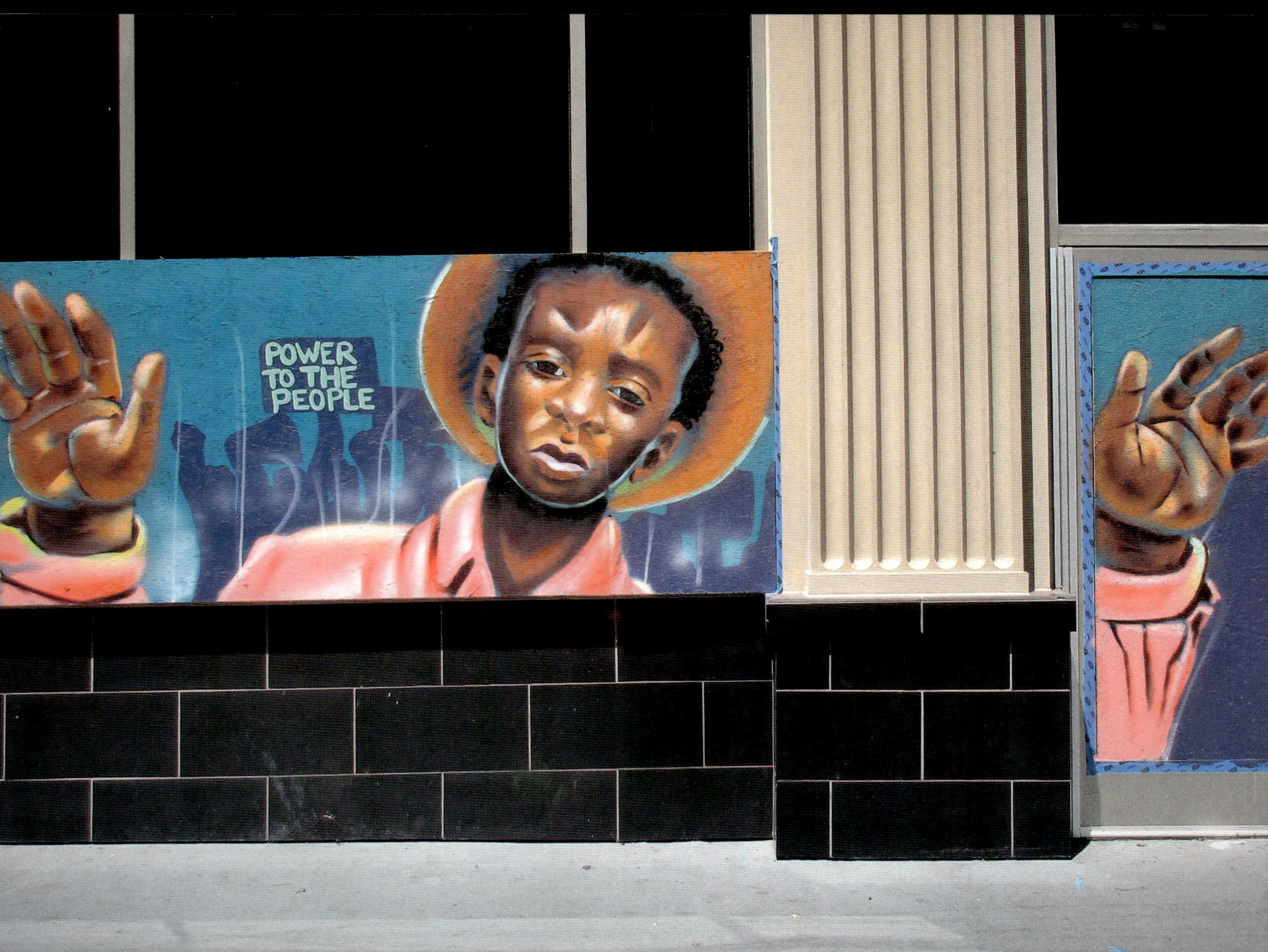



**Downtown Oakland**

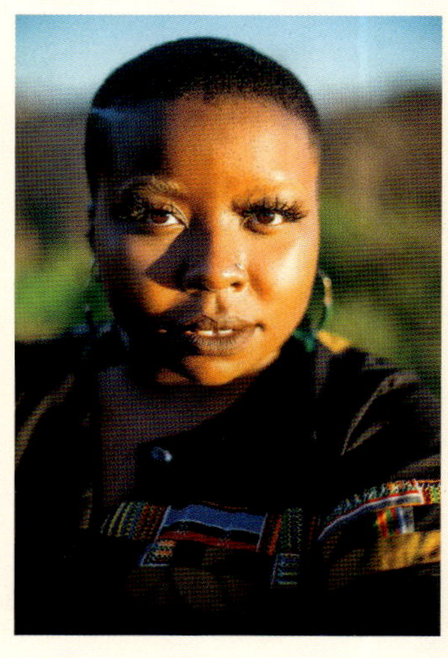

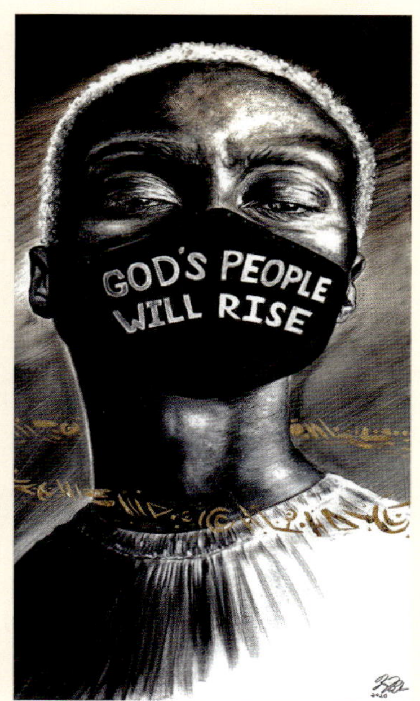


# Zoë Boston

## @ZoeAdiahBoston

*HER NAME IS ZOË BOSTON. Zoë is an artist in almost every sense of the word. She has been drawing for as long as she can remember but did not begin painting until she returned to the West Coast. Born in Los Angeles and raised in Upstate NY, she now resides in the Oakland Bay Area. Zoë's inspirations come from God, life, love, music, food, and everything in between.*

*She is dedicated to being true to herself, which in turn, transforms her work into passion on walls and canvas.*

> **"My goal has never been to be different. My goal is to be myself."**

Just being myself already makes me different. I believe there is a unique power in thriving in who you were created to be, because it will show in everything you do and create. There will never, in all of creation, and throughout time, be anyone like me or you again, so be yourself and love who you are! I enjoy the process of taking the ideas of various clients, and companies, and bringing them to life through murals! Each vibrant piece of work created leaves the environment with more life and in a better state than it was before. As far as what I do on canvas, I call it art to simplify the means of my expression. These pieces were birthed from the passions of life, living freely, being myself, and loving who I truly am. I express myself on walls and canvas and I continue to grow with each new piece. You are not just witnessing art, but pieces of my life's journey. I look forward to being able to share it with you!

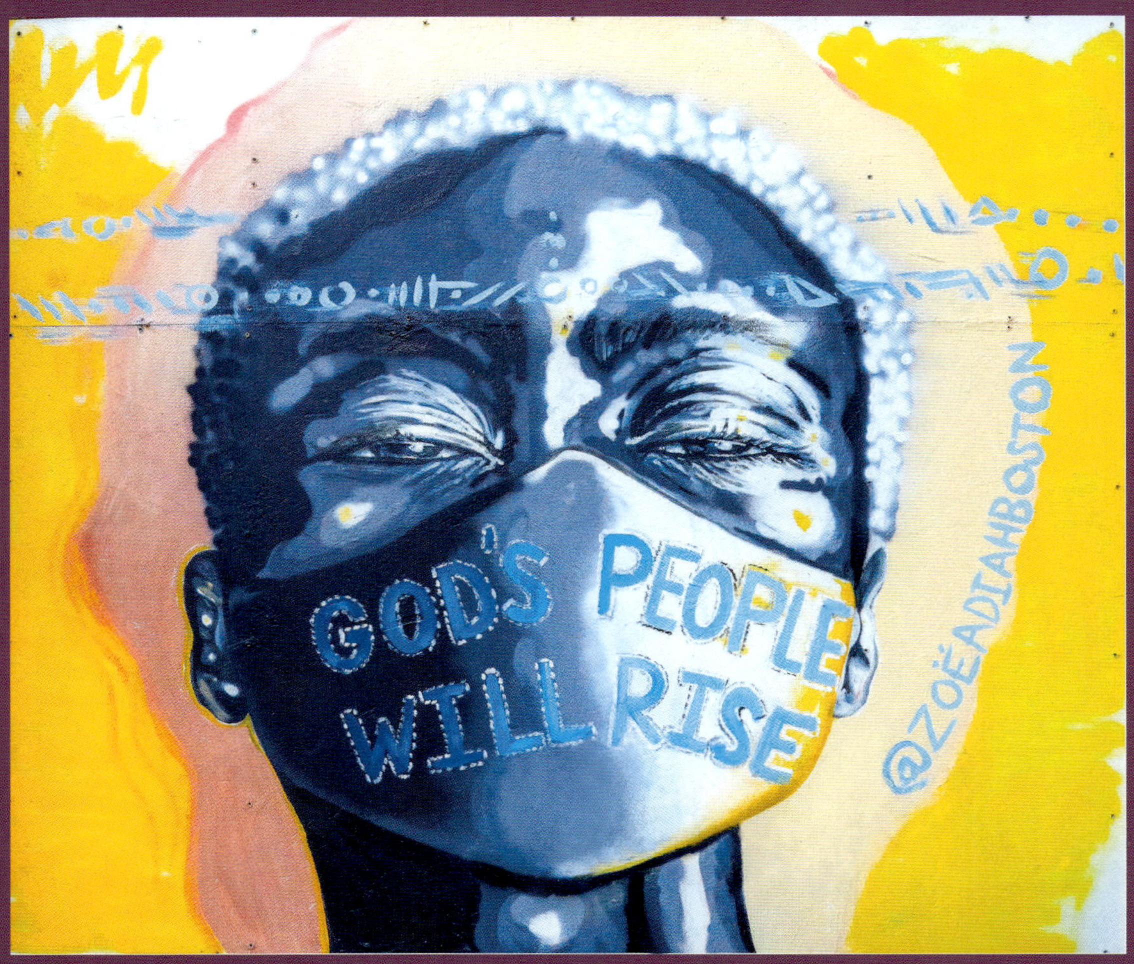


"As long as you take steps that are genuine and rooted in the community and work towards a goal of general elevation, the right doors for you to maximize your efforts will open up as you continue on that path. Don't be afraid to fully be yourself, fully love yourself, and fully embrace your true essence and, as a result, you will also be able to hold that same space for others. Keep going and don't give up. Your voice matters, so use it!"

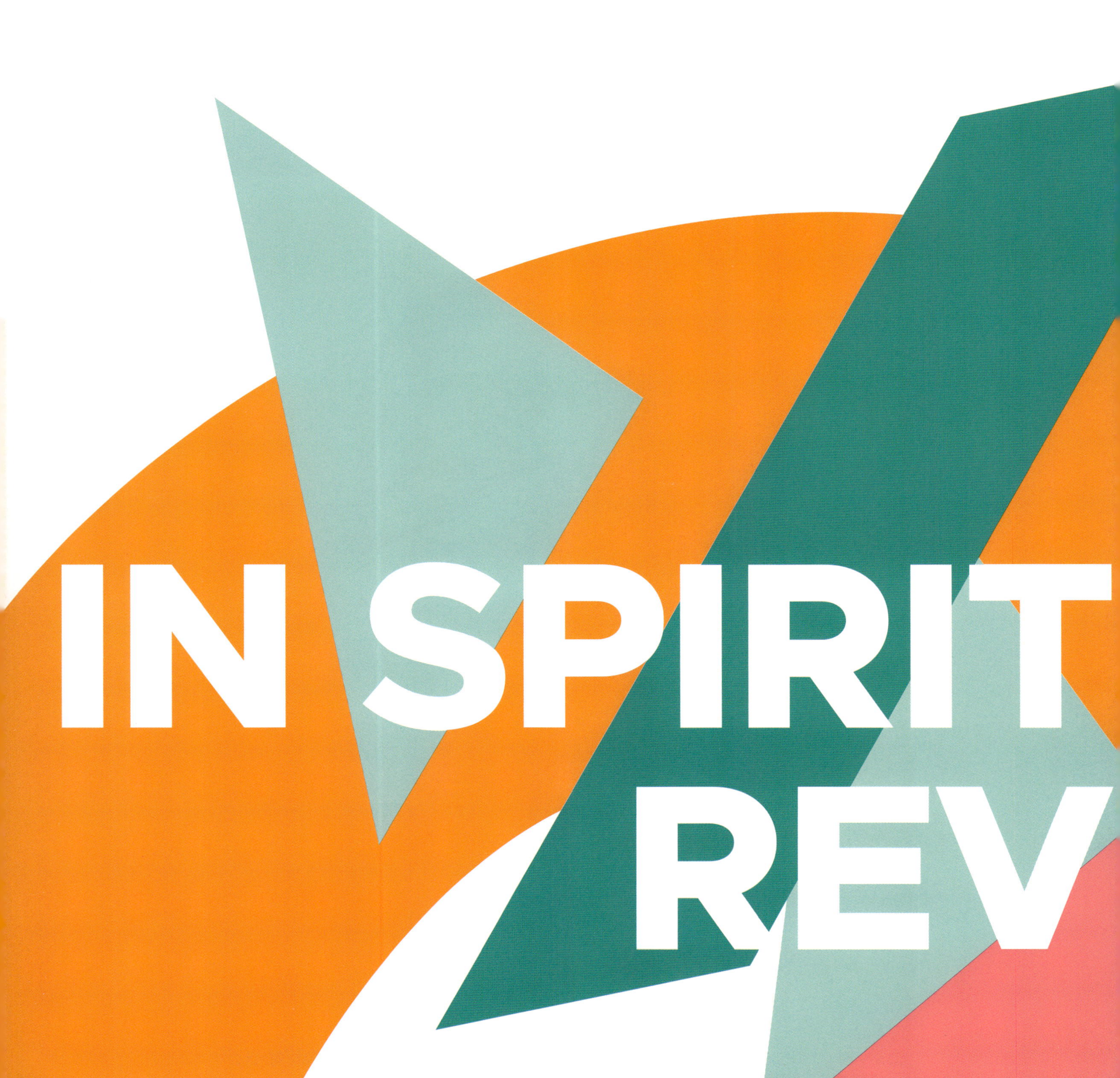

IN SPIRIT
REV

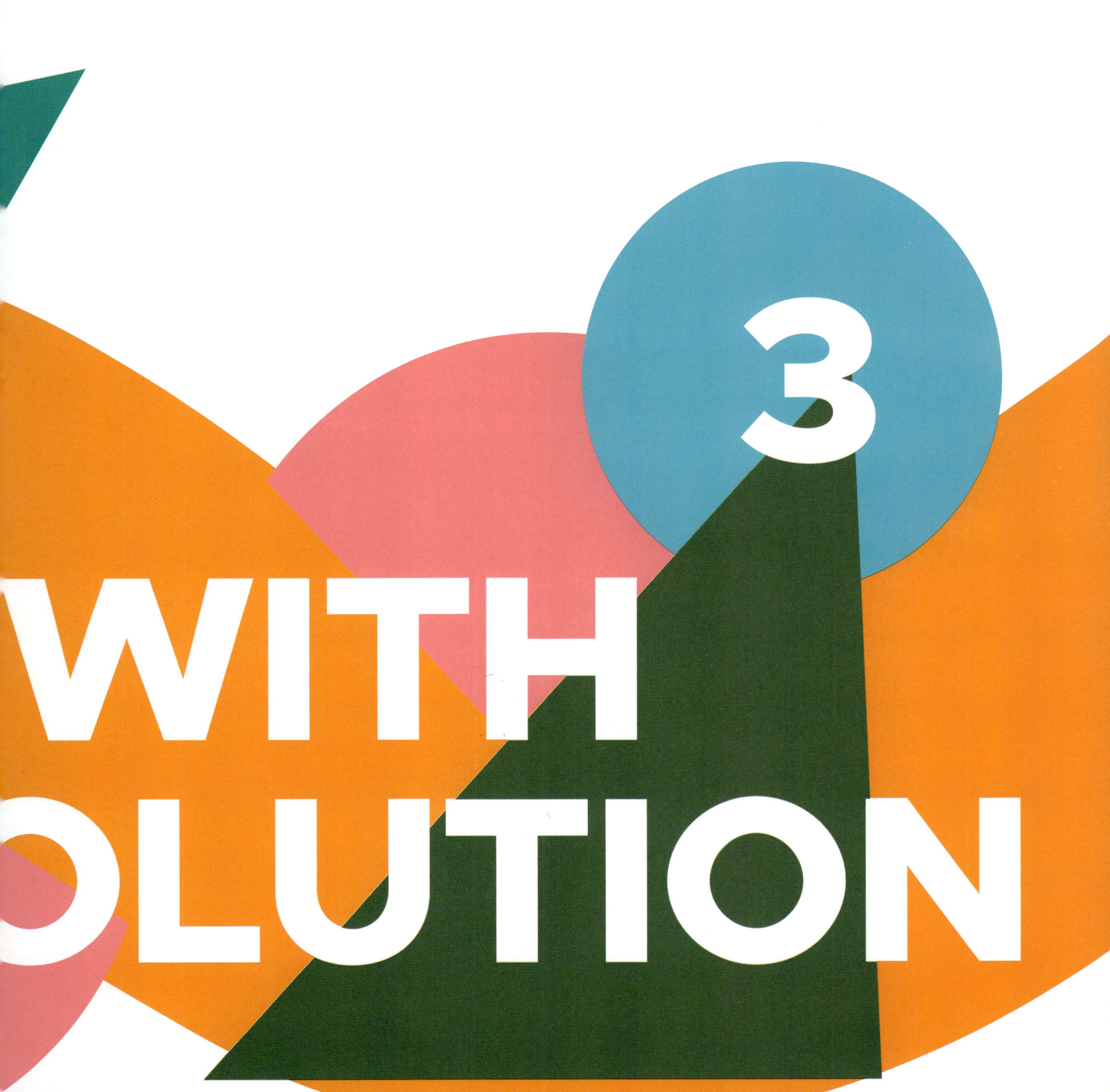
3
WITH
OLUTION

# In Spirit with Revolution

Interview with Emory Douglas
by Tongo Eisen-Martin

## Tongo Eisen-Martin:

*How would you describe life in the Bay Area in 1966? What was going on? What were the people facing?*

## Emory Douglas:

The climate was very intense during the '60s. Because you had police violence as you have today. [Murder and brutality] always being justified. Then you had Black ministers and preachers who would sit at the table with them [the police] to slow down the rebellions that were taking place. They were appointed leaders then...so-called.

That began to change when Black Consciousness came about. Then the people started talking about needing more variables in leadership. You had SNCC becoming more militant. You had the Black Arts Movement. You had the first or second BSU in the country organized at San Francisco State University...

(continued on next page)

At that time 40, 50, 100 people would be killed in those demonstrations by the National Guard. They would send the National Guard into the community. And you had people looting because of lack of resources; or on a deeper level knowing that they were being exploited. Liberating what they needed. And being killed in that process. There were battles back and forth. Gun battles that took place as well.

**Tongo:**
*You see today that we had uprisings, but uprisings in between periods of a mass political nihilism or really entrenched brainwashing. For a long time, politics are barely in everyday conversations. When you all took that evolutionary step, was it similar? Were the day in/day out conversations not about resistance and then things kicked up?*

*Or do you think that people were more primed for involvement back then? Was resistance on people's minds more?*

**Emory:**
It was on young people's minds. The injustice and murders were being discussed. There were debates that were going on in junior college campuses and what have you. And those who had revolutionary consciousness were seeing what was going on with the student movements in South America. And what was going on in Palestine. And there were those who had perspective on what solidarity was about. But that wasn't on a major scale yet.

I think when the Panthers came on the scene, you never had anything like that before. A young Black organization picking up arms, using the law in relationship to patrolling and being able to articulate the law. Pointing out the contradictions of what the government was doing and should have been doing. We were able to capture the masses' attention through the social programs and through self-defense. Critiquing and criticizing those who were sitting on the fence. And getting the attention of the mainstream media. Having those in that Hollywood class, that elite class, who maybe after being blacklisted during the McCarthy era, support us. This organization was a broad youth organization all through the country. Transcending borders as well. I think that brought another level of awareness and consciousness. And support of the people. Even those who talked in public about self-defense as something they wouldn't go along with, behind the scenes, it was a totally different story.

**Tongo:**
*So where the hell did you all come from? How was it possible?*

**Emory:**
I think we caught them off guard at the right time; at the right moment.

**Tongo:**
*How did you touch down in the Party? What brought you in?*

**Emory:**
I was in the Black Arts Movement as an individual in that

wave. Marcus Books printed some of the first political posters that I did. I went to City College of San Francisco and took up commercial art. Which is production art. Hank Jones, who eventually was one of the San Francisco 8, myself, and some others got together to figure out what we were going to do. We were youngsters trying to figure out how to deal with the issues. And a brother in our group said he heard of some brothers that were patrolling in Oakland. But nobody knew much about them at that time.

One day, Hank was going to this meeting. At this time, you had many formations of the Black Panther Party beginning to start. Coming from the south where the symbol comes from. He was going to one of these meetings where they were planning to bring Malcolm X's widow to the Bay Area to honor her. Hank contacted me and asked me if I would come to the meeting and do the poster for the event. And I agreed.

When I went to the meeting, they said there were some brothers coming over who were going to do security. When they came over, it was Little Bobby Hutton, Huey, and Bobby. After that meeting I asked them how I could join. They gave me a card with their number on it. I started catching the bus over to Huey's house. He would show me around the neighborhood. We would go to Bobby's house. That was my first involvement transitioning into the Black Panther Party.

**Tongo:**
*How would you describe the political development of yourself and others once you were in the party?*

**Emory:**
People come in on different levels. Everybody is not going to be one of these intellectual, political giants like Huey or Bobby. People come in because they want change. As they develop, they come to understand what is happening on a deeper level.

Huey and Bobby understood that on a grassroots level those brothers and sisters who were out there in the street on a daily basis; even though they may have been into illegitimate capitalism, were the ones being confronted and brutalized the most. Profiled. Stopped. Jacked up. Talked to out their names. Beaten down. So they were the ones who understood. A lot of them gravitated to the Party based on Huey and Bobby articulating what was the cause of all of what they were suffering.

Huey and Bobby came up with the Ten-Point program. Garvey had one. Nation of Islam had one. But how they wanted to structure and frame it was totally different.

It attracted those youngsters to the party. Fifteen, sixteen, seventeen years old who were out there in the hood. But had some consciousness and determination; and wanted to do something. They gravitated to the organization.

**Tongo:**
*How would you say your art evolved during that period?*

**Emory:**
It was a reflection of the Ten-Point program. It evolved as the Party evolved. You had people who were not in the Party get the Panther paper; and they could tell what direction the politics of the Party was going just by seeing how the art was shifting.

Initially, it was self-defense. It was called the Black Panther Party for Self-Defense. I started with the pig drawing. The pig was the first one. Then in 1968, the name shifted to the Black Panther Party. That was when Huey was incarcerated. Then we had art showing solidarity with people's struggles around the world. Black men and women resisting, showing all aspects of oppression and fighting against it. Artwork that dealt with the social programs. But in any given phase, aspects of every phase of struggle were there.

I also made art out of what we were experiencing. One time, Kathleen, Eldridge, and I had been out organizing, and we came back to the house where he lived on Fell Street [in San Francisco]. At midnight, I was just getting ready to leave and there was a knock. Eldridge asked who it was and they said they were the San Francisco Police. Eldridge said, "Do you have a warrant?" They said no. He said, "Well, you're gonna have to kick the door in." And they proceeded to kick the door in. They were looking for guns to violate Eldridge's parole and send him back to prison. There had been threats on Kathleen's life, so she could legally get a gun. The gun there was in her name. I did a cartoon around that incident.

But ultimately my art was about listening. Hearing what was going on and getting the feeling of what people were feeling. Then I expressed that through the art; captured that in art form. That's what I was fortunately able to do. The art itself took on a life of its own. The pig drawings transcended the Black Panther Party; became a national and international symbol. Went beyond boundaries became a world symbol in the context of identifying those who were abusing their power and abusing the people. A universal symbol in the sense of how power was used to define the oppressor and those who were oppressing us. I couldn't believe it. You even had some people who we would call bootlickers. They liked the work. It was transcendent.

**Tongo:**
*Your art could never have been alienated from the struggle, but at the same time, having to put so much time in, what was that dance between the struggle activities and the art activities? How did they work together? Did they contradict?*

**Emory:**
As we evolved, we lived in collectives. We were committed to the organization. We had structure. We had responsibilities.

It was never quite easy, but "you got me and I got you." Huey always used to say though, "Give Emory his space. He needs time to create and design."

You had others who admired the work, but they wanted expediency. They wanted it right now. I had to balance that, too. During the production work, it wasn't just the newspaper. I also had to work on stuff concerning the health clinics and for the school. Or if there was some kind of action we were doing and we needed to put out information. So you had to deal with all those things as well as the community printing we were doing. You had to figure out how to get it all done.

**Tongo:**
*What was your approach? Were you relaxed or were you digging in?*

**Emory:**
Well, I was relaxed once my cadre developed. You have to understand that in the beginning, it was just myself. We had what we called those "colossal events." Sacramento. When Huey got shot and the policeman got killed. People wanted to join the party. We had to figure out who these people were. Setting up these chapters. Having the political education classes. Evaluating our work and how we could improve it. At the same time, you got fundraising going on at certain levels. Talking with Hollywood types and others who wanted to donate and make contributions to the organization. But once my cadre developed, it took some of the pressure off.

**Tongo:**
*Your art emphasized the foundational heroism of women in the revolution. And you created some really strong heroic women figures in the art. Can you speak to that?*

**Emory:**
We used to study and look at the struggles around the world. The Cubans had women in the revolution. African liberation movements had women in their revolutions. In Vietnam, you had women intricately integrated into the resistance. Same thing in Palestine. We were inspired by that. Not in the context of trying to duplicate, but being in spirit with.

**Tongo:**
*You all didn't pull any punches. What were the impacts that you all had on mass culture?*

**Emory:**
We were radical. We were beyond. But we had a language. A powerful language. Street language. Integrating the politics into a street language that people could understand.

**Tongo:**
*Some Panthers were Vietnam War war veterans. How did they come to the party?*

*Today there is an abundance of soldiers because we have basically had perpetual war since 9/11. What would that outreach look like now?*

**Emory:**

It has to come out of what exists. You can be inspired by and be informed about what took place in the past, but you can't duplicate it in that context. So it has to come out of what exists today. You couldn't do some of the stuff that we did back then. They would wipe you off the map. They would call you terrorists. The Vietnam veterans came into the Party because they realized that they were fighting the wrong war. Geronimo Ji Jaga, he talked about it when he was in the infantry. He was in a plane. And they want him to shoot people in Detroit. Veterans became informed and enlightened by the devastation that they were unfortunately involved in. That's one of the ways that we were able to get houses. They were able to get GI loans. We took those GI loans and bought houses. They were the ones that helped us secure our locations. They wouldn't have survived a 16-hour stand-off and five-hour shoot-out in LA if there were not veterans in there who understood stuff.

**Tongo:**

*What was the early life of the paper?*

**Emory:**

I was able to do production work on the paper because that's what I was taking up at City College. I took up commercial art; learning production skills, how to put publications together. If I took up fine art, I may have been a fine artist, but I wouldn't have been able to work on the paper.

We wanted to have a lot of photographs, artwork, and big captions in the paper so that those who weren't going to read the long articles could still get the gist of what was going on. We also made the captions big enough for the seniors to read. The first issue was in early April 1967. Not long after, I go to the Black House one evening. Eldrige is leaving. And he says, "We're going to Sacramento tomorrow. Do you want to go?" I said, "Yeah." He said, "Well, I'll be here at 7 o'clock so we can meet up with everybody in Oakland." So now the second issue of the paper is about going to Sacramento.

**Tongo:**

*That's the second issue?*

**Emory:**

That's the second issue—the first "tabloid" issue of the Black Panther newspaper is [about] Sacramento. We had a meeting before we went where it was explained why Bobby was going and leading the delegation. Huey wasn't going because they felt like it was gonna be a "colossal event." A lot of activity around it. With the press there and what have you. And setting up this young organization, we needed somebody to stay back to talk about why we went. And so that was why Huey didn't go and Bobby did. What people didn't seem to see was that there were a lot of men and women in that delegation. You see the men. But you had the Denzel Dowell family. Some of them went. Some of his sisters and brothers went. Bobby Seale's first wife, Artie Seale was a part of that delegation as well. We had Mark Comfort; brother who introduced Bobby to the Denzel Dowell's family. Who felt that the Panthers could help them. He also was a civil rights activist in the south and knew the historical context of the Panther. Folks from East and West Oakland.

**Tongo:**

*There are some groovy radical publications these days, but can you speak on the importance of a publication being tied to an actual organization?*

**Emory:**

It's better if it is because you want everybody, whether they're tied to the organization or not, to be able to talk and reflect on what needs to be done.

That was the important thing about the Black Panthers—we were the vanguard organization. We led by example. We had the vision. You had people who were inspired by that vision. That began to stimulate ideas. What you're doing is you're spreading the message, regardless of how much an individual was going to participate. But gave them a vision of how to participate.

**Tongo:**

*What was the influence that Malcolm X had on you all?*

**Emory:**

Bobby and Huey would always talk about the influence [of Malcolm X]. They identified with Malcolm. Even more so after he came back from Mecca. Because then he had a broader scope and perspective. They were inspired by him. We used to play Ballot or the Bullet in our office on Fillmore on loud speakers all day long at people trying to get down the street.

**Tongo:**

*As politics were becoming more militant back then, what was the strategy you all arrived at?*

**Emory:**

Early on, some organizations were talking about starting the struggle from the underground. But Huey would say that's not what we are going to do. He mentions that in "To Die for the People." He says if you go underground and the people don't know who you are, they are not going to support you. They are just going to look at you as a terrorist. And they are going to say, "We not supporting terrorists." So he said we are going to have the social programs, enlighten and educate people about who we are and what needs to be done. He said people are going to gravitate towards those who serve their interests.

**Tongo:**

*What were some of the biggest challenges for the Party?*

**Emory:**

In the early days, it was the intensity of the patrols. And you had challenges when Huey got shot and the Free Huey movement started.

**Tongo:**

*What year was that escalation of police antagonizing you?*

**Emory:**

By late '67/early '68. Before Eldridge left the country and before Lil Bobby was murdered.

**Tongo:**

*How was it living with that intensity of attack
from police?*

**Emory:**

You know they will try to do terrible things to you, but you're
still committed. You are just committed to what you're doing.
Now of course you had people who can only go so far in the
context of external repression. That is understood. But for
the most part, we continued doing what we were going to do.
And it wasn't like we were just sitting there, lame ducks. They
knew that we would defend ourselves. Defend ourselves if it
was favorable, and we would put our hands up when it wasn't.

**Tongo:**

*That is a lot of heat to organize in spite of.*

**Emory:**

You had to be a little crazy; whether you knew you were crazy
or not. But it wasn't like we were in isolation. We always had
some civil rights and human rights support that were always
there. And we set the table by having great communicators
who came into the Party like Kathleen Cleaver and Eldridge.
Great articulators like Bobby and Huey. You had publications,
magazines, universities, wanting them to come talk; laying
out the Ten-Point platform. Being invited around the world by
different liberation movements because like I said, this never
happened before in this country. Black organization, young
people. And we were inspiring people around the world. You
had Dalit Panthers in India who were inspired by the Panthers.
You have the Polynesian Panthers; who actually came out to
the 50-year anniversary and stayed in my home.

**Tongo:**

*If you are up to it, can you speak
about the decline?*

**Emory:**

Well number one, you have to understand that there were
external forces always playing on our limitations, on the fact
we were young. You had state infiltration orchestrating things
like the murder of Fred Hampton. This young brother steals
a car and takes across state lines. Now he has a federal beef.
They make a deal with him to infiltrate the Chicago chapter
and he becomes a higher-up security; then he sets up the
whole assassination of Fred Hampton and Mark Clark; and
sets up other Panthers to be shot.

**Tongo:**

*What can an organization not do without?
What does an organization need to do and to
have in order to be effective?*

**Emory:**

You have to have constructive evaluation. See how you can
improve it, make it work better. Having political education
classes, those kinds of things. Being in tune with what's going
on in the real world. You have to constantly be aware of your
limitations and your shortcomings and try to overcome those
things. Have a system in place to overcome internal obstacles
to moving forward.

**Tongo:**

*What was a good way of instilling discipline to deal with the growing tasks?*

**Emory:**

That was a big part of the political education classes. And also part of discipline was critiquing. Analyzing our work. The Little Red Book had a lot of universal principles that we applied.

When we started chapters and branches, those who wanted to start a chapter or branch had to come to the Bay Area. And they had to sit in on the political education class, to see how things were done. They had to go out and sell the paper; all of that to get a feel. If it felt like they weren't the right ones, then we didn't allow them to start the chapter. If they were right for it, we would send people from headquarters to check it out, observe how they were set up and what they were doing. There had to be a uniformity of things that took place in each chapter. They had to carry out what was done at central headquarters—political education classes, and critiquing, criticism, self-criticism, all those things, evaluations of the work. Overcoming internal contradictions—all the squabbles—you have to do all those things.

There were always shifts. We used to read Frantz Fanon and the Red Book. All kinds of reading and critiquing and evaluating. You had people talking so much intellectual theory, Huey said, "Well, now we have to put down those books and go out there and put it into practice." We were getting caught up in theoretical things with no practice in the real world. There's always shifts too, in being one with the people. We thought there was going to be the revolution, and that the people were going to join in and start shooting and defending themselves,

and that didn't happen, and it just became the police and the Panthers in these shootouts with the community on the sidelines saying, "Right on." Huey would say, "Well it's time to put down the guns, take off them uniforms, and become one with the people."

**Tongo:**

*What do you think about this current political reality with the uprisings? What's your analysis of these movements and what is your prescription?*

**Emory:**

You have some powerful scenes. But you don't have any organizations to come behind that and reinforce it. People are being confronted by a beast that they thought didn't exist. And other people are not inspired by the resistance they see. They think of themselves as being a part of the system. When repression comes down, it blows their minds. They can't deal with it.

Some people want to do something about it, but they don't have the discipline. We're dealing with Americanism. We're dealing with people being Americanized. So you have to develop that discipline in an organization. So it's not just an individual engaging struggle by themselves. And it's through an organizational structure that embraces a broader scope that you can have the discipline required for struggle.

The analysis is that now you are living in a whole different time than when there were the Black Panthers. You have 50 years since it started. The system has studied its demise. And have think tanks on how to make sure that it never happens again.

We have to break the chains of a Western colonial mindset, and that's a process. This is a racist, bigoted country but it has manipulated people into believing that it isn't. People believe that it can be reformed. People have to decide if social justice is to truly help others or to be integrated into the exploitative system.

**Tongo:**

*What would be your advice to revolutionary artists today?*

**Emory:**

A revolutionary artist is about change. That's what they have to understand. What change means to you. What contribution do you want to make to change? I was part of an organization. So everything that came about, came out of that collective living. I carried that collectivity on as I evolved. You've got creative folks now and they have to determine what contribution they can make on a consistent basis and how they can come together collectively.

**Tongo:**

*You're a revolutionary still in motion in a way that probably no other figure from that time has gotten to be having your art have a modern engagement. What does it say about the visual medium that it has this kind of timeless quality to it?*

**Emory:**

I think it expresses a feeling, a connection, and captures the invisible aspect of what people see and feel and touch and think. It just has that link between those who are struggling today and yesterday. That's the only way I can explain it because it came out of this movement that already had great communicators. I was listening and interpreting that spirit of resistance and defiance and being provocative in ways that never were before. I think deep down people felt that way and they got to see it not only being talked about, but put into practice at the same time.

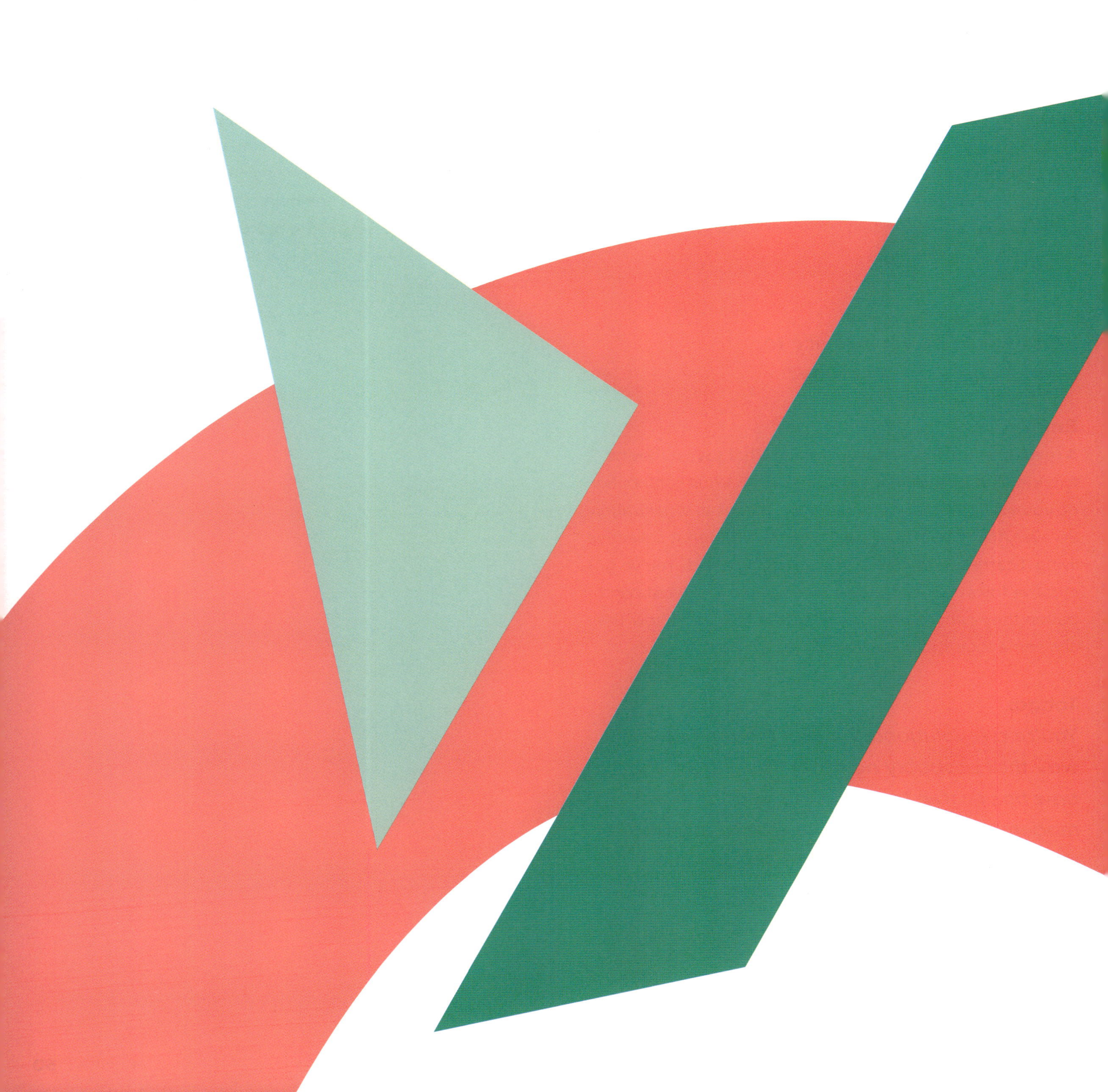

# MURALS

4

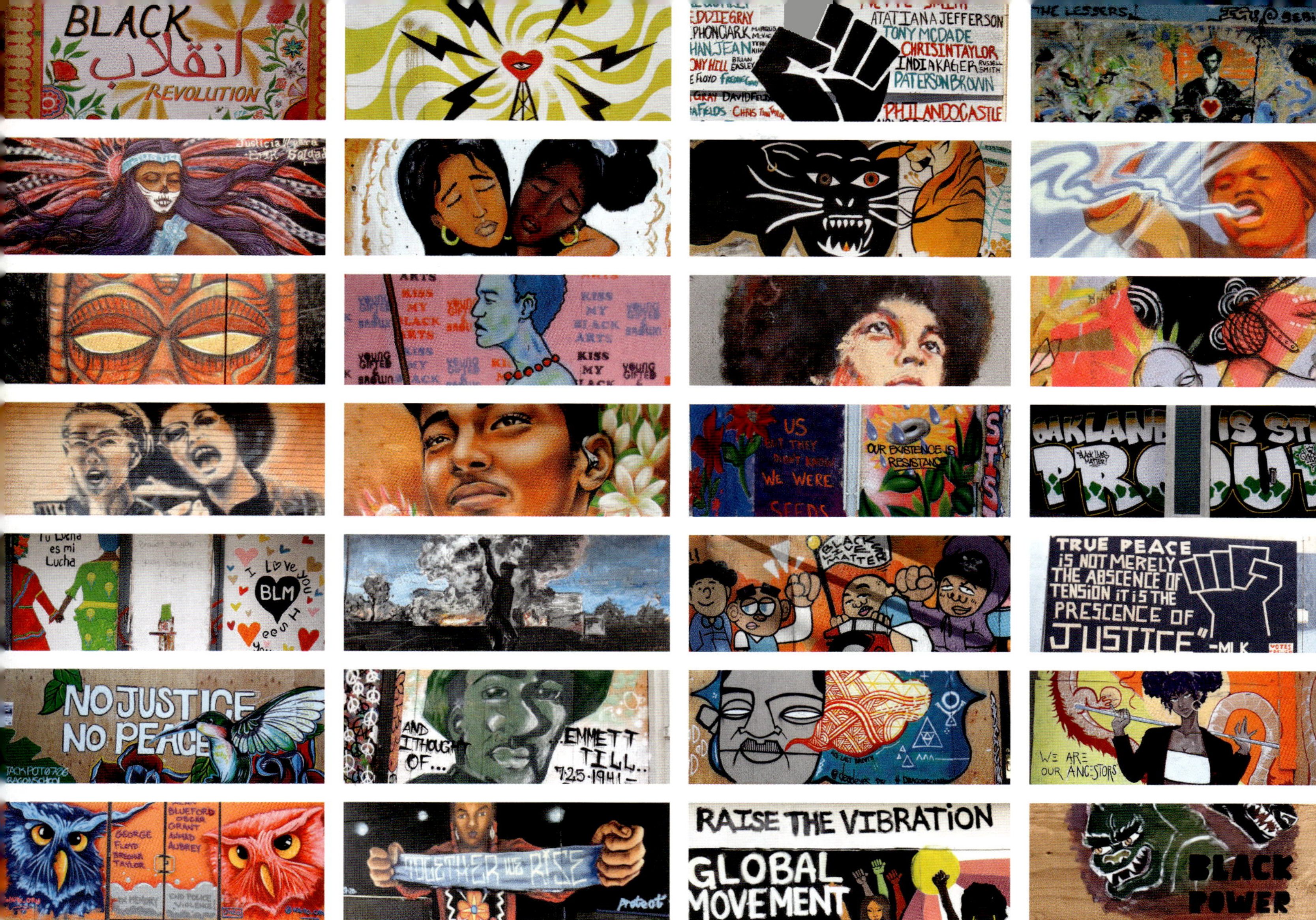

**With much love and thanks to Patricia Garcia, Kari Barnes, Edsel Rivera, and Eddie Kochiyama for allowing us to reproduce these photo**

1. @kakikasi @mirzazeher @fragrant _hawa **2.** TEM Banditas **3.** Unknown **4.** @sebity **5.** @panchopescador **6.** @jackieq_designs
**7.** @spatchgela @peweezey @nabeaner **8.** @wolfe_.pack **9.** @worthyfoe **10.** @lacocinaloca **11.** @jaroldcadionart
**12.** @paloma_in_black **13.** @rchoi.art **14.** @misterbouncer **15.** @shishimadriz @ireneshiori **16.** delPhresh
**17.** i.luv Phoenix (upcoming second grader) **18.** Unknown **19.** @darinpaints **20.** Unknown **21.** @Jackpot0706  **22.** Unknown
**23.** @deadeyes_ptv **24.** @sebrinapham **25.** @naito.oru **26.** @panchopescador **27.** @dragonschool99 Megan Lewis @babyylumpiaa
**28.** @rumplingz

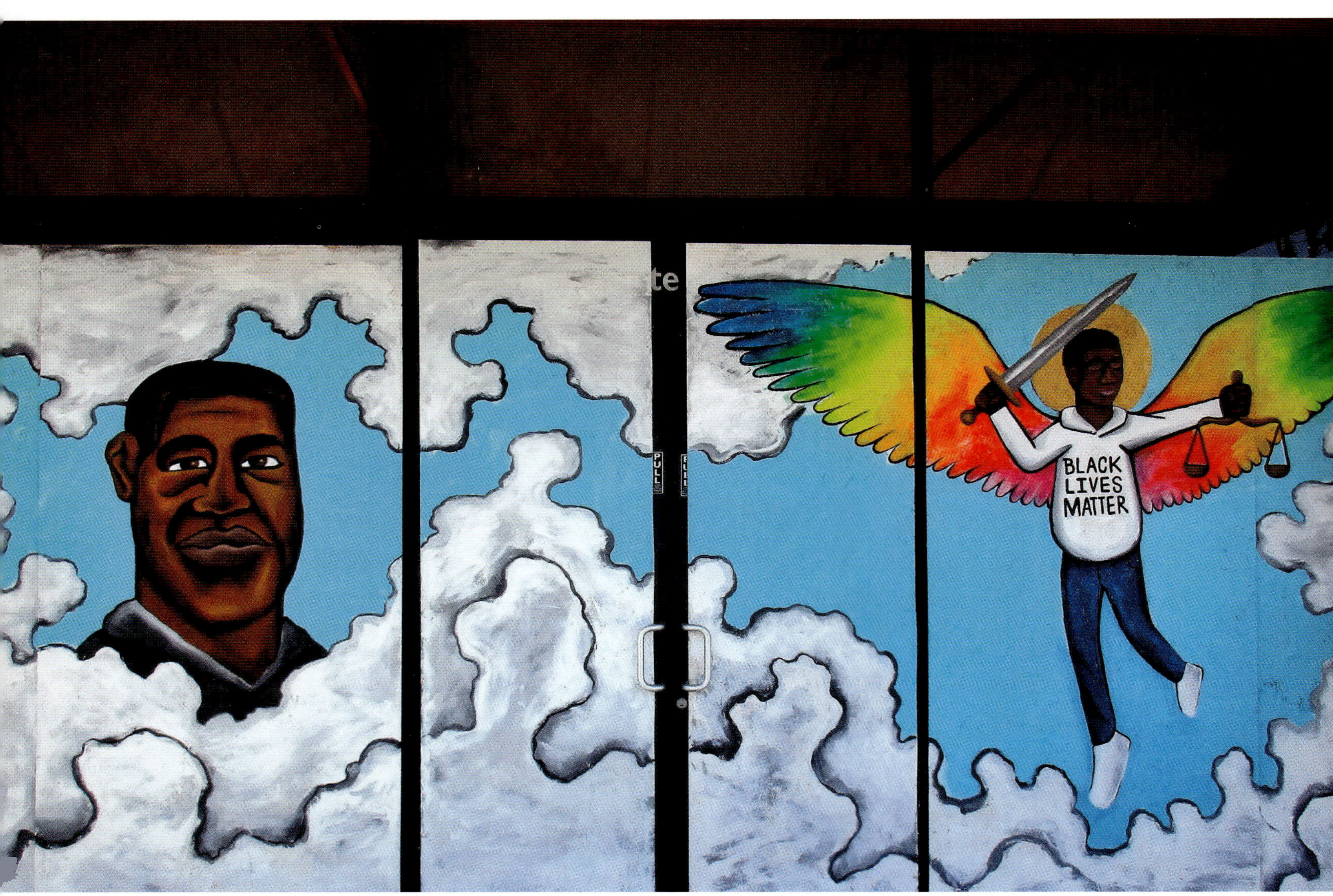


**Fruitvale**
Fruitvale Village

# Alex Sodari

@sodapaints

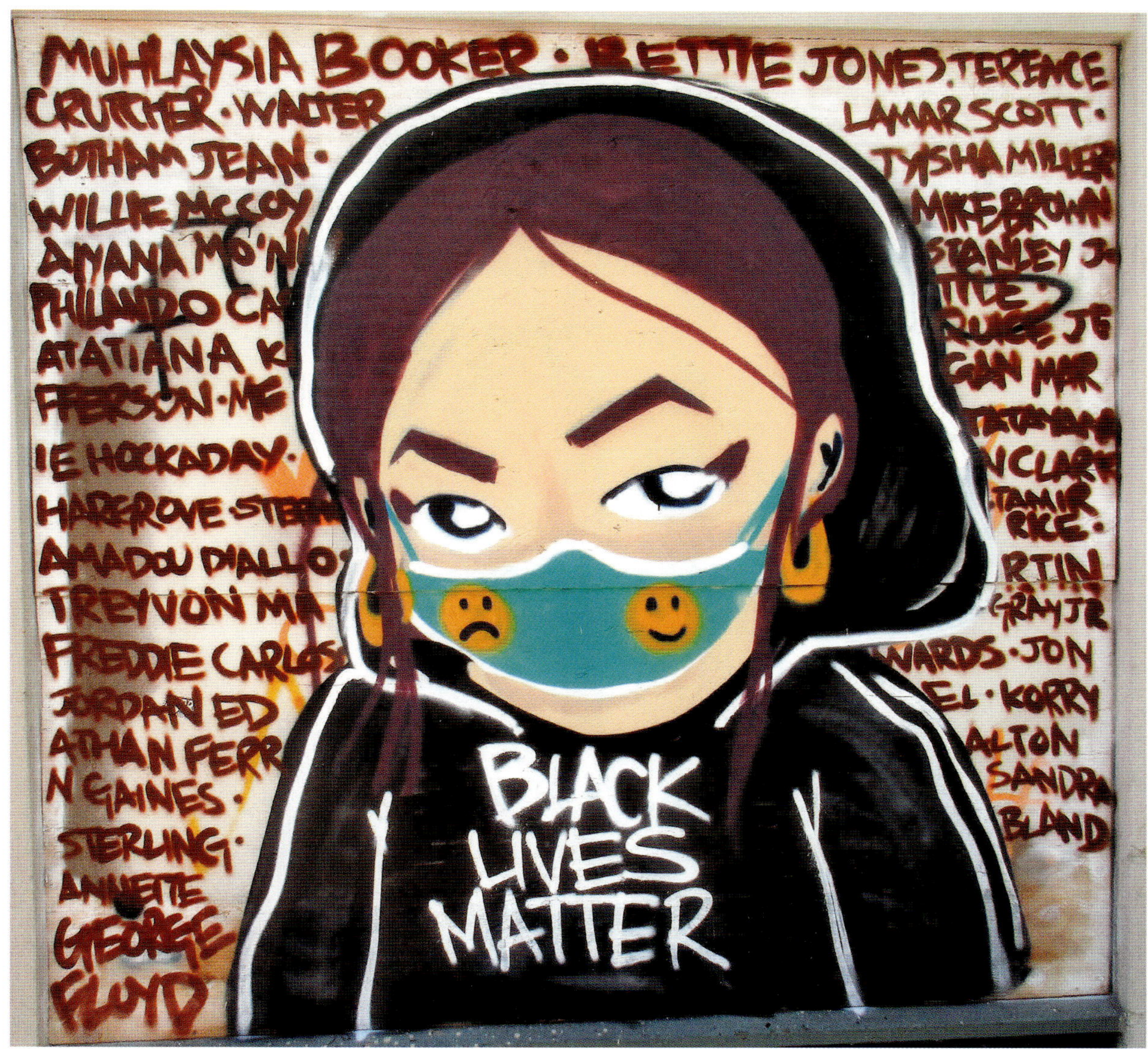


**Downtown Oakland**
1615 Broadway

# Alrad

@dimebagdarla

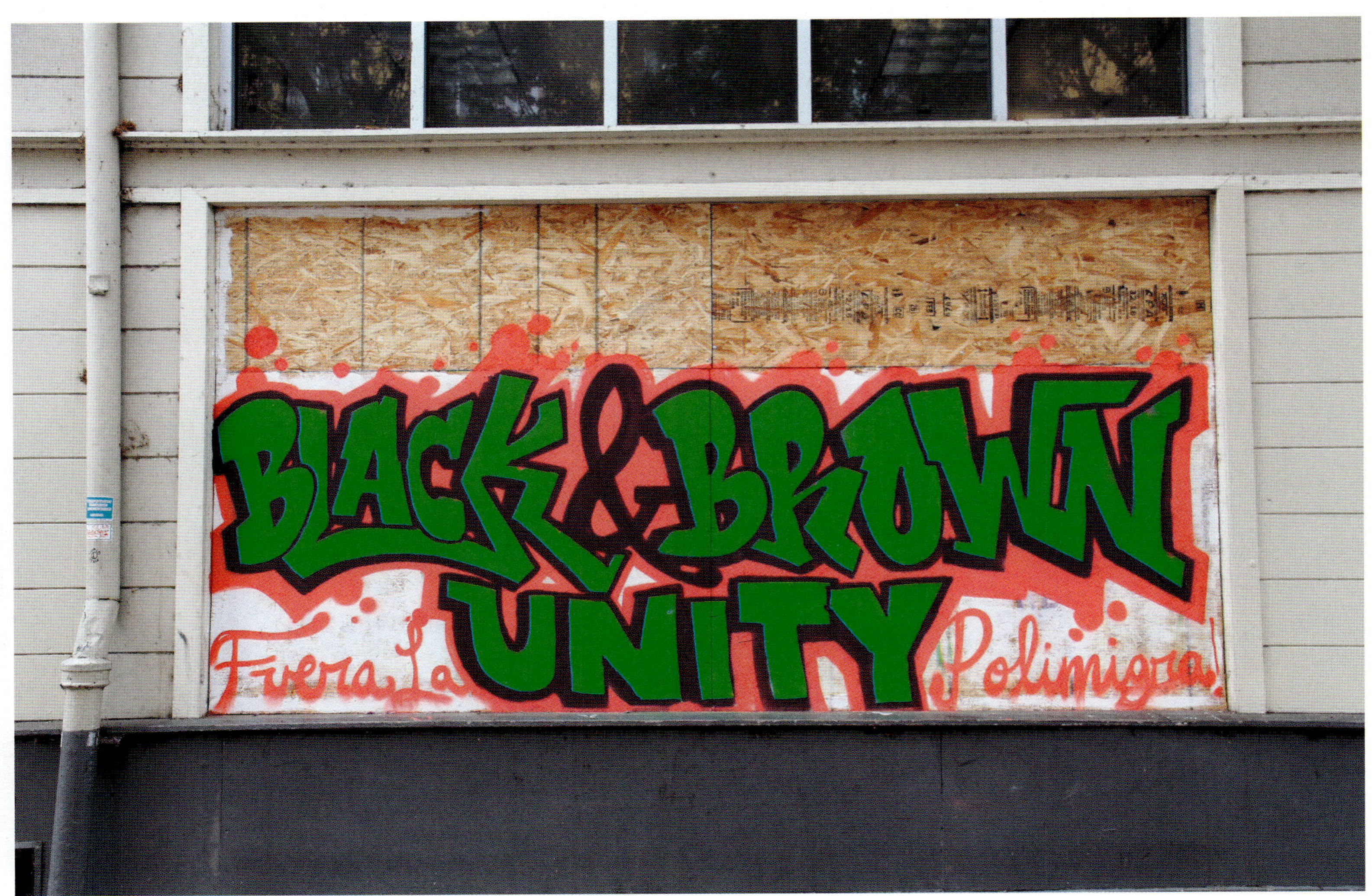





# Angelica Lopez

**in collaboration with:** @visual.cole and @m0th.gurl

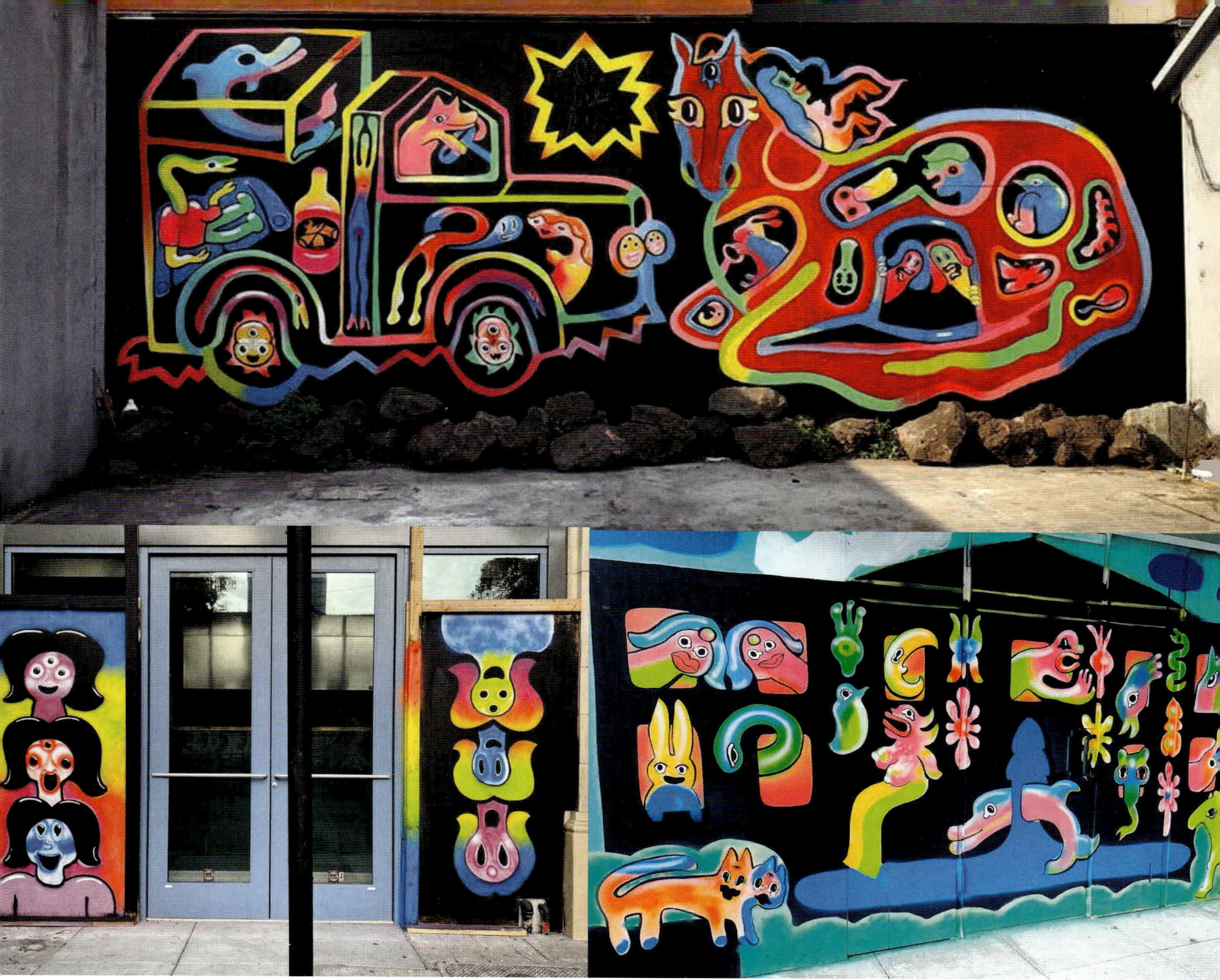

# Bud Snow

@bud_snow

**Downtown Oakland**
Jack London Square
3rd Street at Jackson

**Fruitvale**
Ford St at 29th Ave

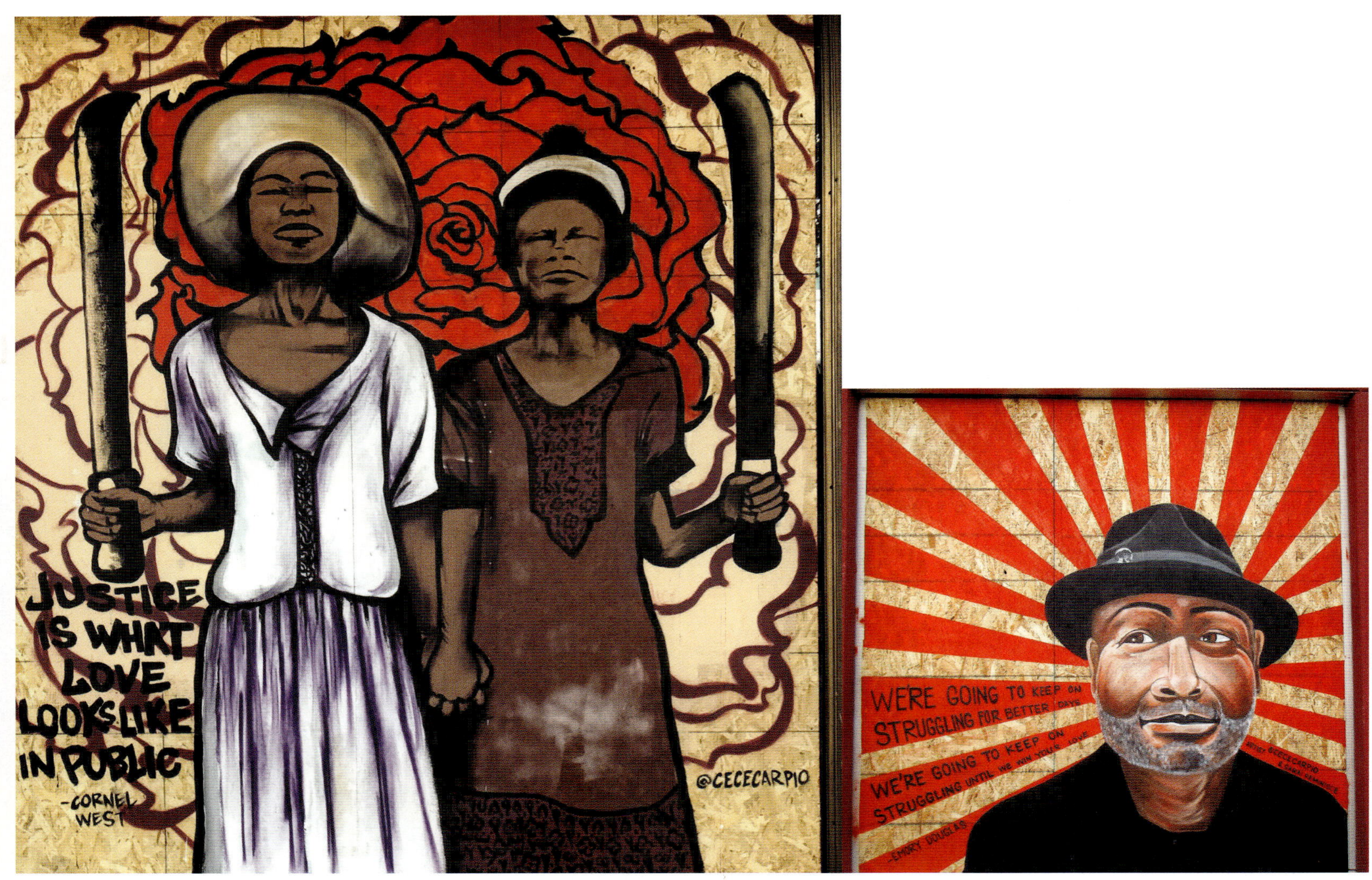


# Cece Carpio

@cececarpio

**Chinatown (Oakland)**
8th and Broadway

**Downtown Oakland**
20th and Broadway

**in collaboration with:** Sarai Reminisce

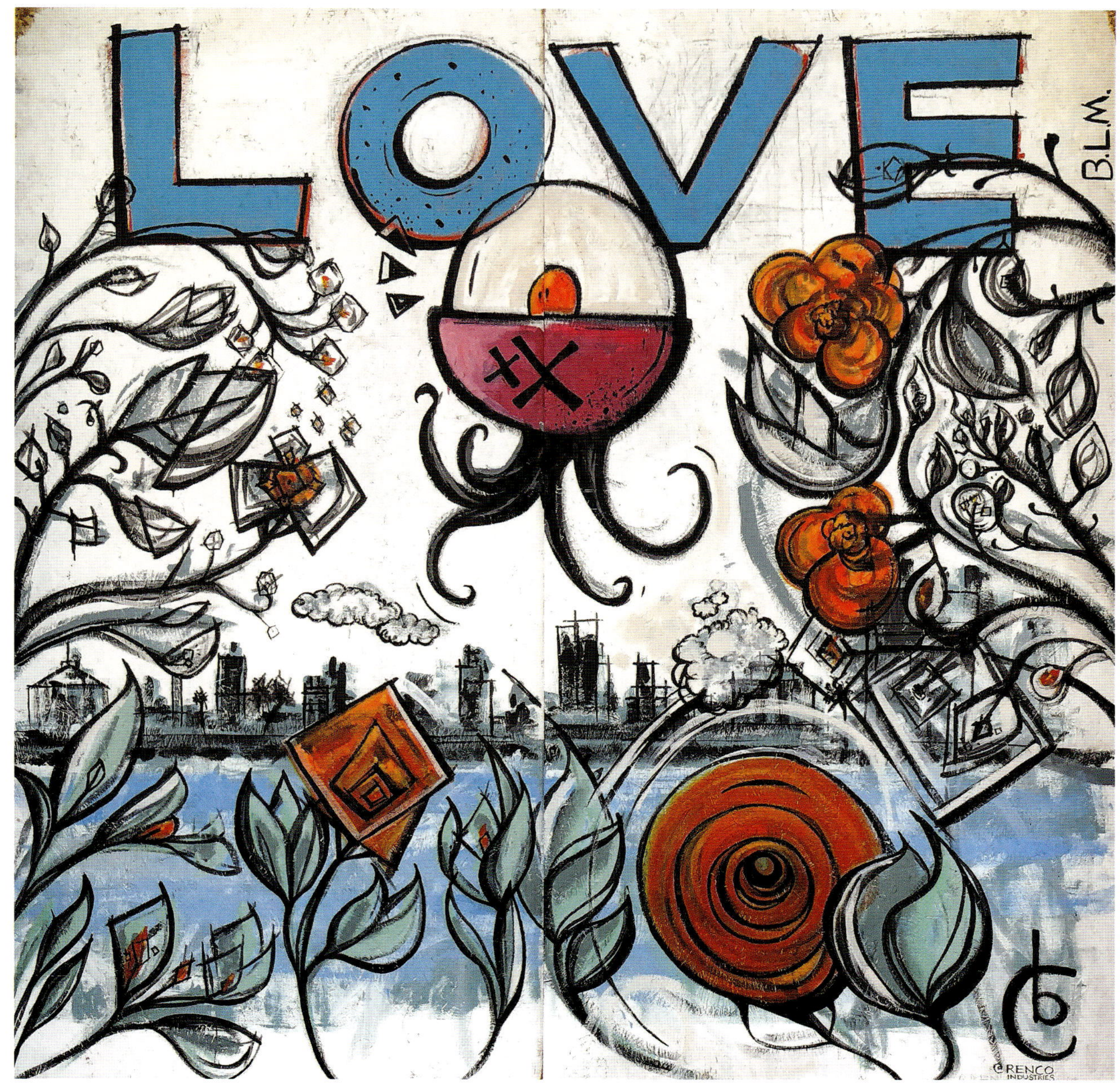


# Chip F. Beal

**Downtown Oakland**
Franklin between 12th and 13th

@rencoindustries

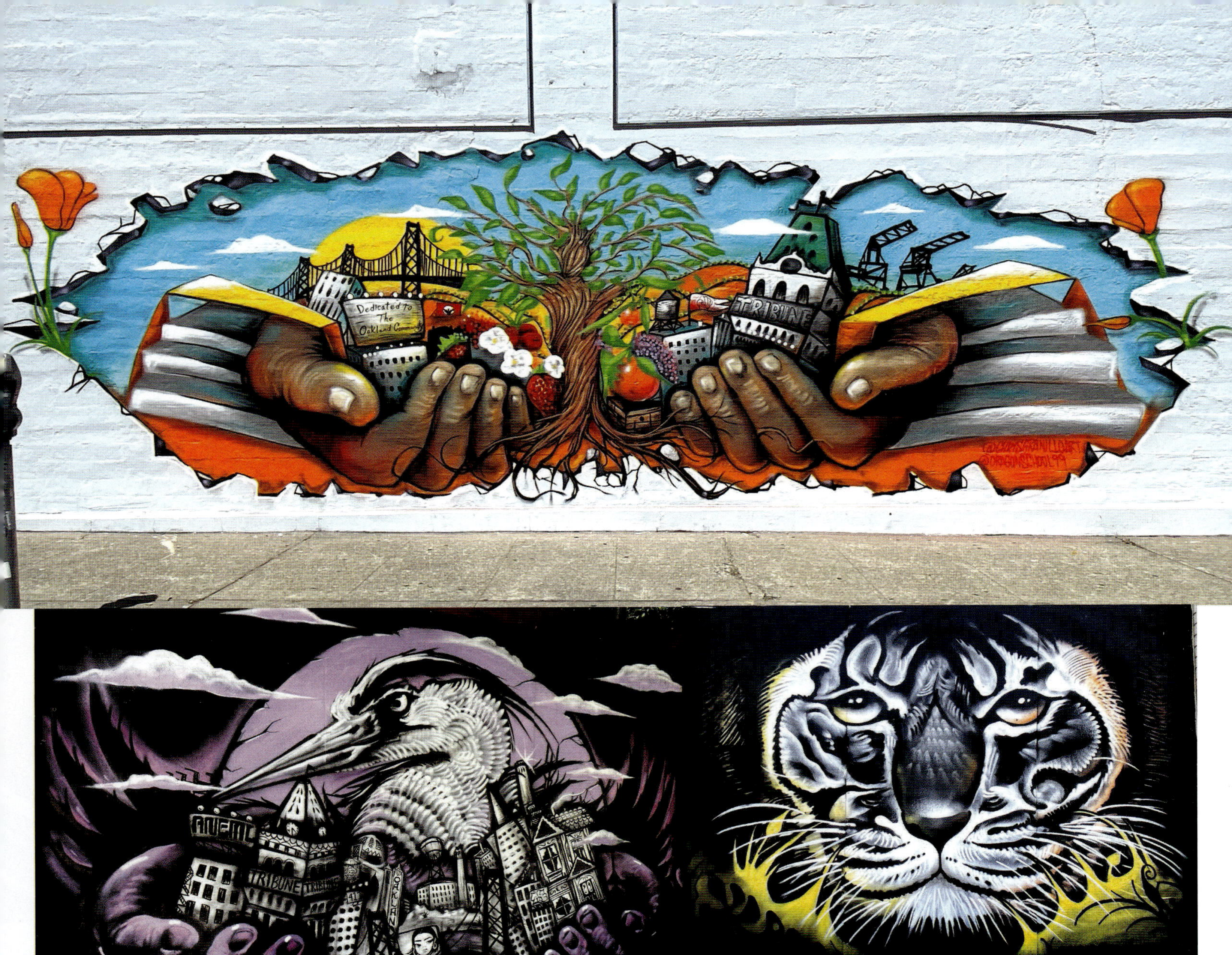


# Chris Granillo

**Downtown Oakland**
Broadway

@chrisgranilloart

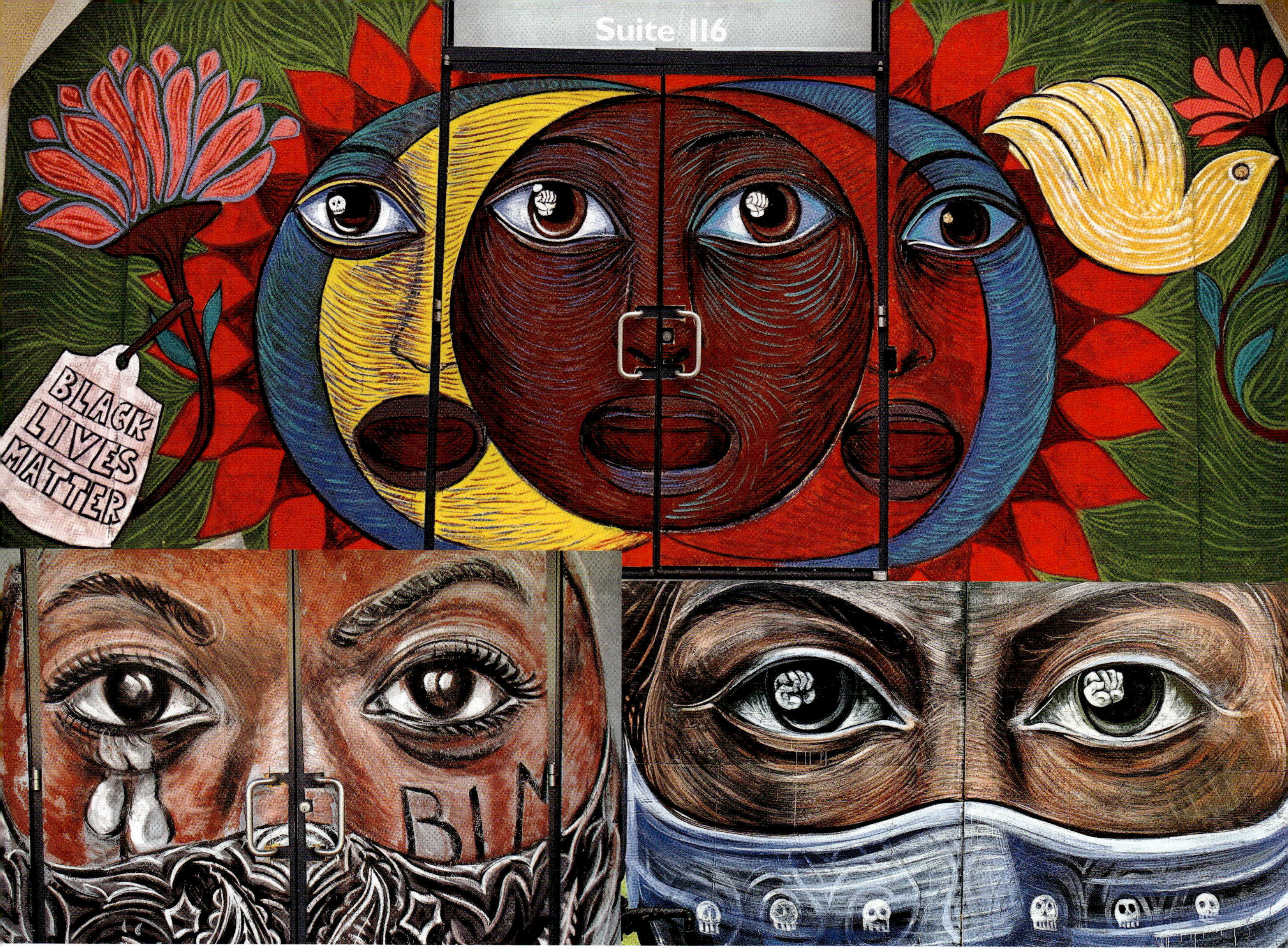


# Daniel Camacho

@danielcamachoelpintor

**Fruitvale**
Fruitvale Village

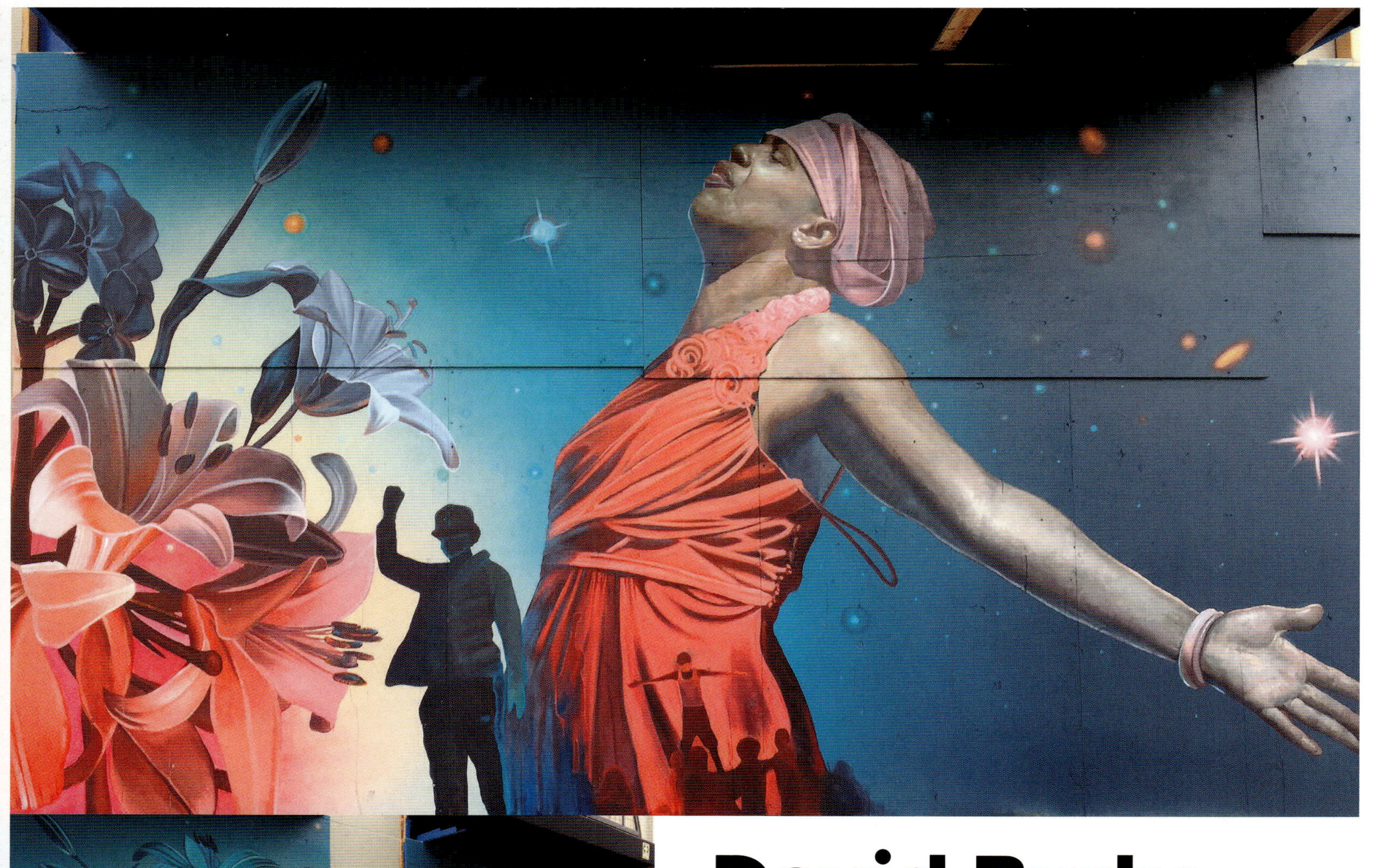

# David Burke

## @hungryghoststudio

**Downtown Oakland**
22<sup>nd</sup> and Broadway

**in collaboration with:** Joevic Yeban @joevicyeban,
Dorias Brannon @dorias_brannon

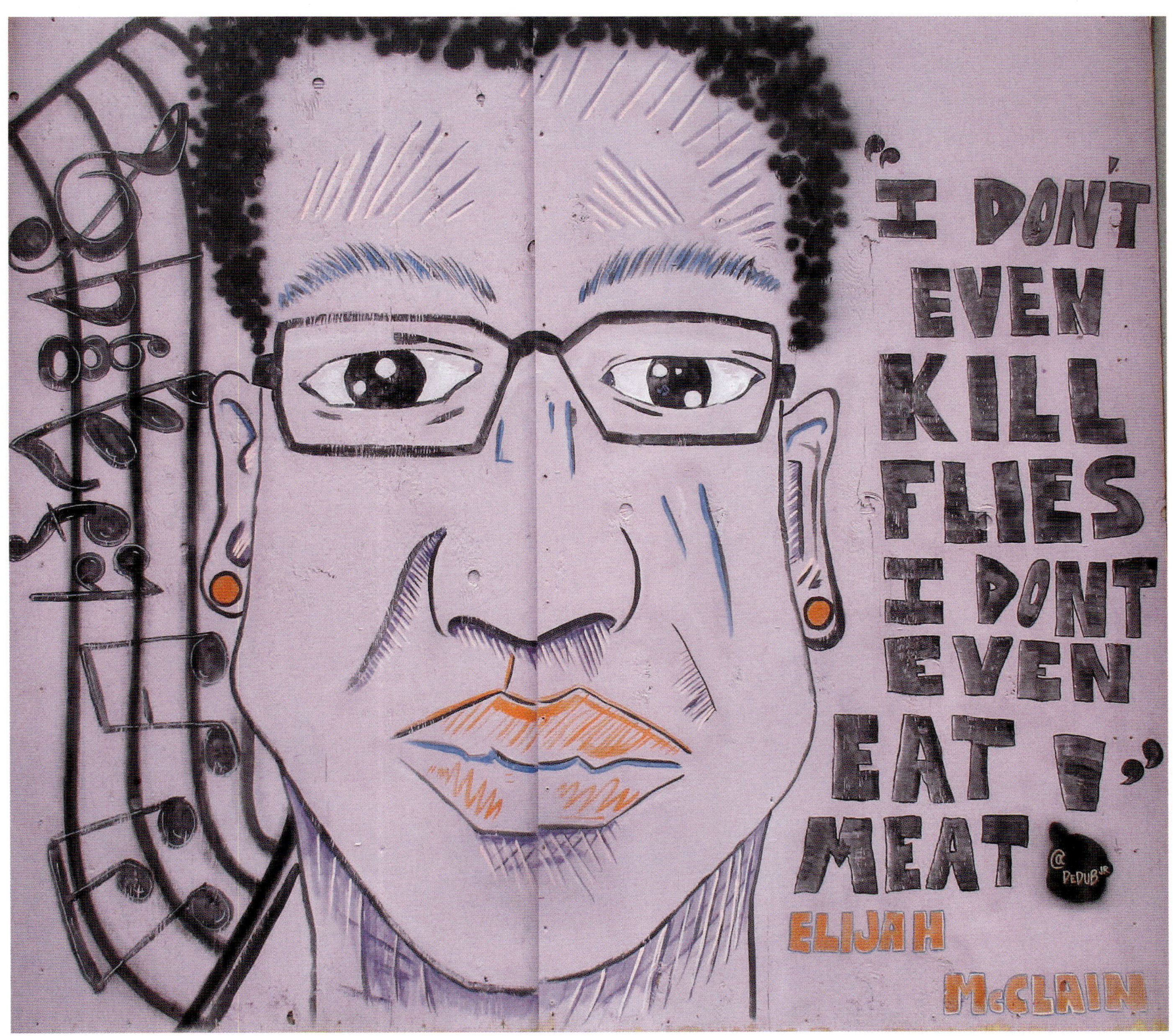




# David Foreman

@dedubjr

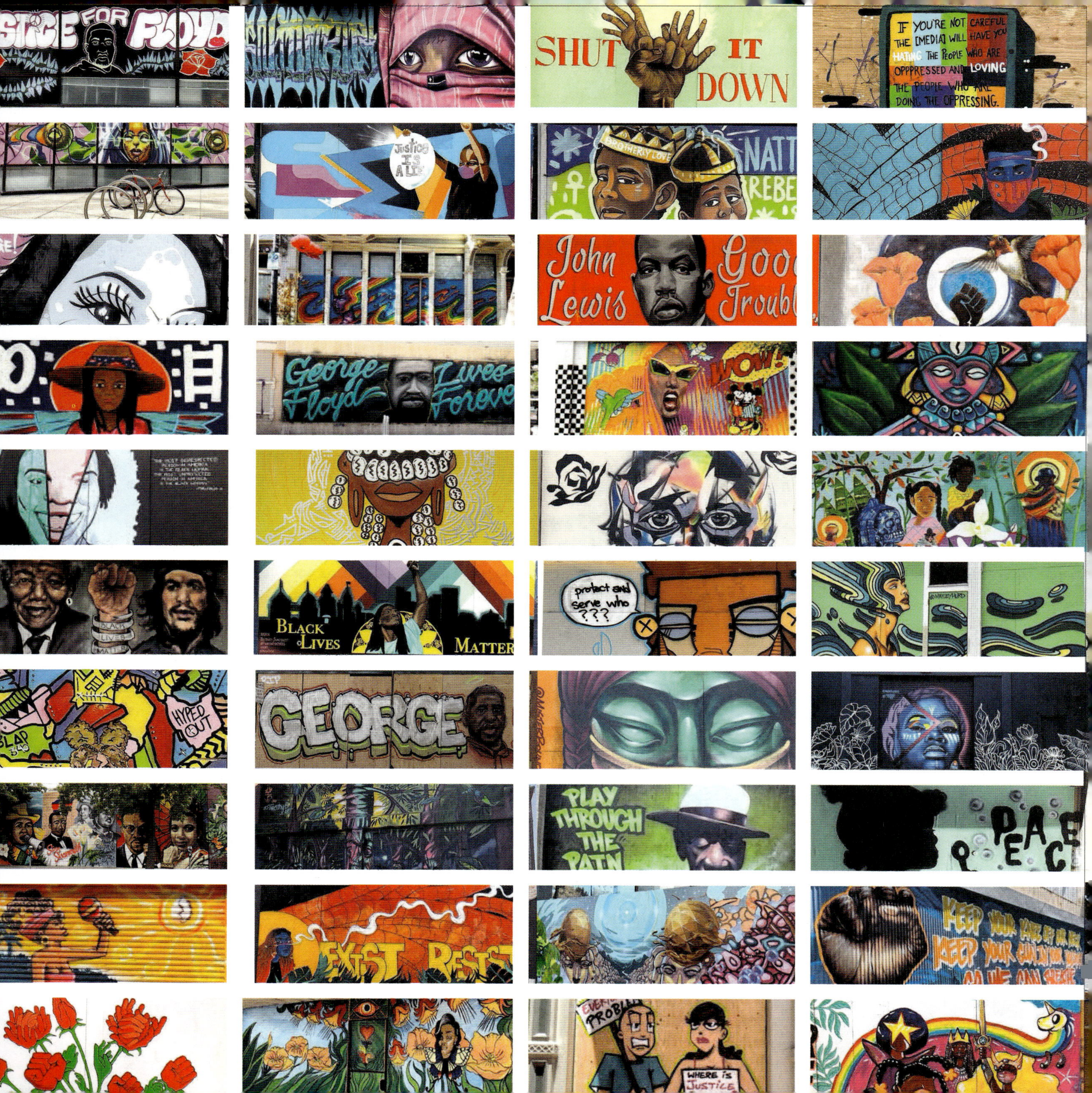

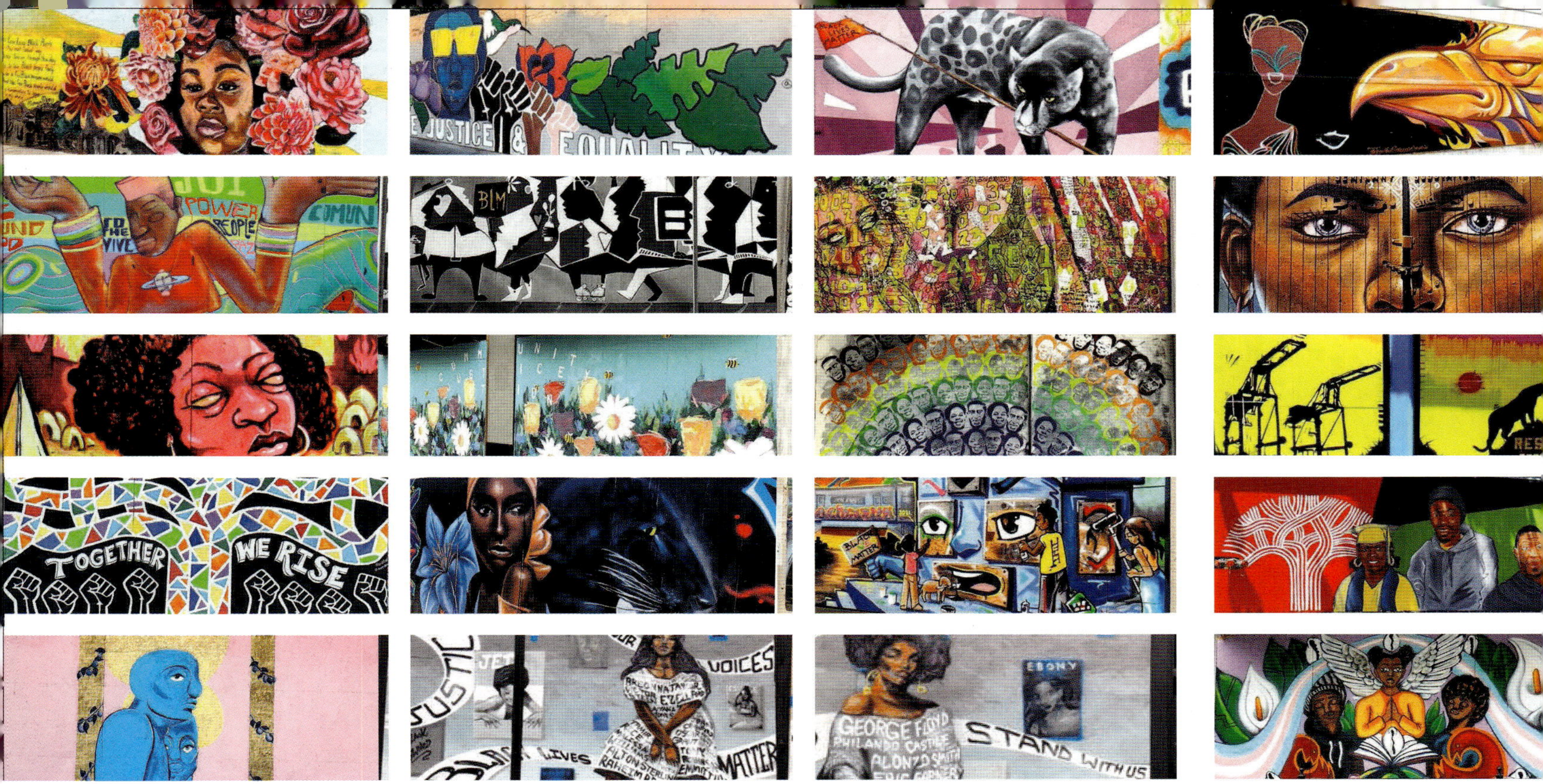

**With much love and thanks to Patricia Garcia, Kari Barnes, Edsel Rivera, and Eddie Kochiyama for allowing us to reproduce these photo**

## Page 65

**29.** @girlmobb **30.** @panchopescador @dayinthelifeofninjashoes **31.** @twinwallsmuralcompany **32.** @piecesbypeezy

**33.** @timothyb_art **34.** @juliocrodriguez__ @casket.sheep **35.** @nattyrebelart **36.** @hellafutures

**37.** @thee_angler **38.** @matleyhurd **39.** @matthuntering **40.** @bali_

**41.** @adisa_ayo **42.** @deredwrk **43.** @sheldon_greenberg **44.** @lamakina510

**45.** @yungcoconut **46.** @artbyshido **47.** @junyarts.kr **48.** @lospobresartistas @breakfast_burritoo @frederickoalvarado @hooperarts @lamakina510 @jgberumen @niko93.tilinifinity **49.** @3nolam **50.** @frozenfeathers **51.** @deadeyes_ptv **52.** @matleyhurd

**53.** @iamkingbeitia **54.** @timothyb_art @t1ffanyrart **55.** @wolfe_.pack @iamkingbeitia **56.** @keenevisions

**57.** @beastoakland @ireneshiori @chrisgranillo **58.** @timothyb_art **59.** @stevenanderson_art **60.** @t hee_angler

**61.** @honey.of.myrrh **62.** @hellafutures @thesamaniist **63.** @wolfe_.pack @joshuamaysart **64.** @kemest510 @stevenadnerson_art

**65.** @amandabliss.art **66.** @thewastelandgrows **67.** @theezy6 **68.** @scepterarts @kweenovartz

## Page 66

**69.** @robinlogie @the8sun @nicolegervacio @ebonysun @g.theartist510 @_stonesky @lalamaria2155 @_xiomaralima @thepeoplesconservatory **70.** @jackpot0607 @deadeyes_ptv @angelicamckinley @pkaf_510 **71.** @kilimunoz **72.** @trustyourstruggle

**73.** @breakfast_ burritoo **74.** @artistmrblack **75.** @leeloo_levay **76.** @panchopescador

**77.** @orundide **78.** @stevejaviel @andrealeecosta **79.** @sirbenedictb **80.** @abstract_oakland

**81.** @brittsatt **82.** @ireneshiori **83.** @paintedladder **84.** @kissmyblackarts @nattyrebelart @wolfe_.pack @bayareamuralpro

**85.** @clarence_lives **86.** @paintedladder **87.** @paintedladder **88.** @lamakina510

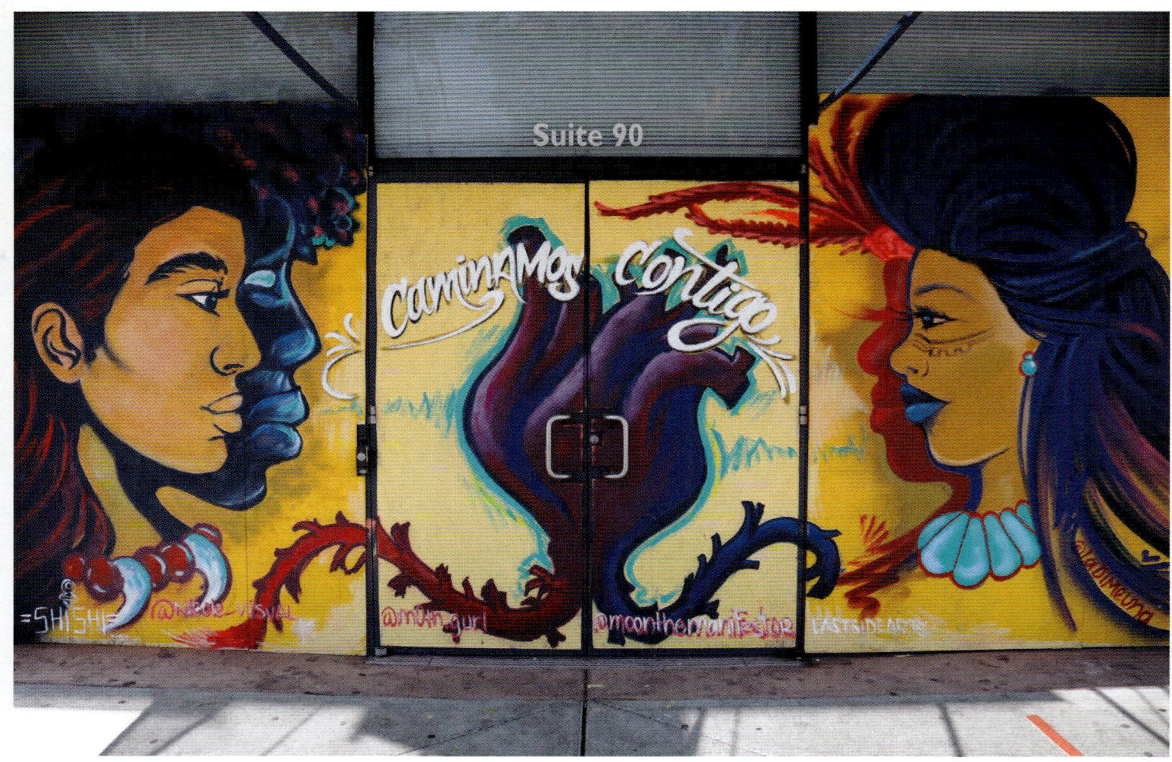


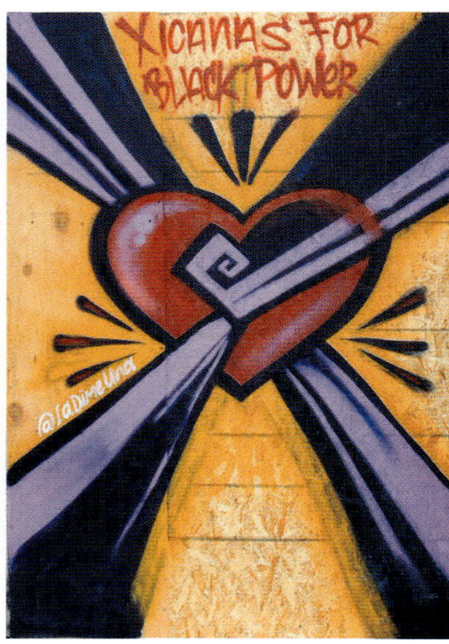


**Fruitvale**
Fruitvale Village

# Dime

@ladimeuna

**in collaboration with:** Yazmin "Shi Shi" Madriz @shishimadriz,
Kenya Akbar, @visual.cole, @m0th.gurl

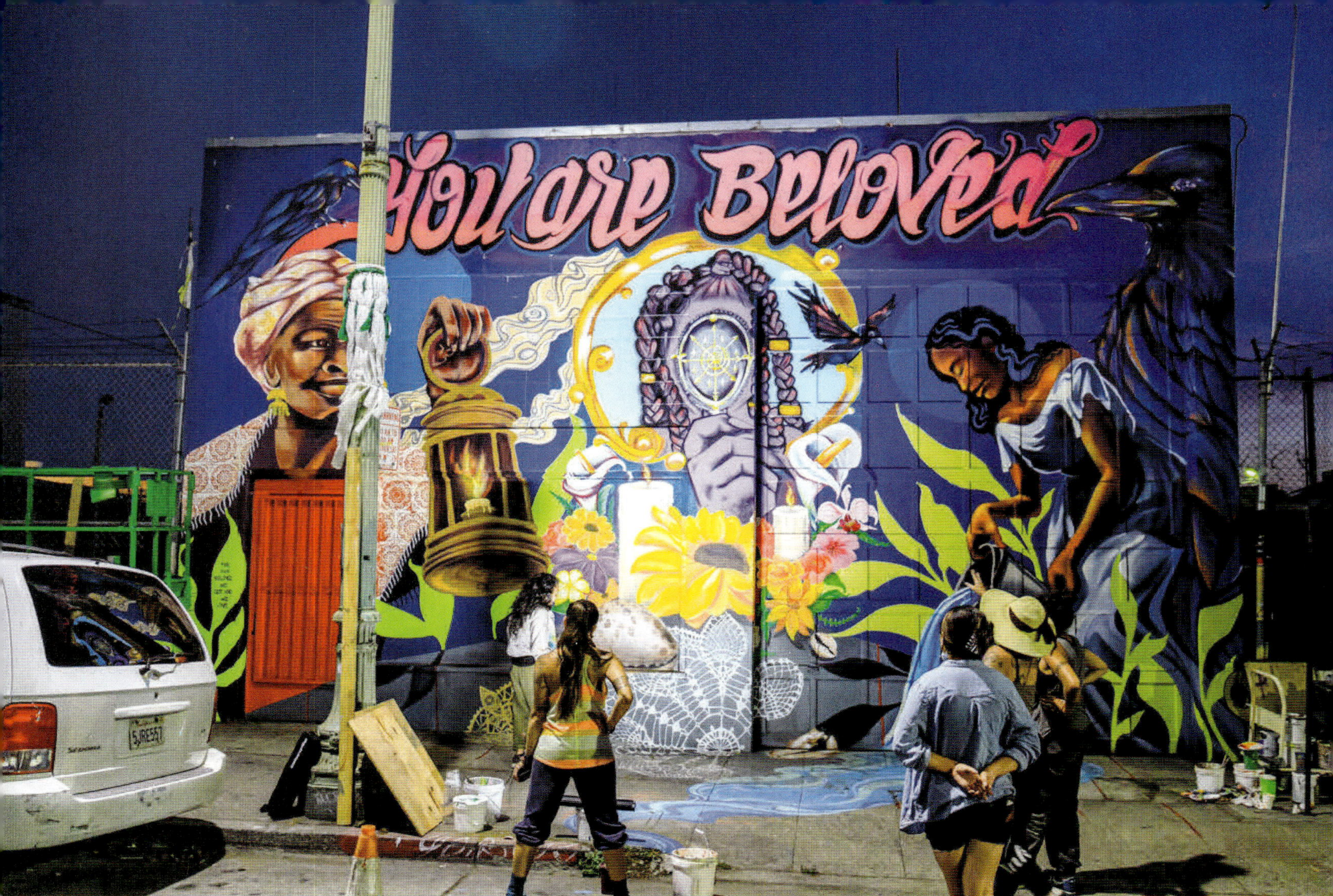


photo by Joe Keefe



# Eastside Arts Alliance

@eastsidecultural

**in collaboration with:** Leslie "Dime" Lopez (@ladimeuna),  Angela López, Cece Carpio @cececarpio, Franceska Gámez @franceskagamez, Priya Handa @priya.k.handa, Inbal Rubin @Inbalrubinart, and Sarai Reminisce

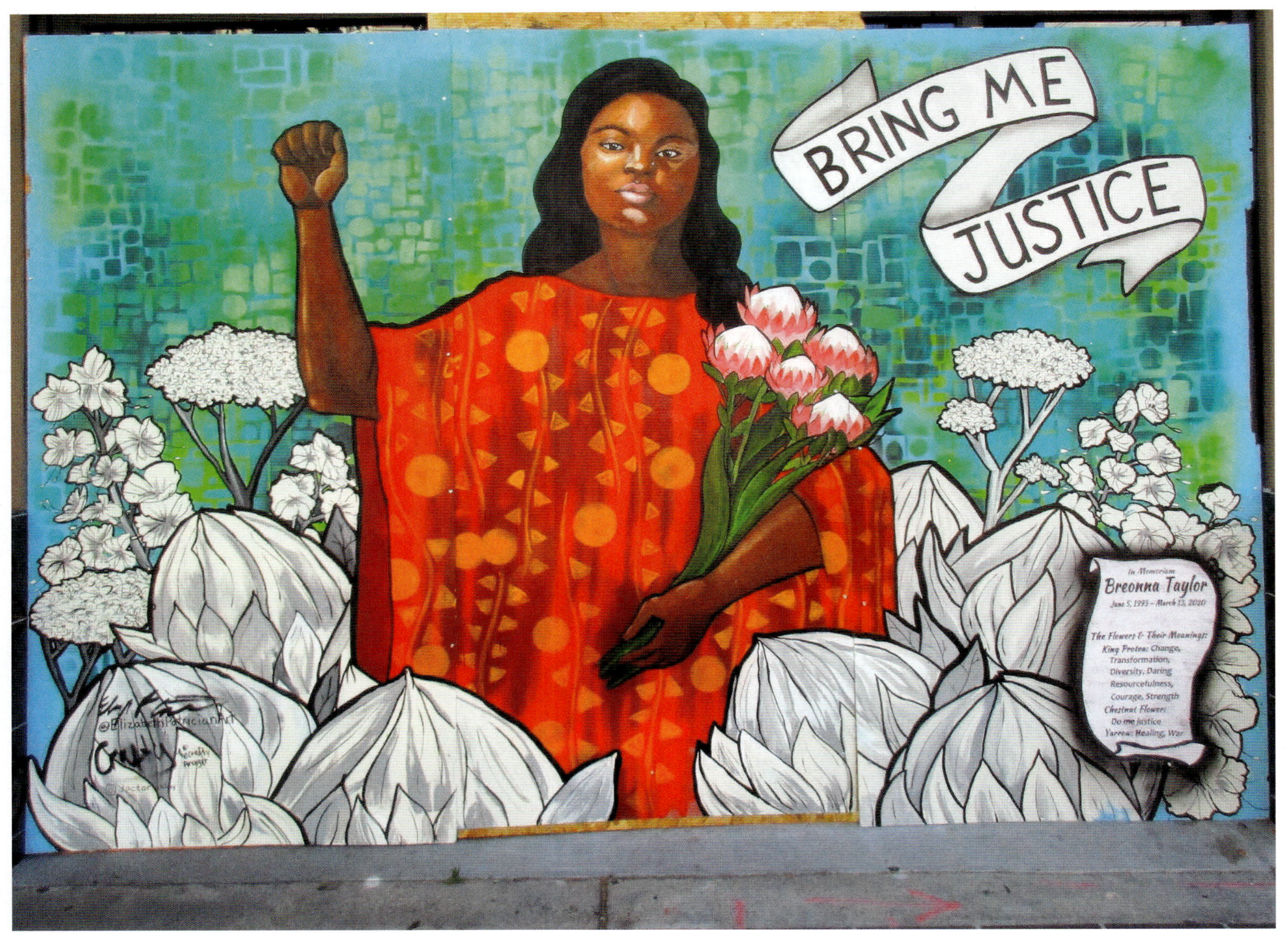


# Elizabeth Patrician

**Downtown Oakland**

@elizabethpatricianart

**in collaboration with:** @thecraftyavenger, @doctorshiny

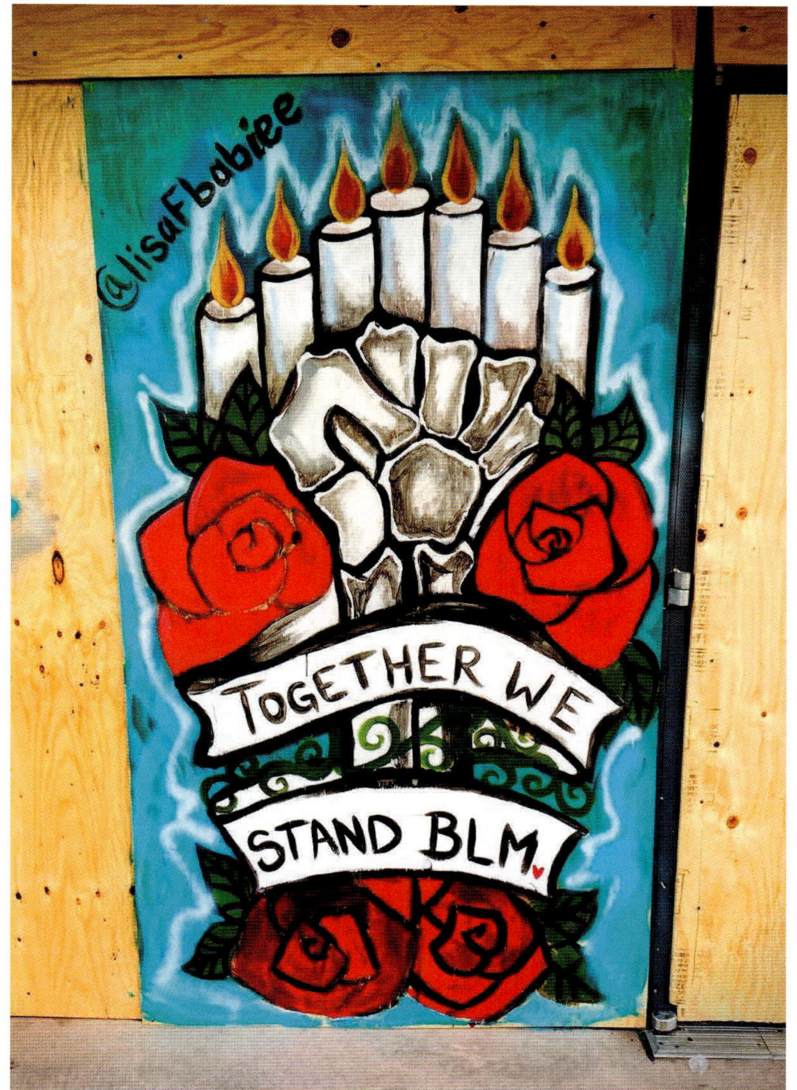




# Elizabeth Peña

@lisafbabiee

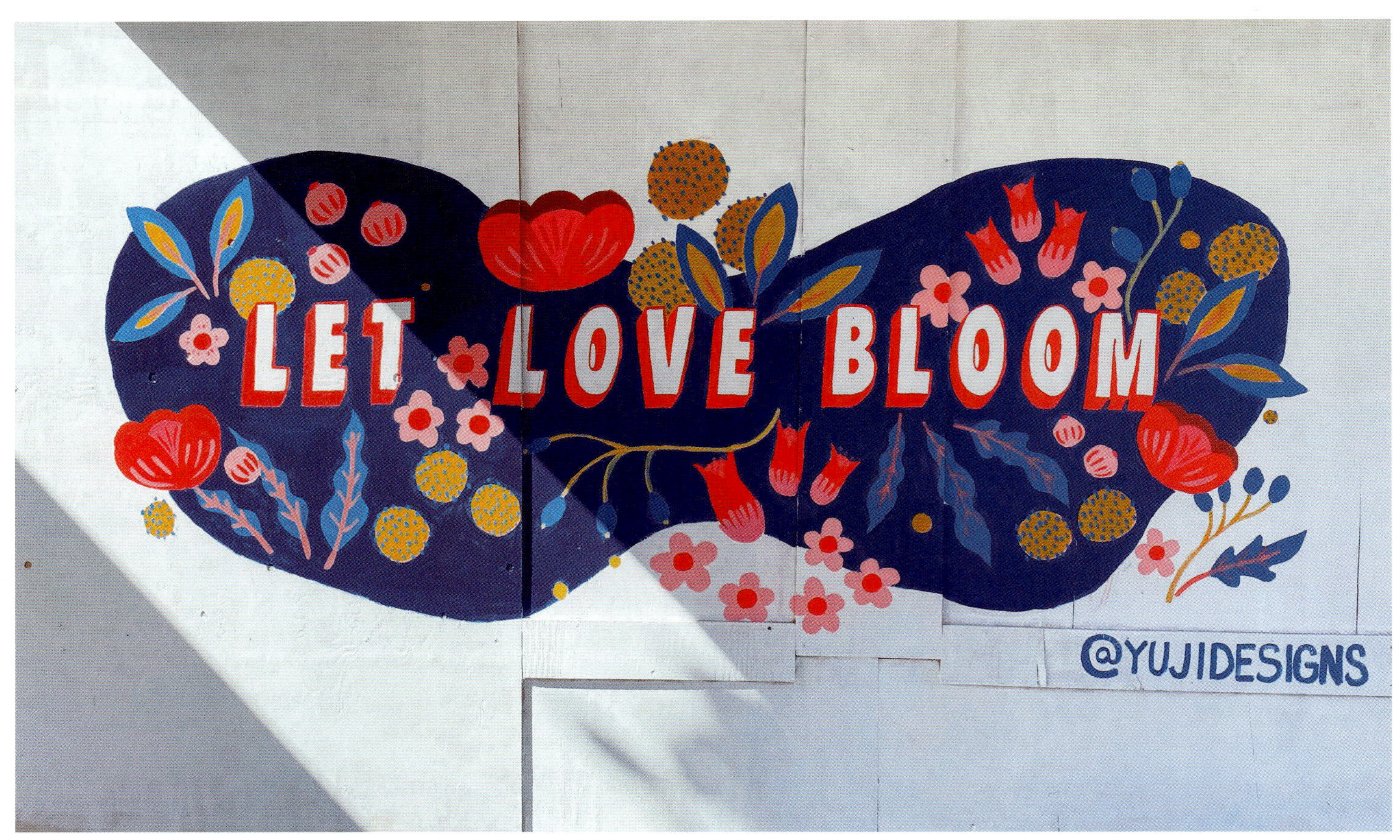


# Eugenia Ho

**Chinatown (Oakland)**
9th and Webster

@yujidesigns

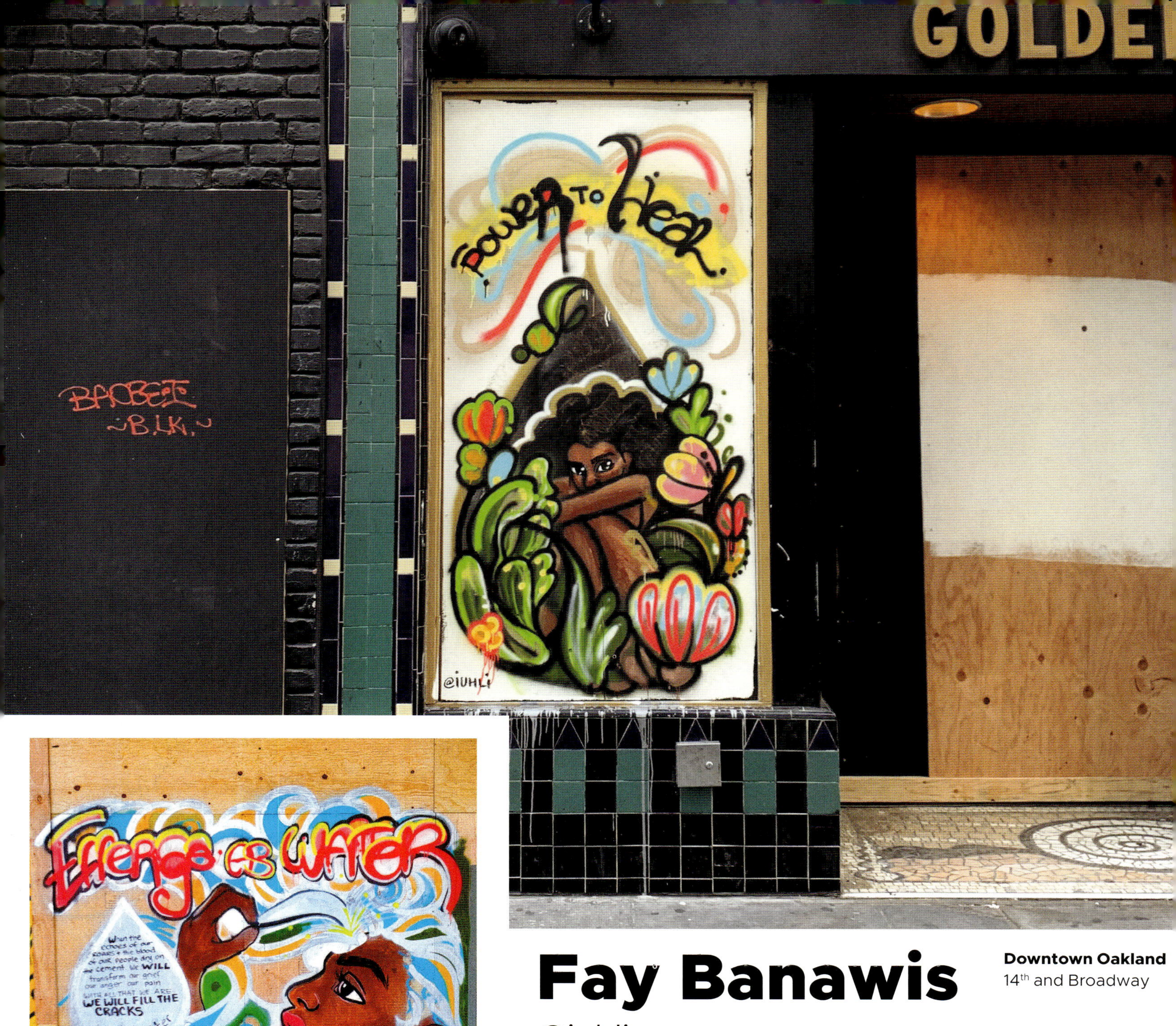


# Fay Banawis

@iuhli_

**Downtown Oakland**
14th and Broadway

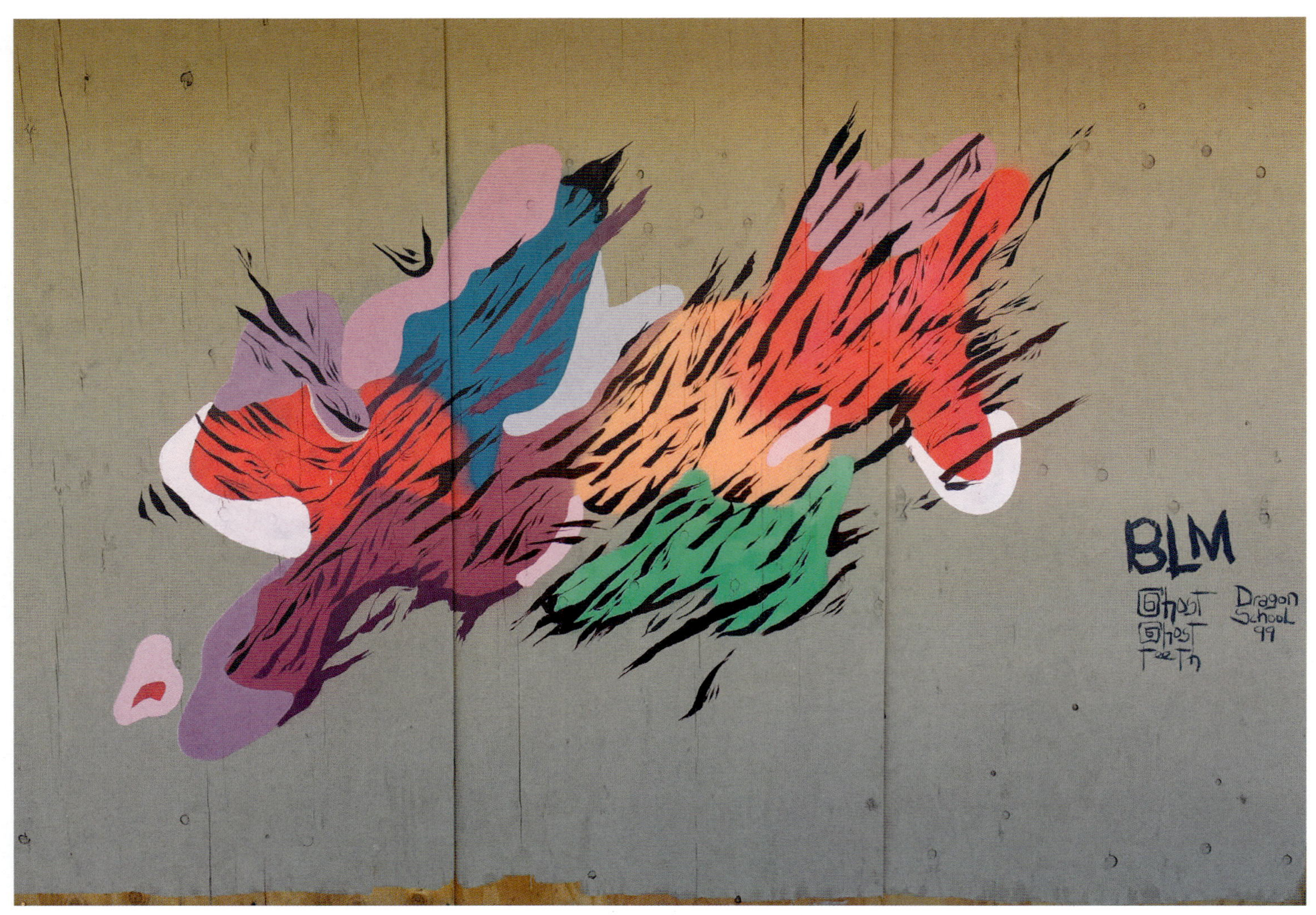


# ghost ghost teeth

**Chinatown (Oakland)**
345 9th Street

@ghostghostteeth

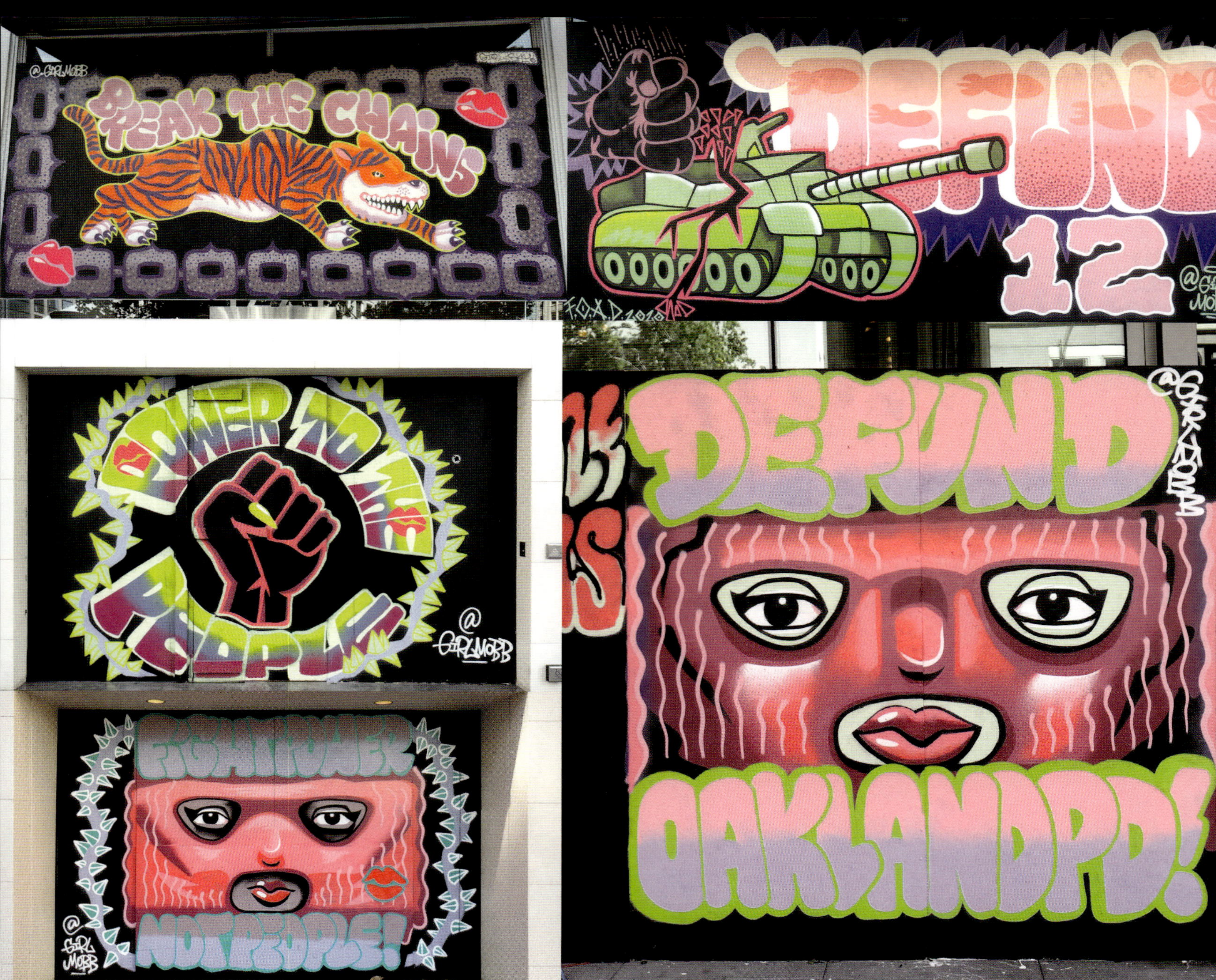


# Girl Mobb

@girlmobb

**Downtown Oakland**
Broadway and 12th

**Uptown Oakland**
Broadway and 27th

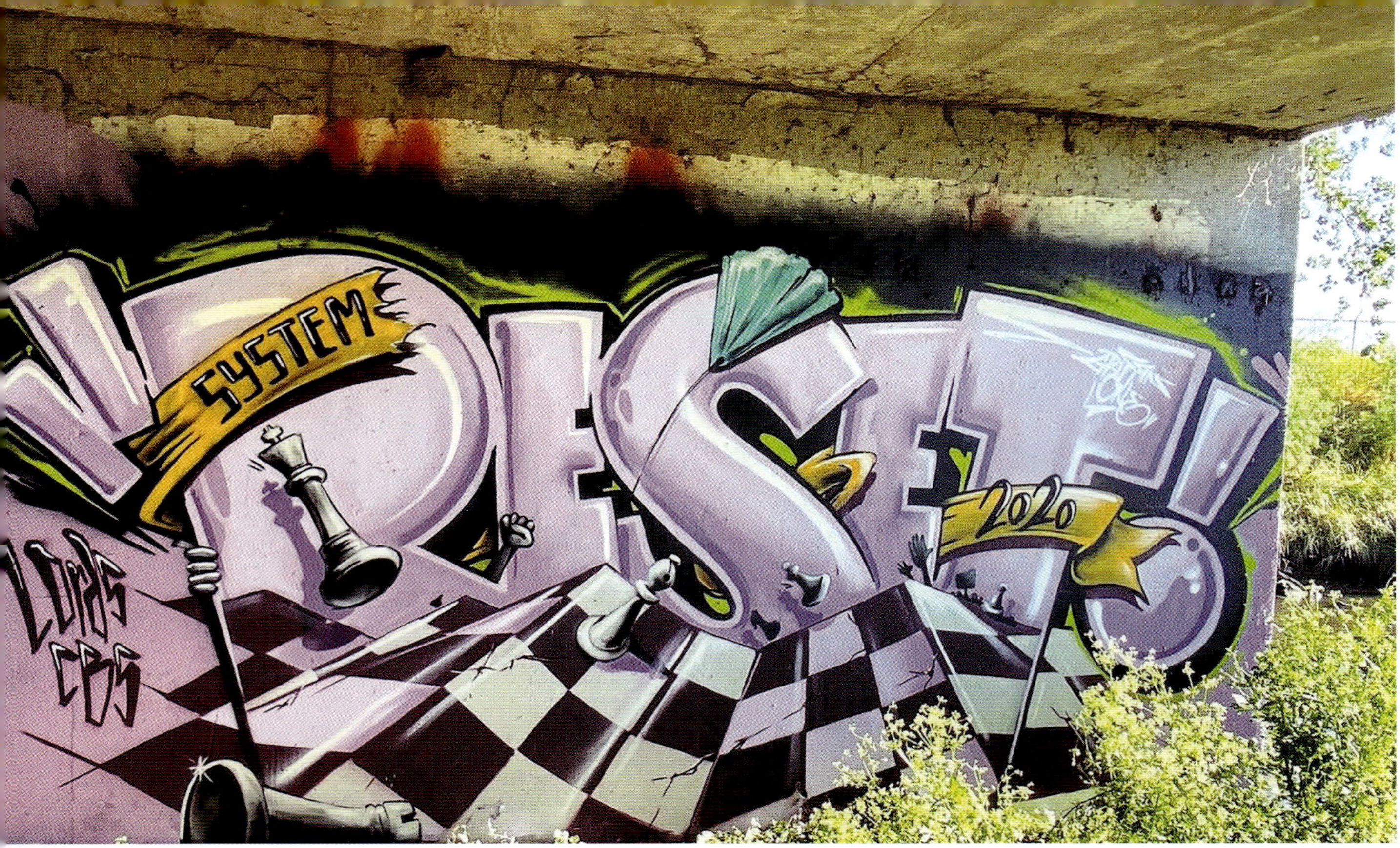

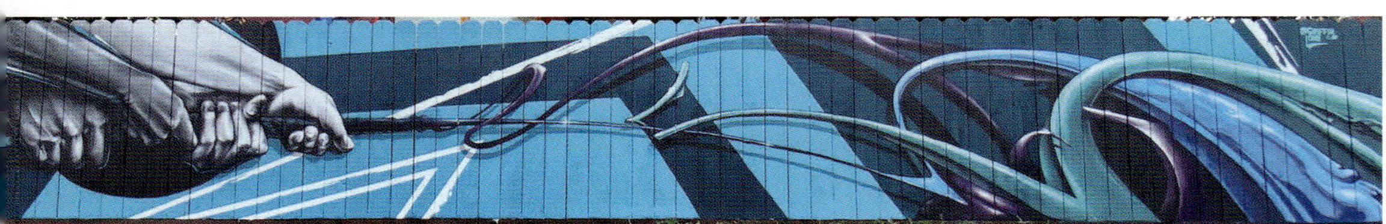

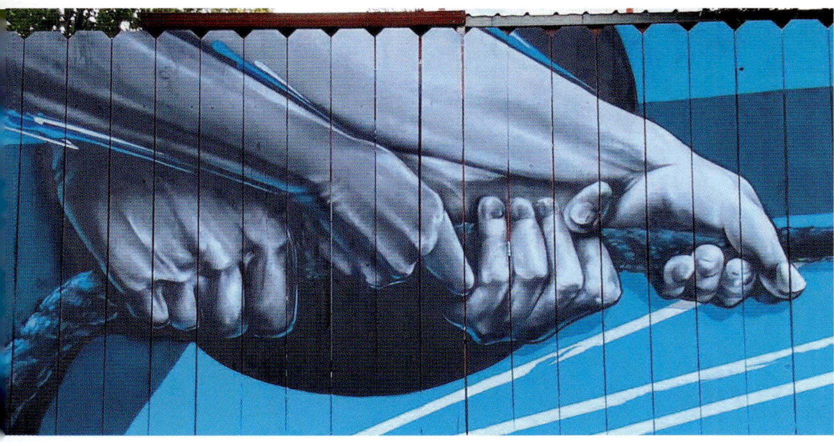



**Downtown Oakland**
Jack London Square
2nd and Broadway

# Griffin One

@griffinone

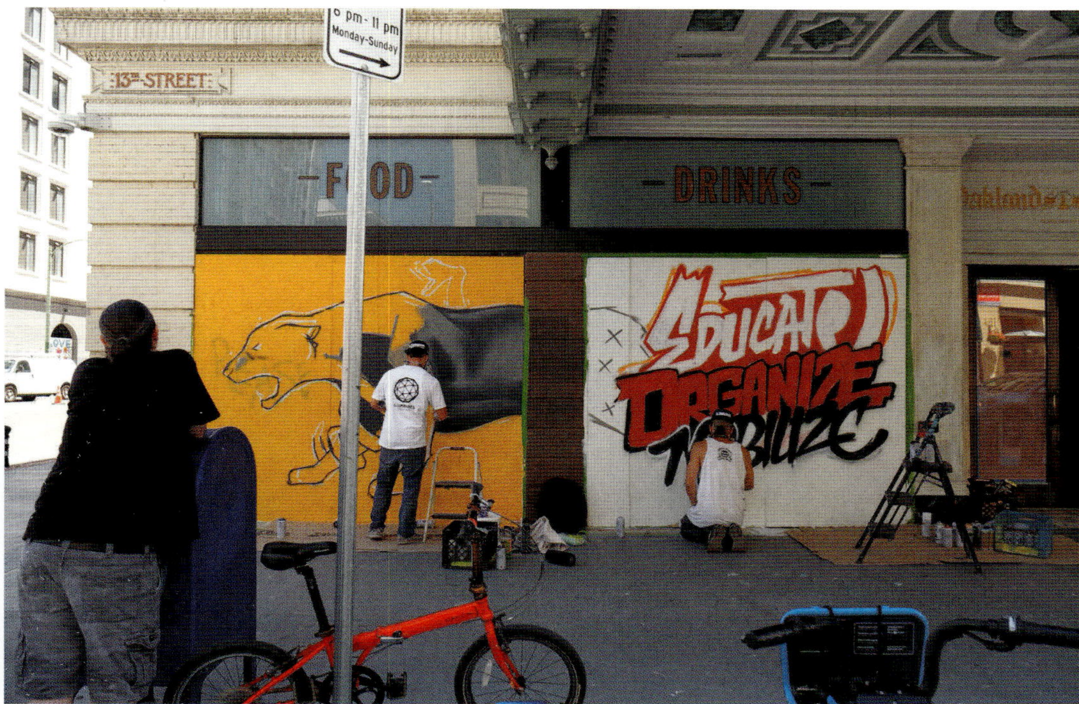


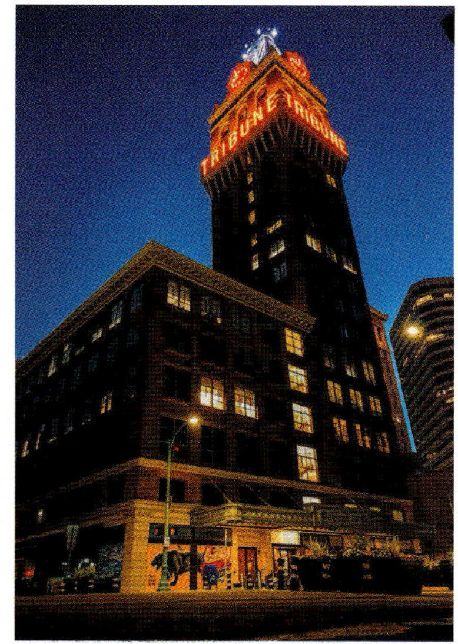


**Downtown Oakland**
Tribune Tower
13th and Broadway

**a collaboration between:**

@flavorinnovator, @kruptdotcom,

@chrismlinden, @mikekukreja

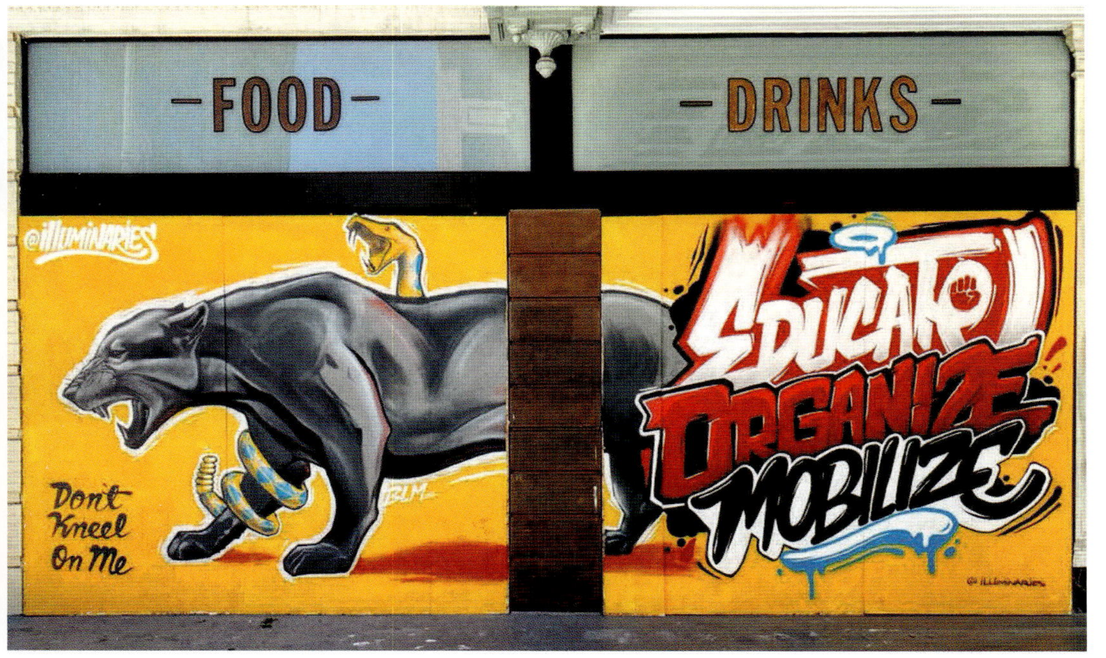


# Illuminaries

@illuminaries

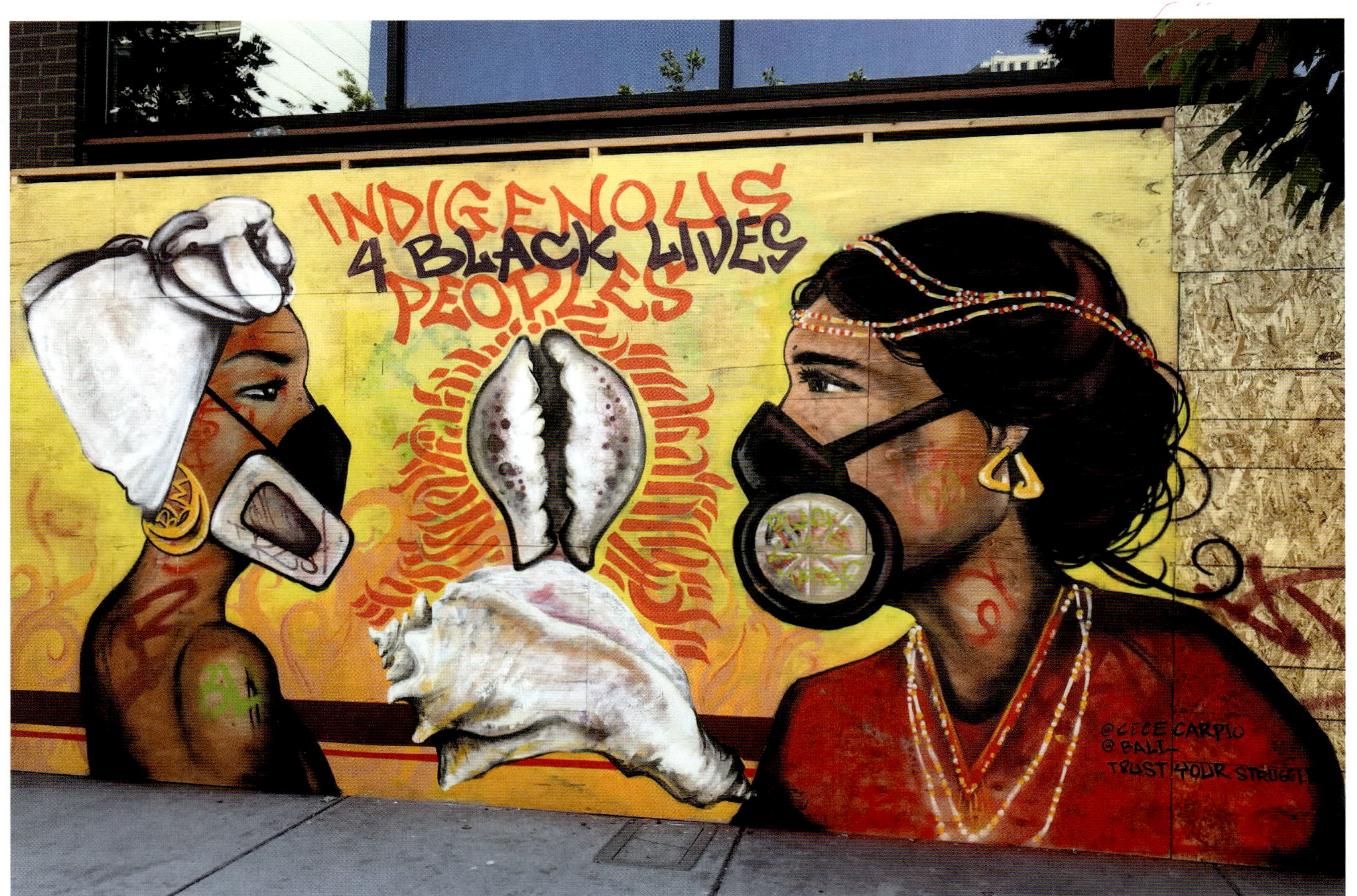


# Inbal "Bali" Rubin

@inbalrubinart

**Fruitvale**
Fruitvale Village

**in collaboration with:** Cece Carpio @cececarpio

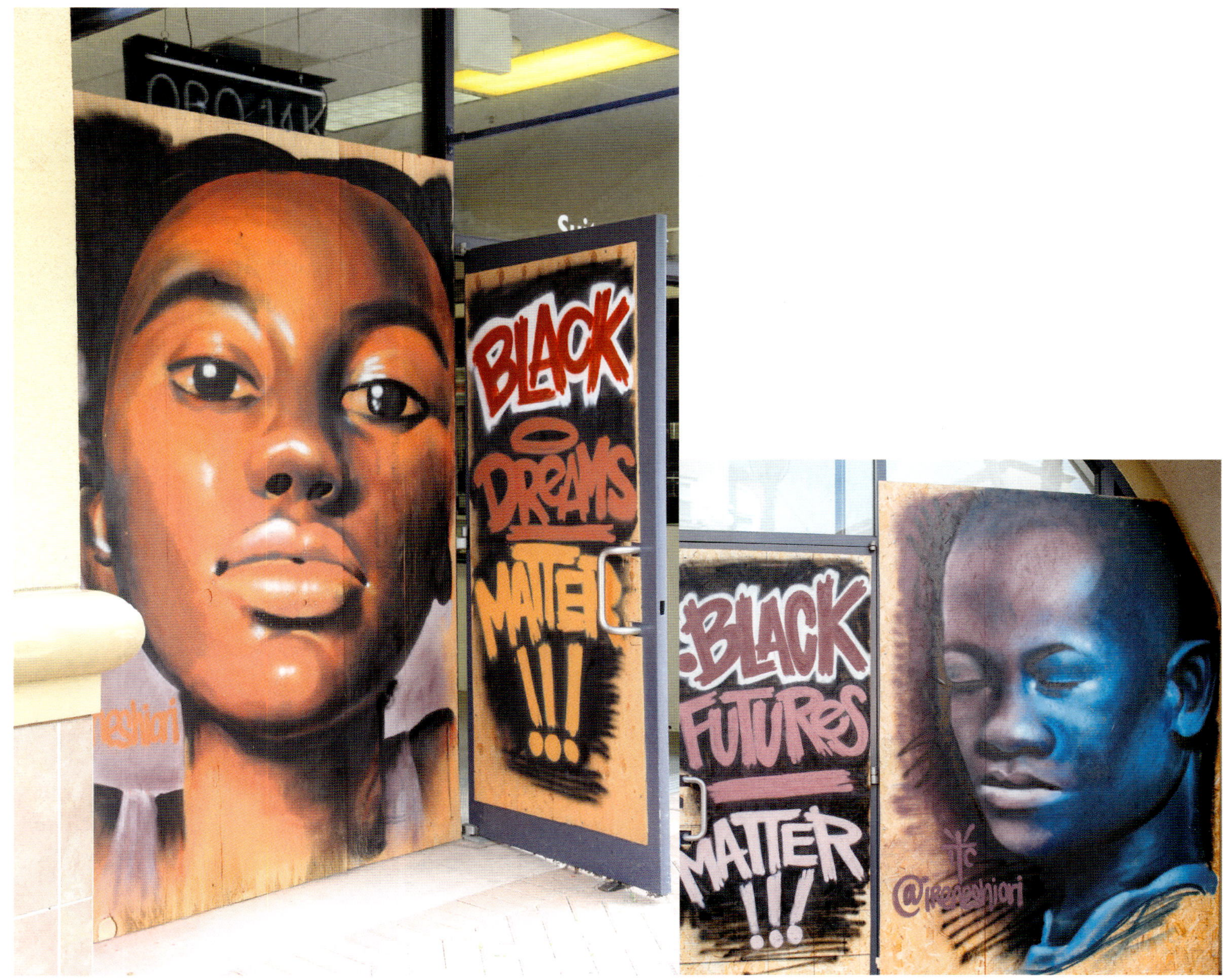


# Irene Takahashi-Coker

@ireneshiori

**Fruitvale**
Fruitvale Village

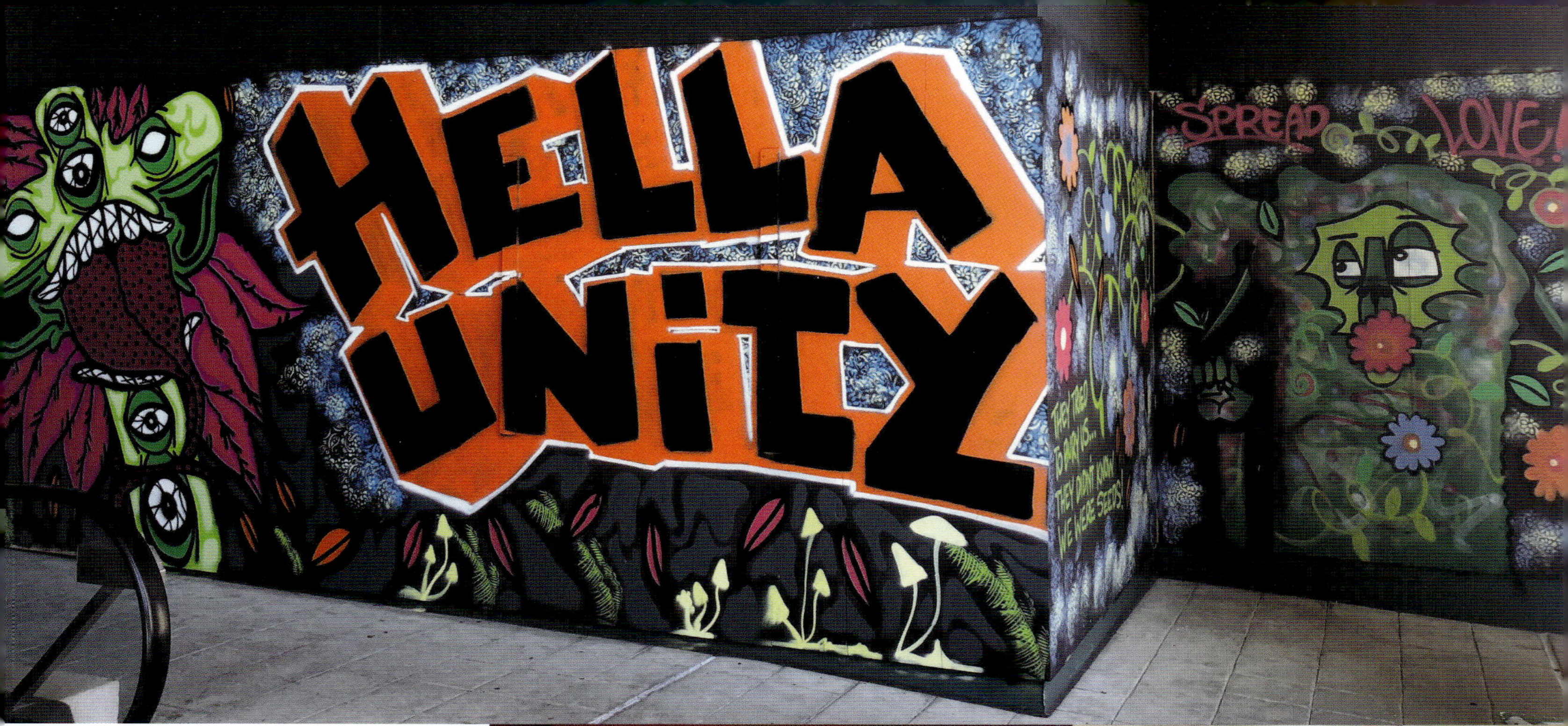

# Jude Capili

@freshcoastphotos

**Chinatown (Oakland)**
8th and Broadway

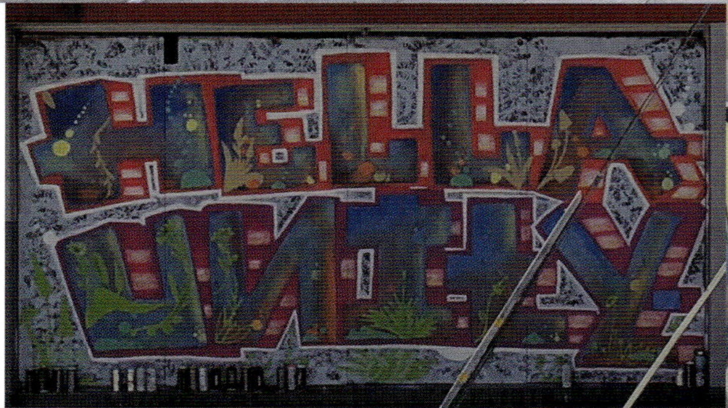

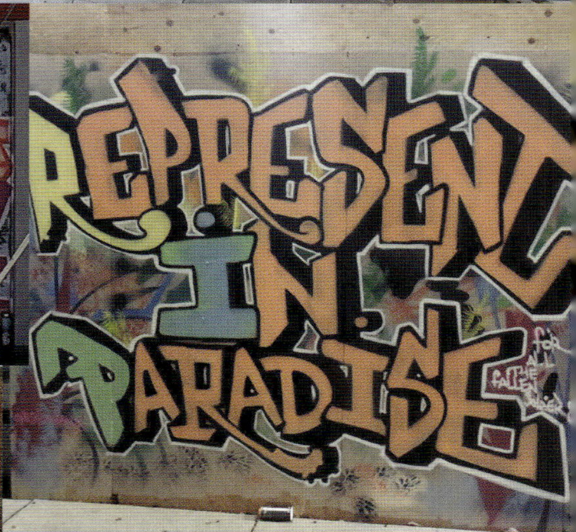

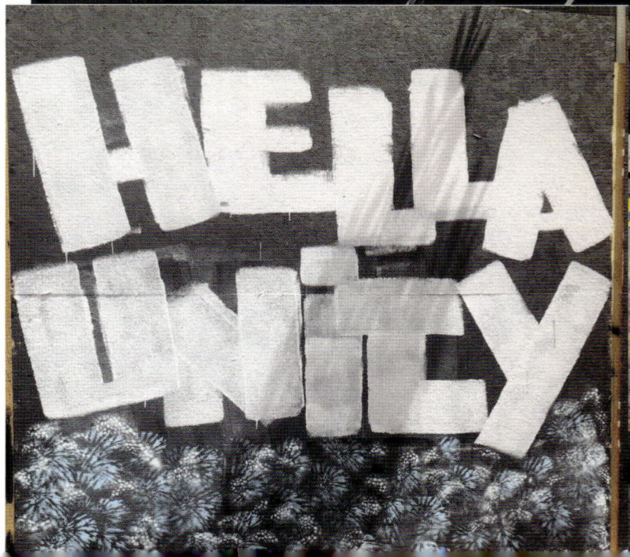

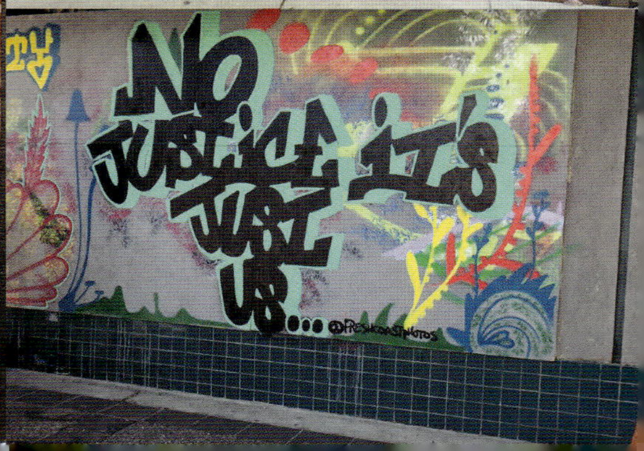

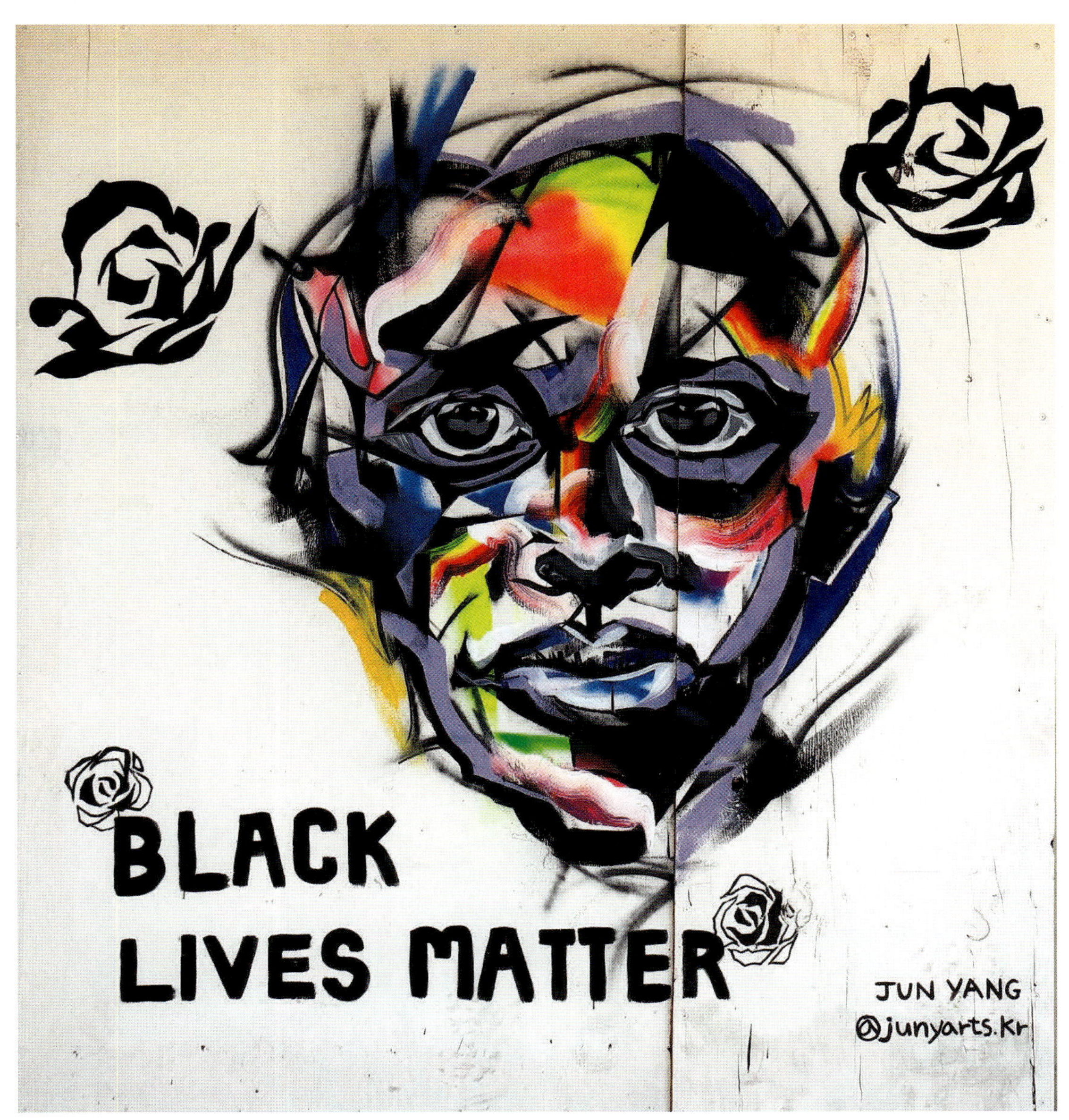


# Jun Yang

@junyarts

**North Oakland**
Tip Top Bike Shop;
48th and Telegraph Ave

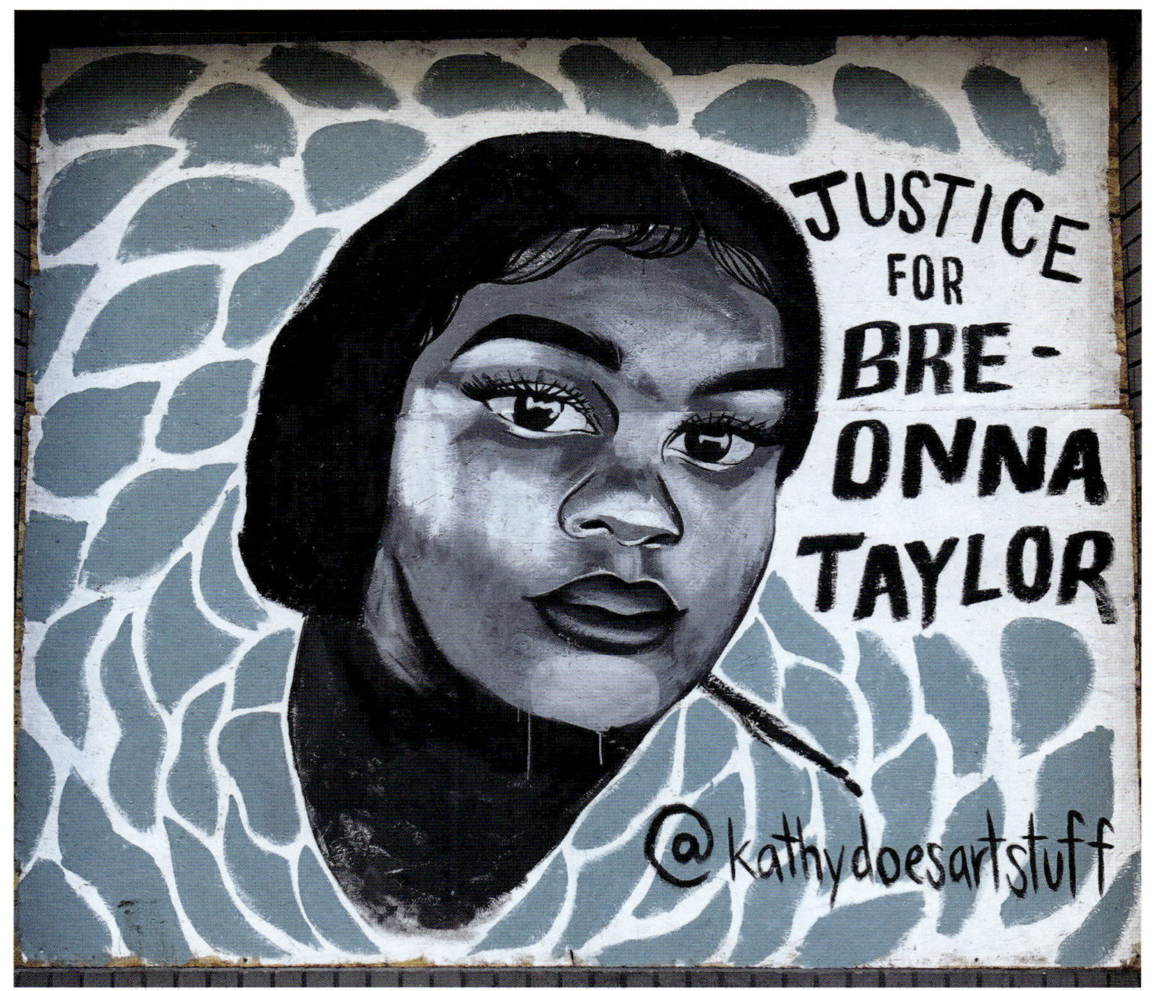


# Kathy Liang

@kathydoesartstuff

**Downtown Oakland**
12th and Franklin

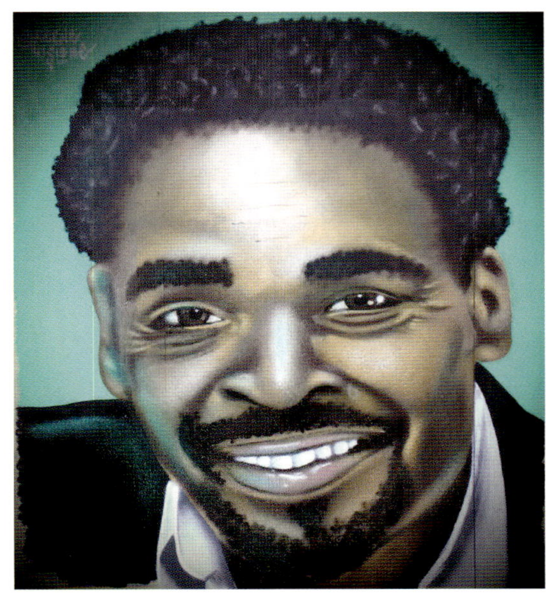
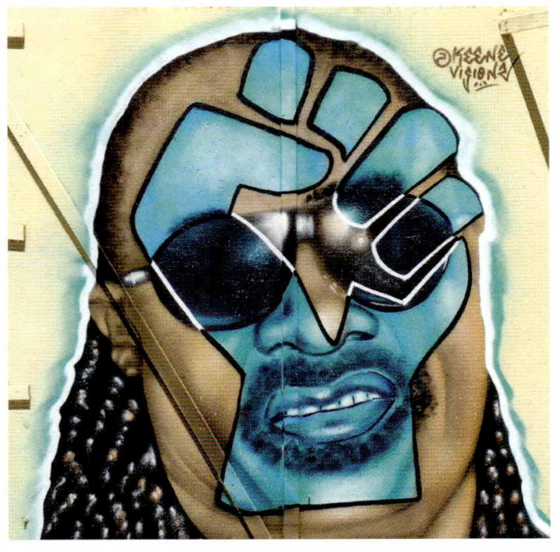
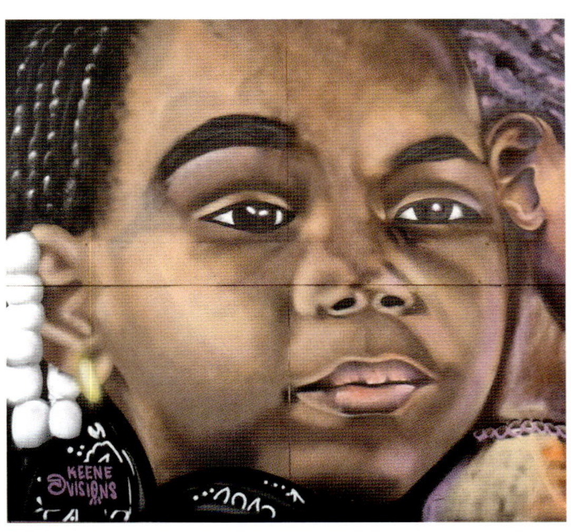
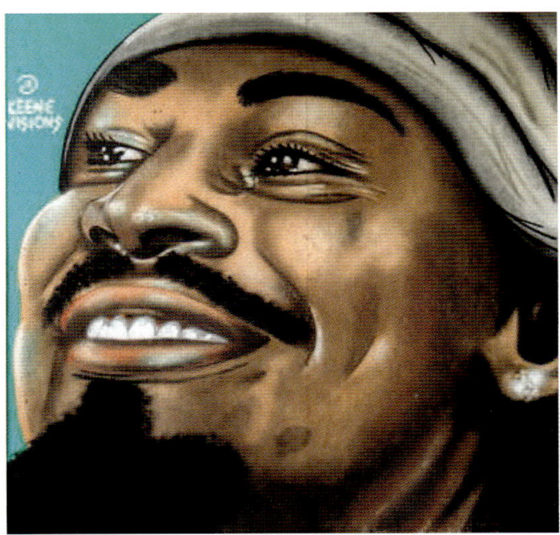

# KeeneVisions

@keenevisions

**Downtown Oakland**
Broadway and 12th

**Downtown Oakland**
Broadway and 17th

**Downtown Oakland**
Broadway

**Downtown Oakland**
Broadway and 14th

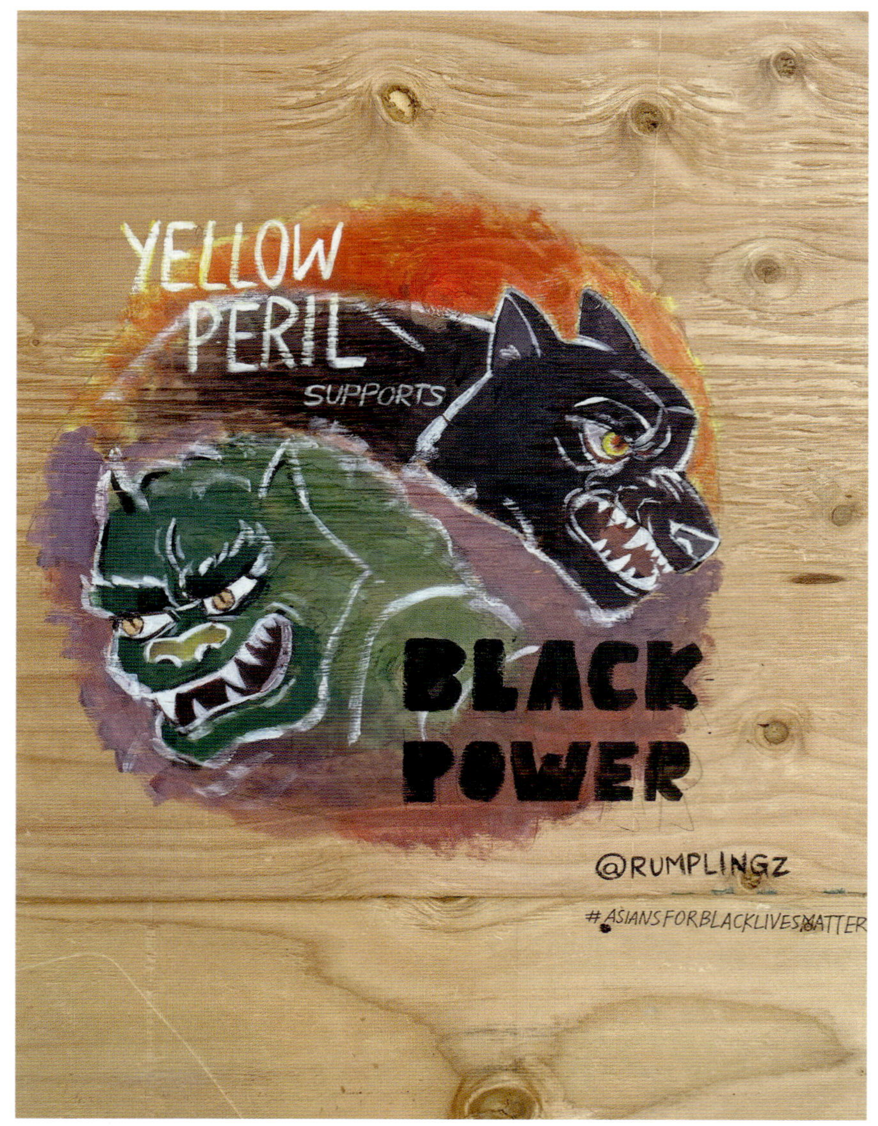




# Lynn Huang

@rumplingz

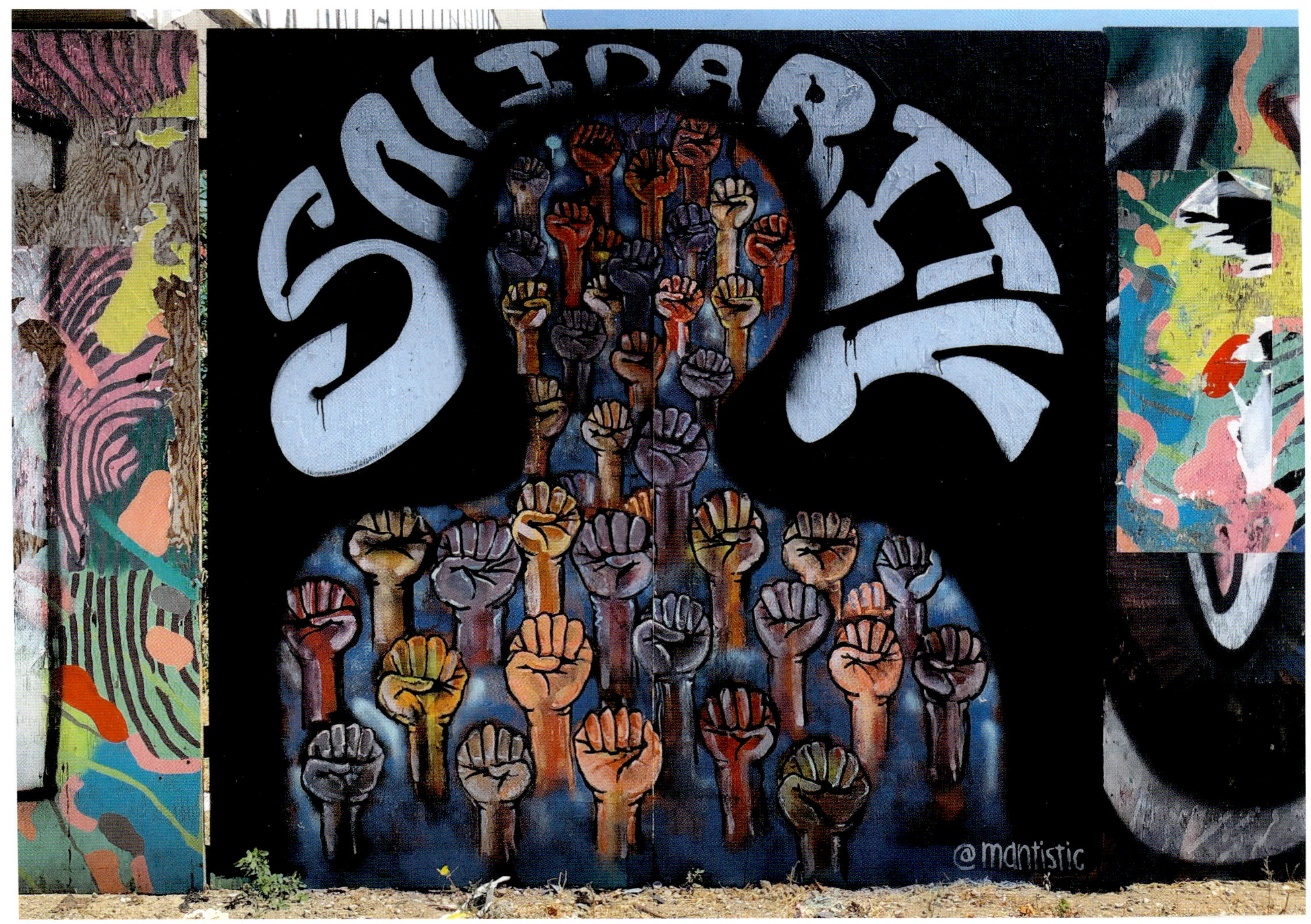


# Mario Navasero

@mantistic

**Chinatown (Oakland)**
8th and Broadway

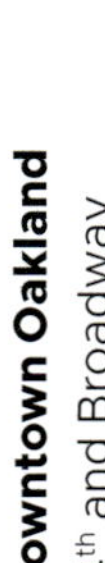

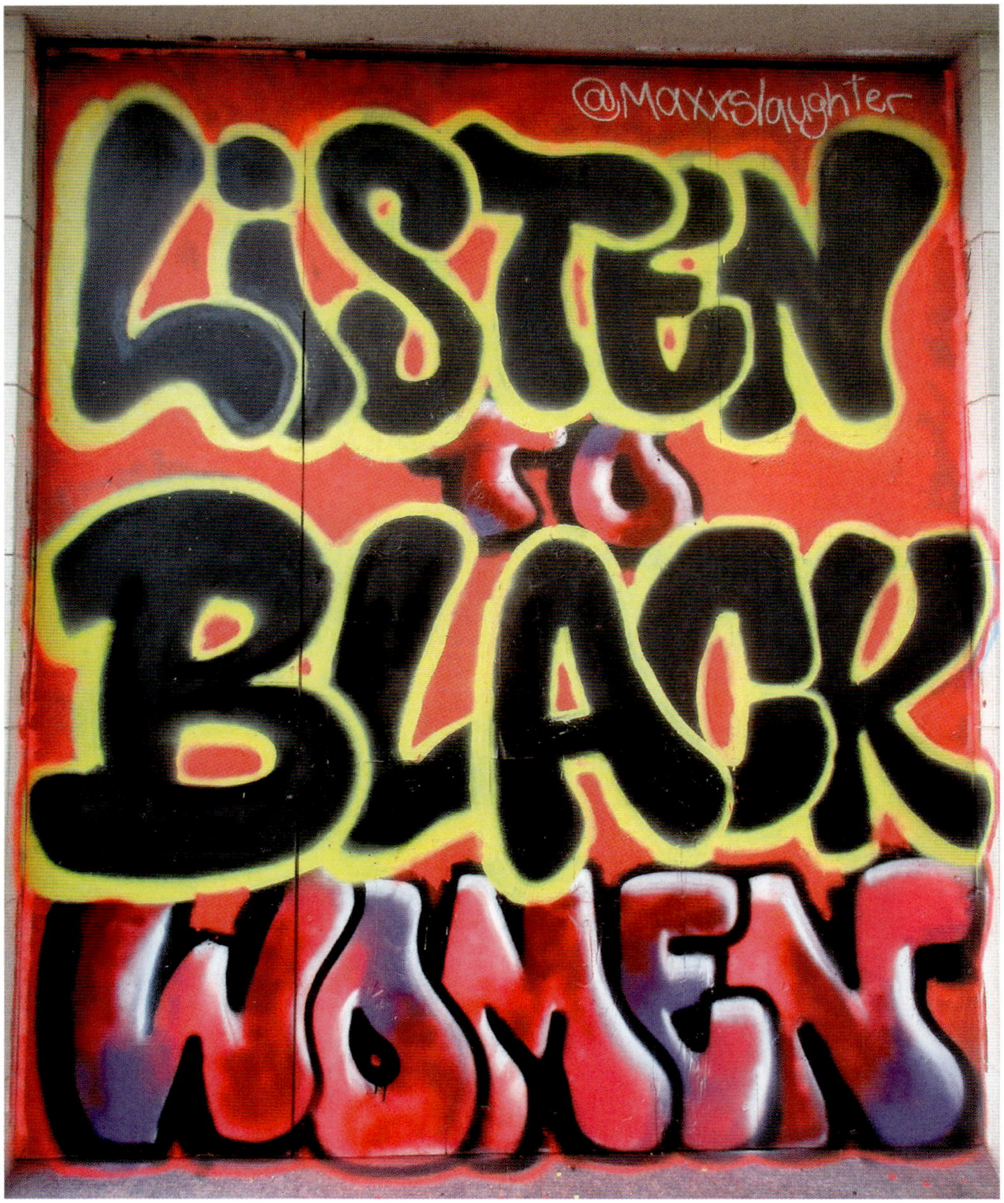

**Downtown Oakland**
14th and Broadway

# Maxx Slaughter

@maxxslaughter

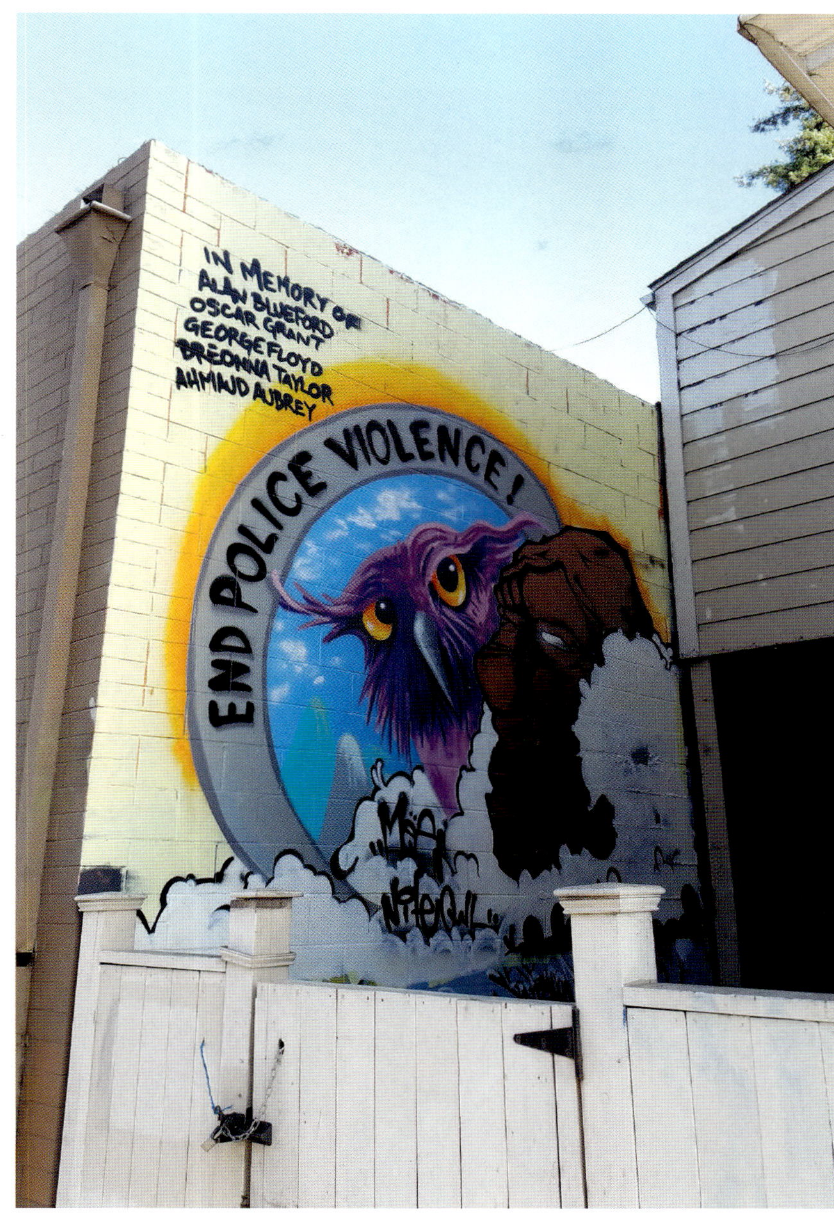


**Uptown Oakland**
Broadway and 27th

# Nite Owl

@naito_oru

**in collaboration with:** @shakebranches_barber

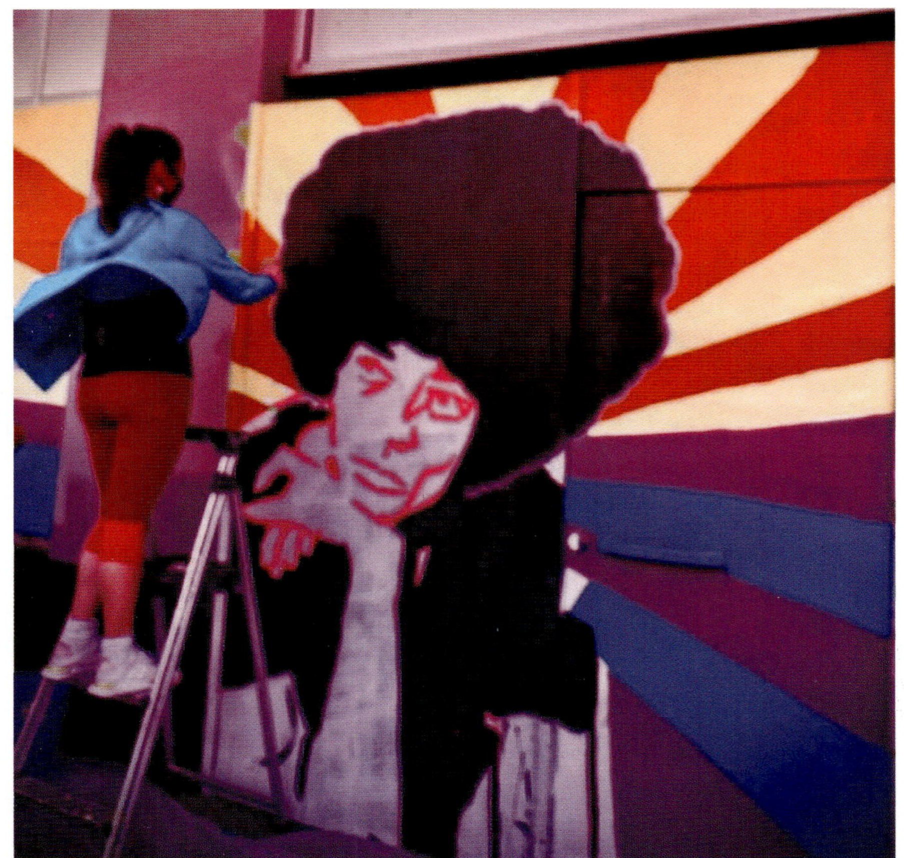



# Nyia Luna

@mushroombeatz

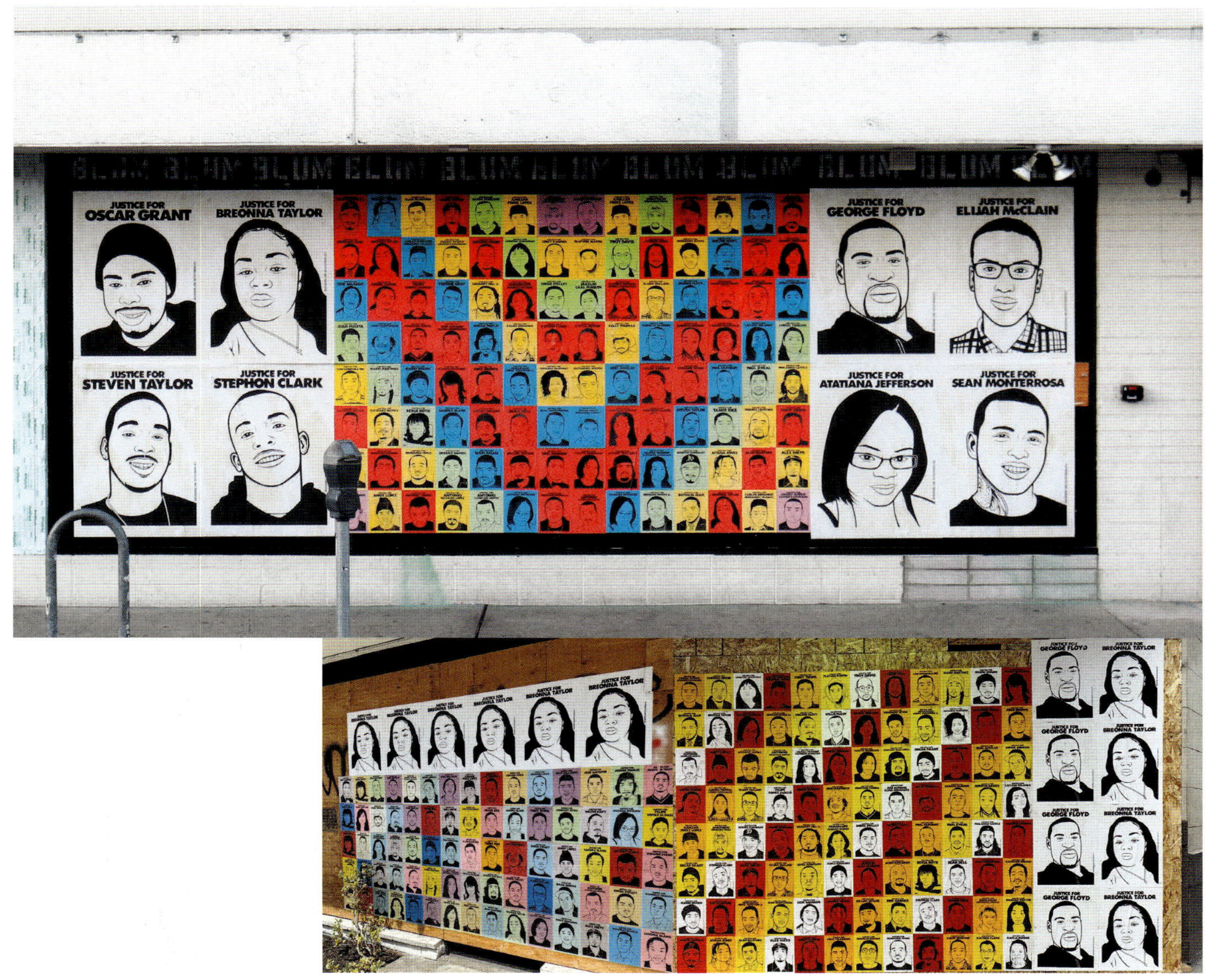


# Oree Originol

@oreeoriginol

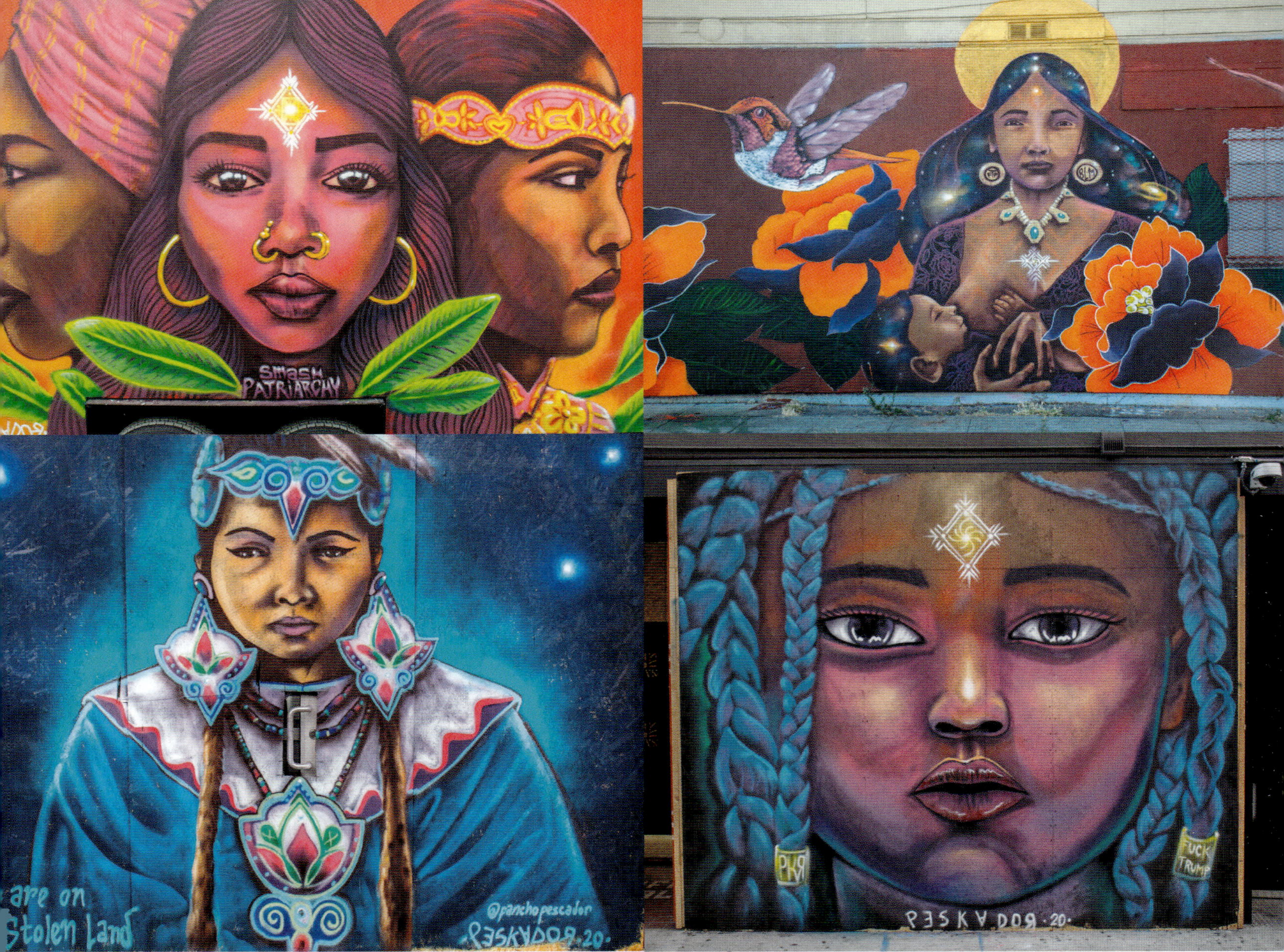

# Pancho Pescador

@panchopescador

**East Oakland**
Youth Spirit Artworks
Tiny Home Village

**East Oakland**
International and 34th Ave

**East Oakland**
International and 92nd Ave

**Downtown Oakland**
Cosecha Restaurant

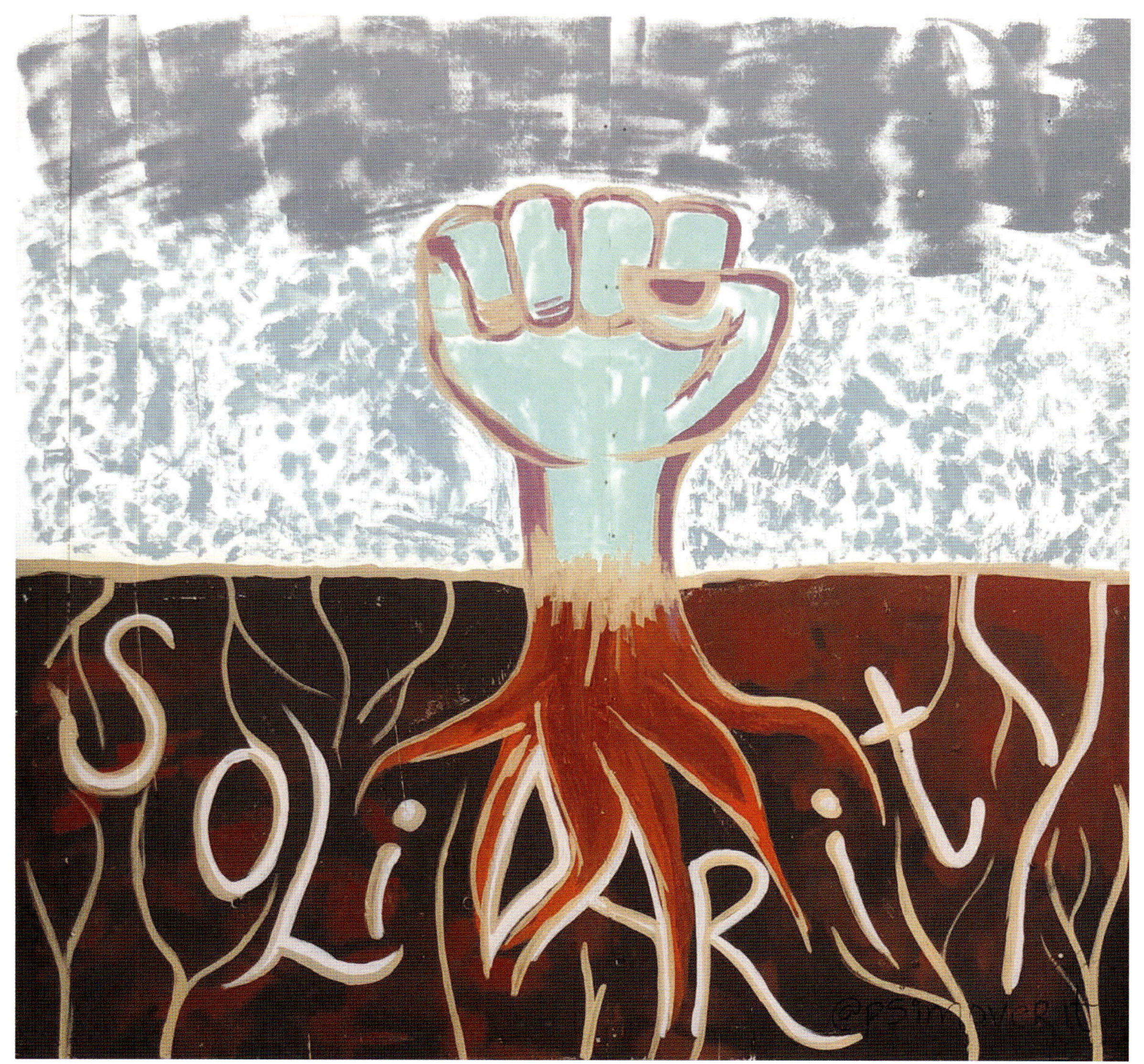


# Parul Sharma

**Downtown Oakland**
14th and Broadway

@psimoverit

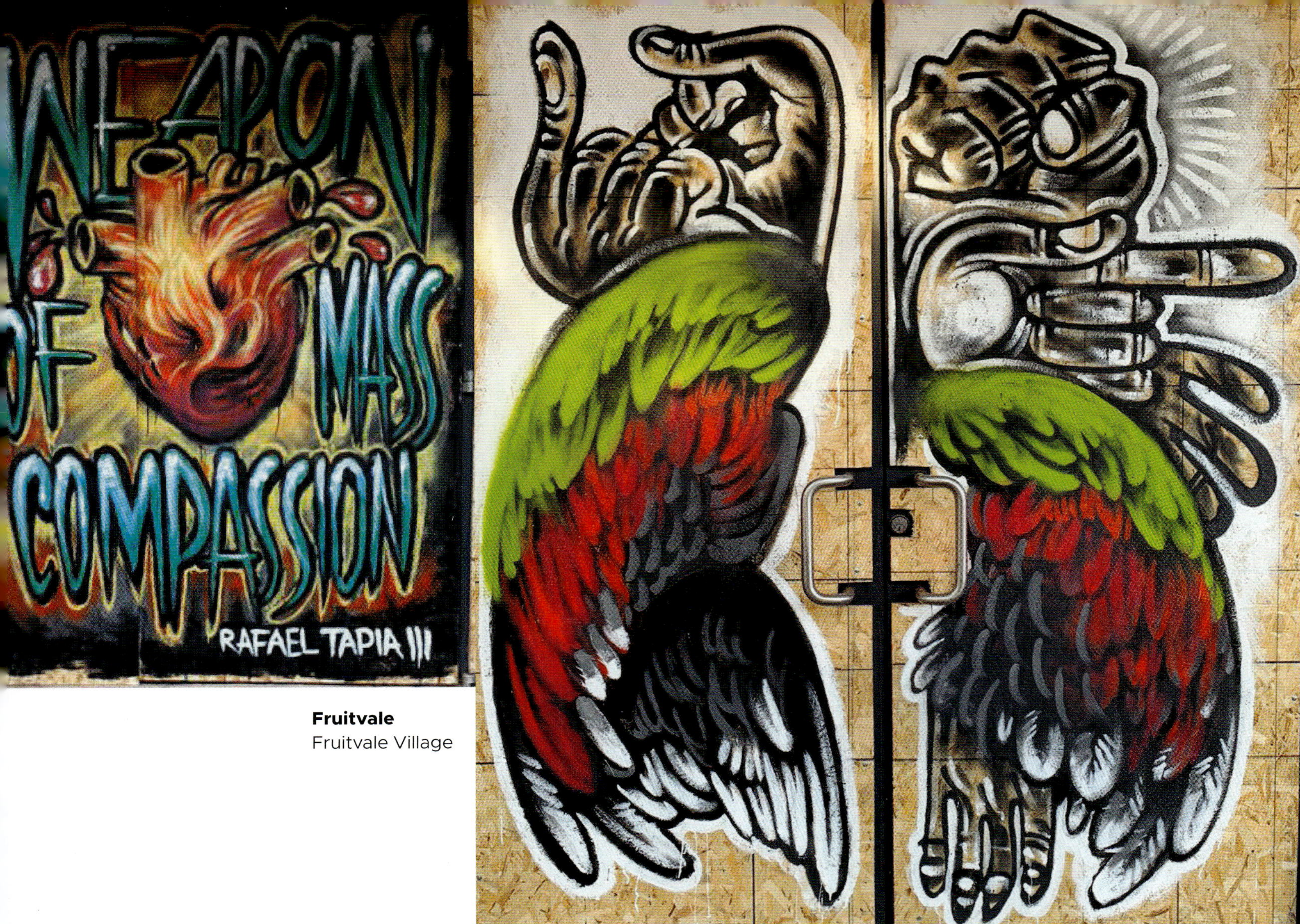


**Fruitvale**
Fruitvale Village

# Rafael Tapia III

@RustySaltBabies

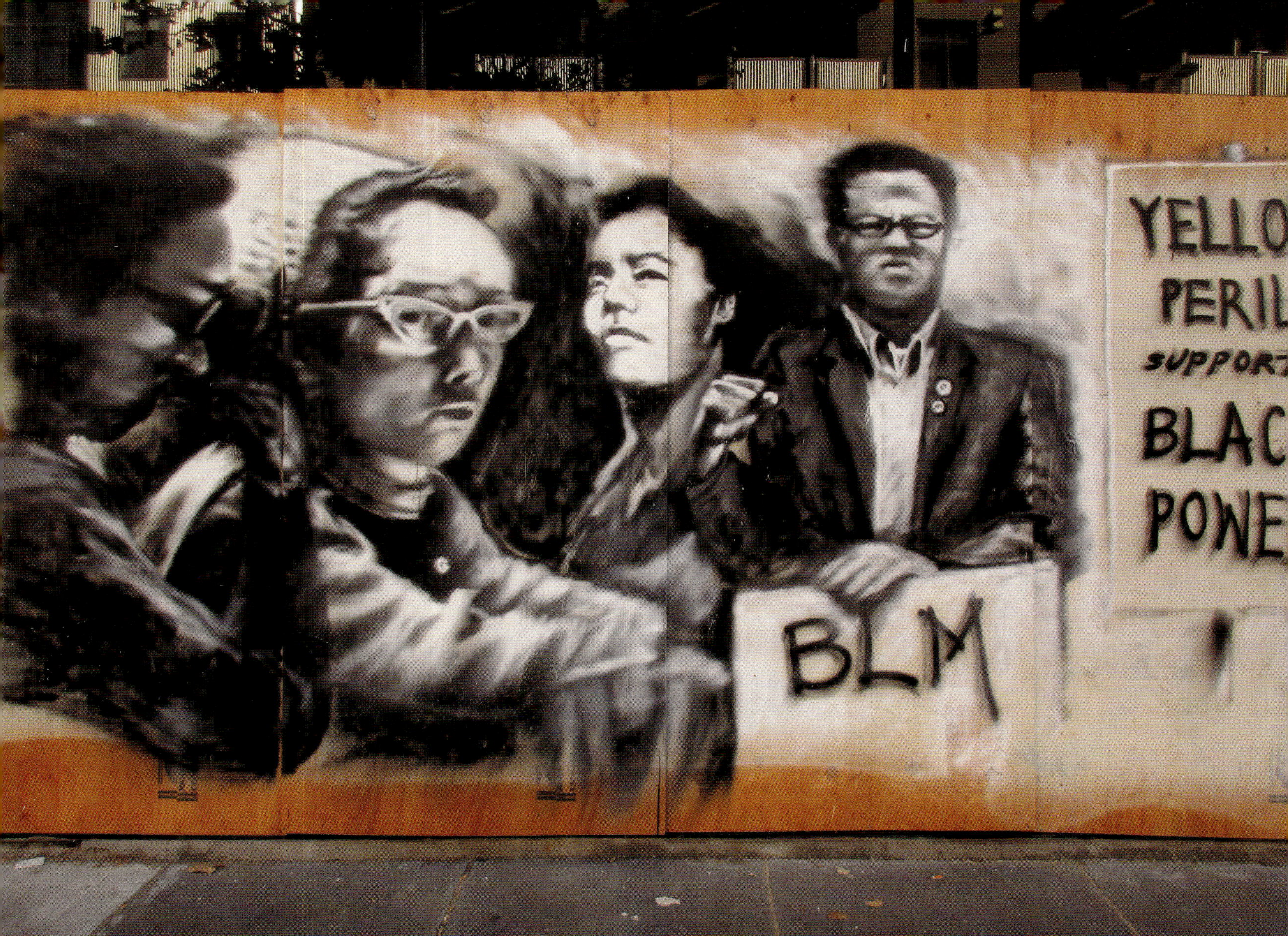


**Oakland Chinatown**

# Richard Choi

@rchoi.art

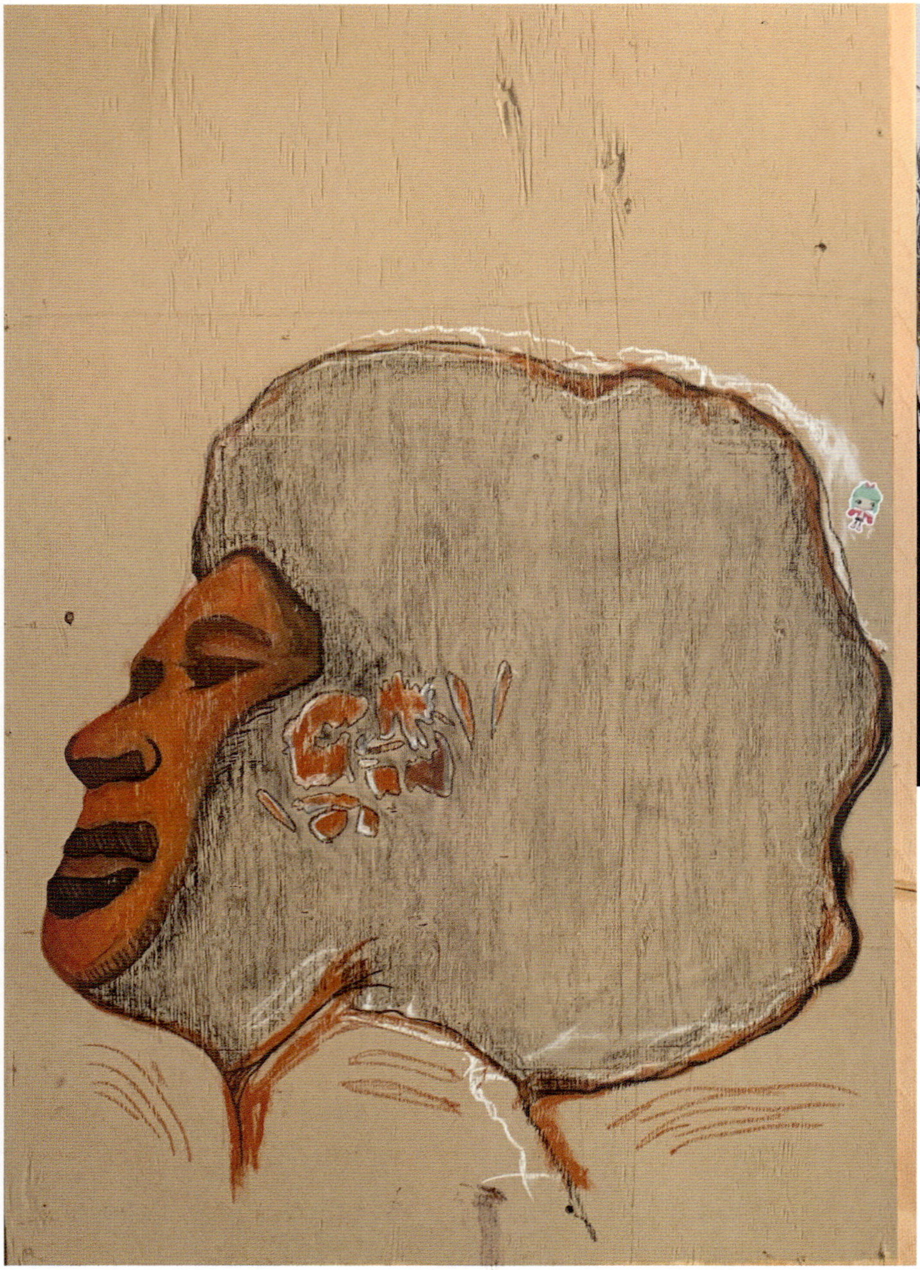

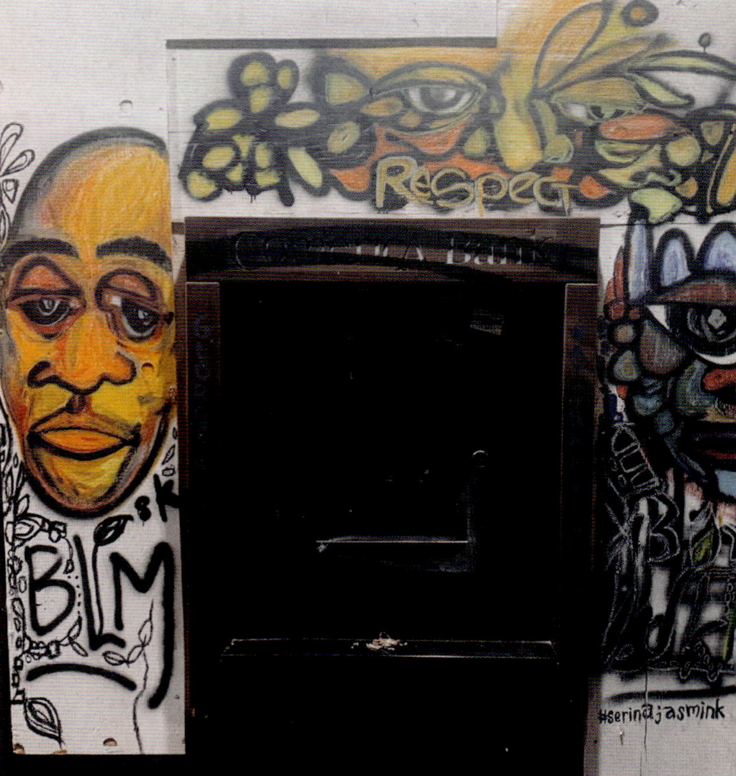


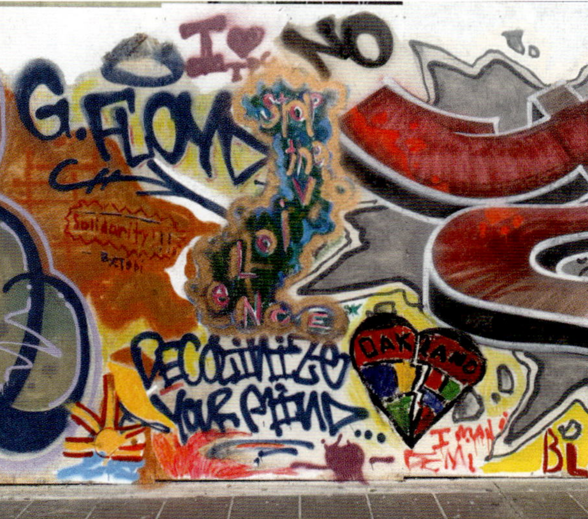


**Downtown Oakland**
12th and Broadway

# Serina Jasmin Koester
@serinajasmink

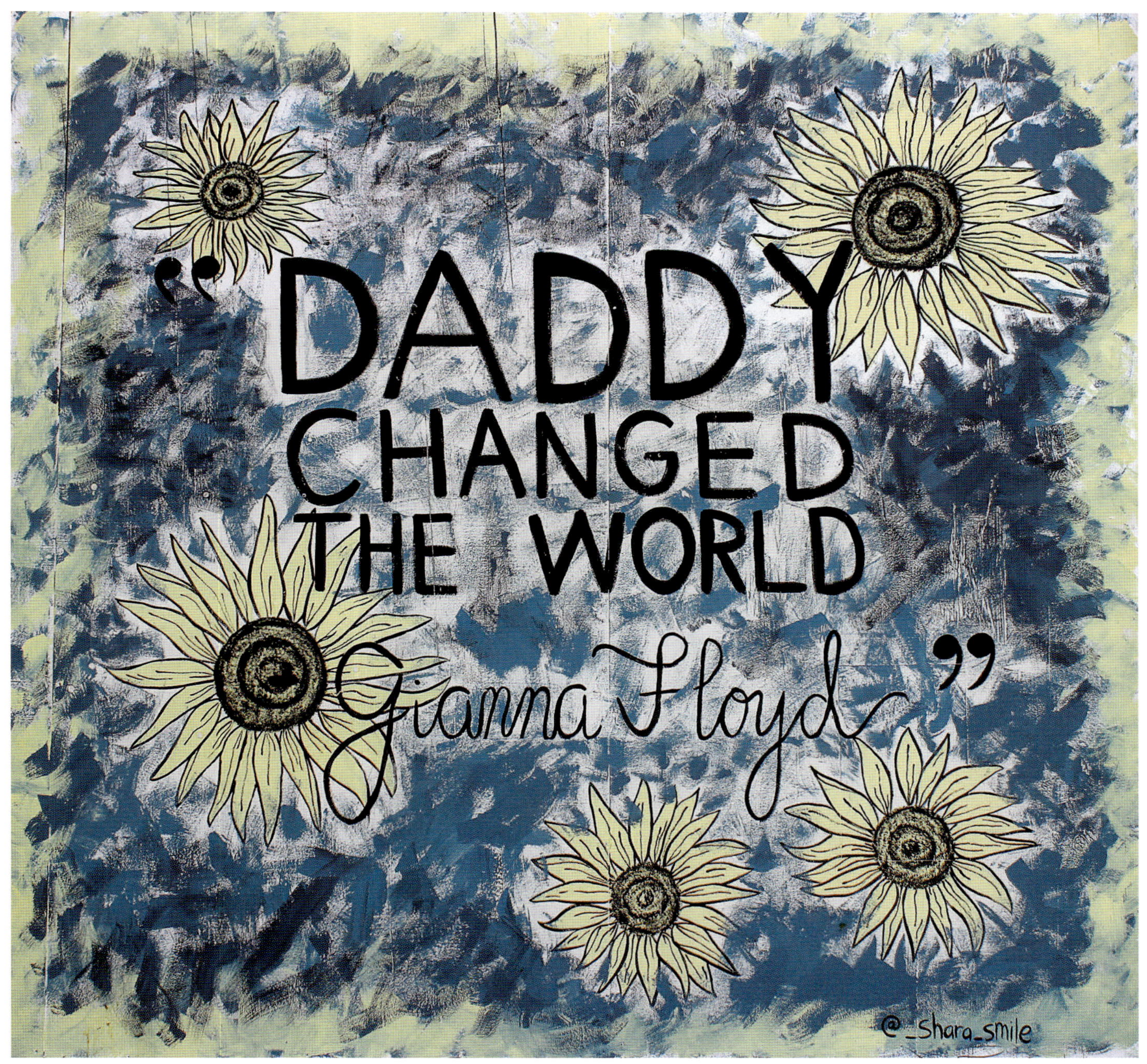


# Shara Shimabukuro

@_shara_smile

**Downtown Oakland**
14th and Broadway

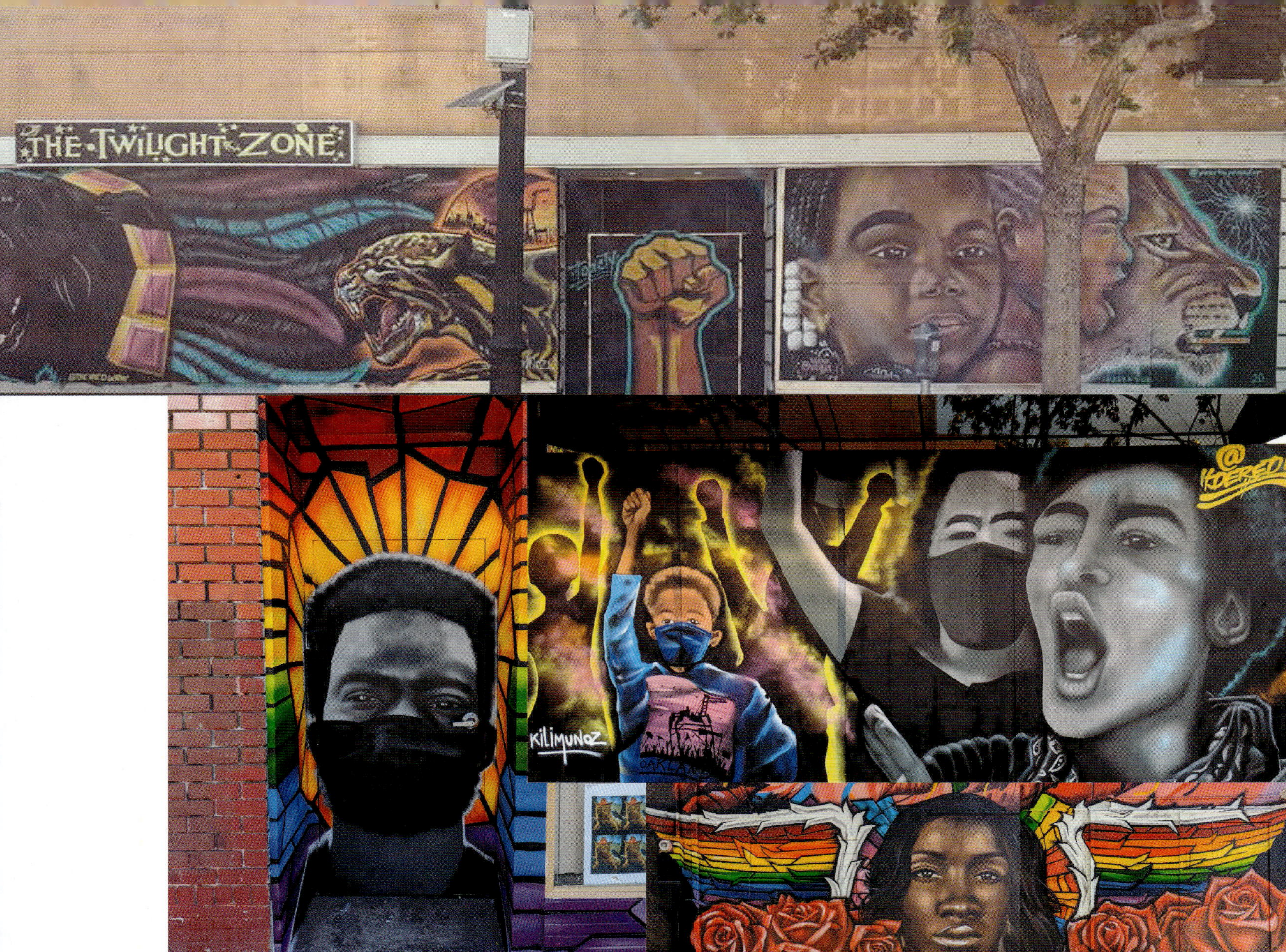


# Shawn Gibson

**Downtown Oakland**
Broadway

@deredwrk

**in collaboration with:** Cristian Munoz @kilimunoz

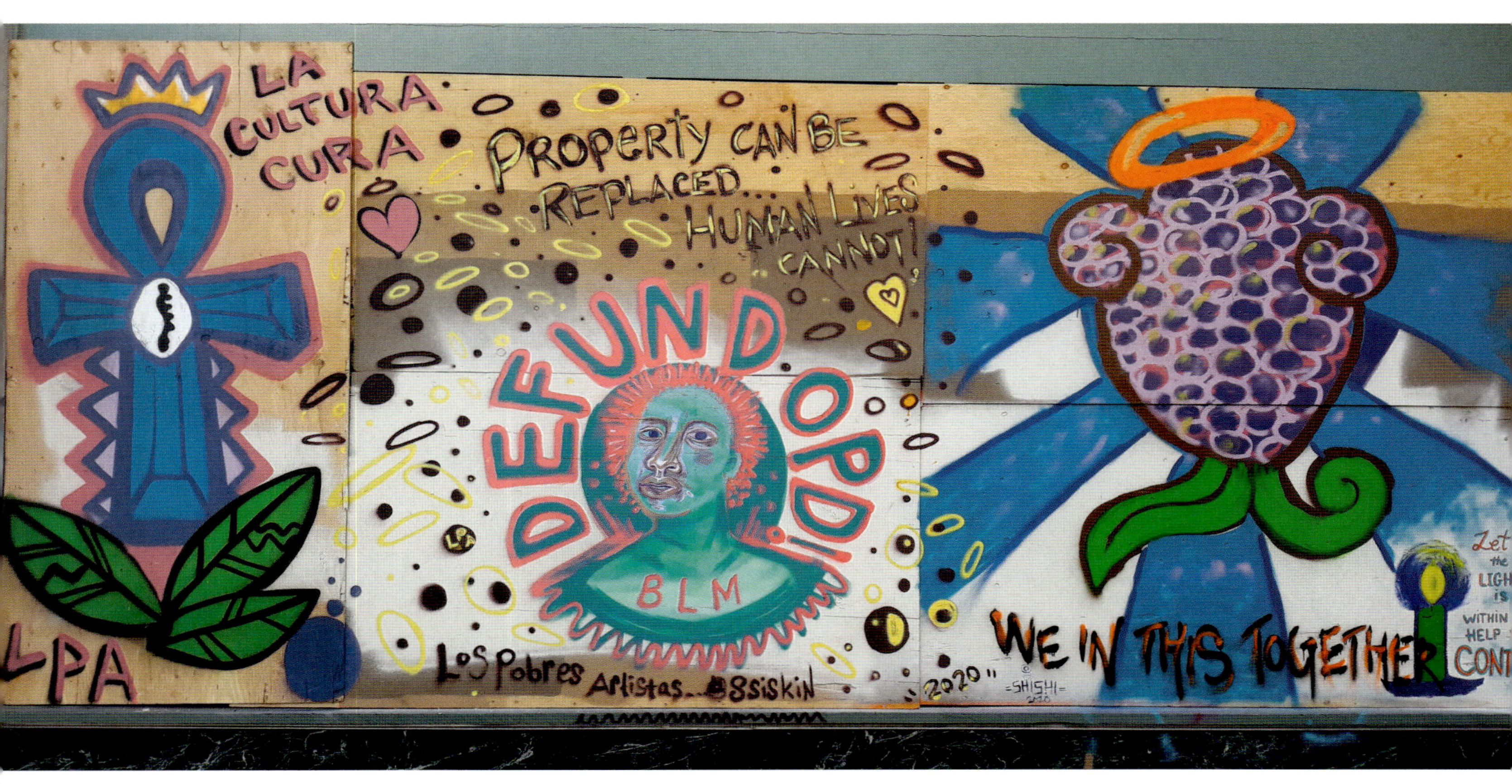


# Shi Shi

@shishi.madriz

**Downtown Oakland**
Tierra Mia Coffee
20th and Broadway

**in collaboration with:** Los Pobres Artistas

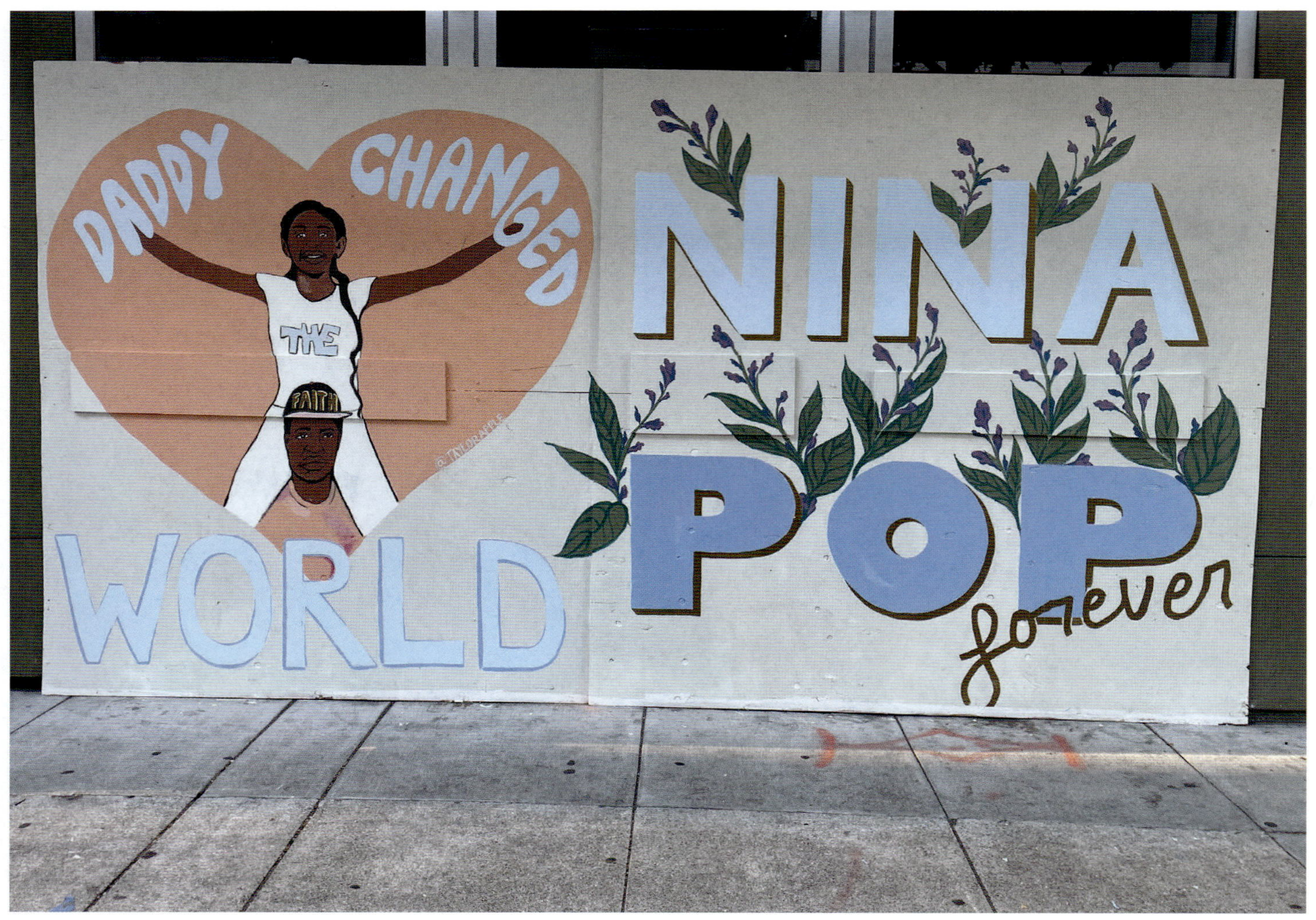


# Taylor Apple

@taylorapple

**Downtown Oakland (Lakeside)**
1401 Jackson Street

**in collaboration with:** Laura Dickie, Holly Hapka, Natasha Rosenberg, Sarah Cobillas, Tatiana Dannenbaum

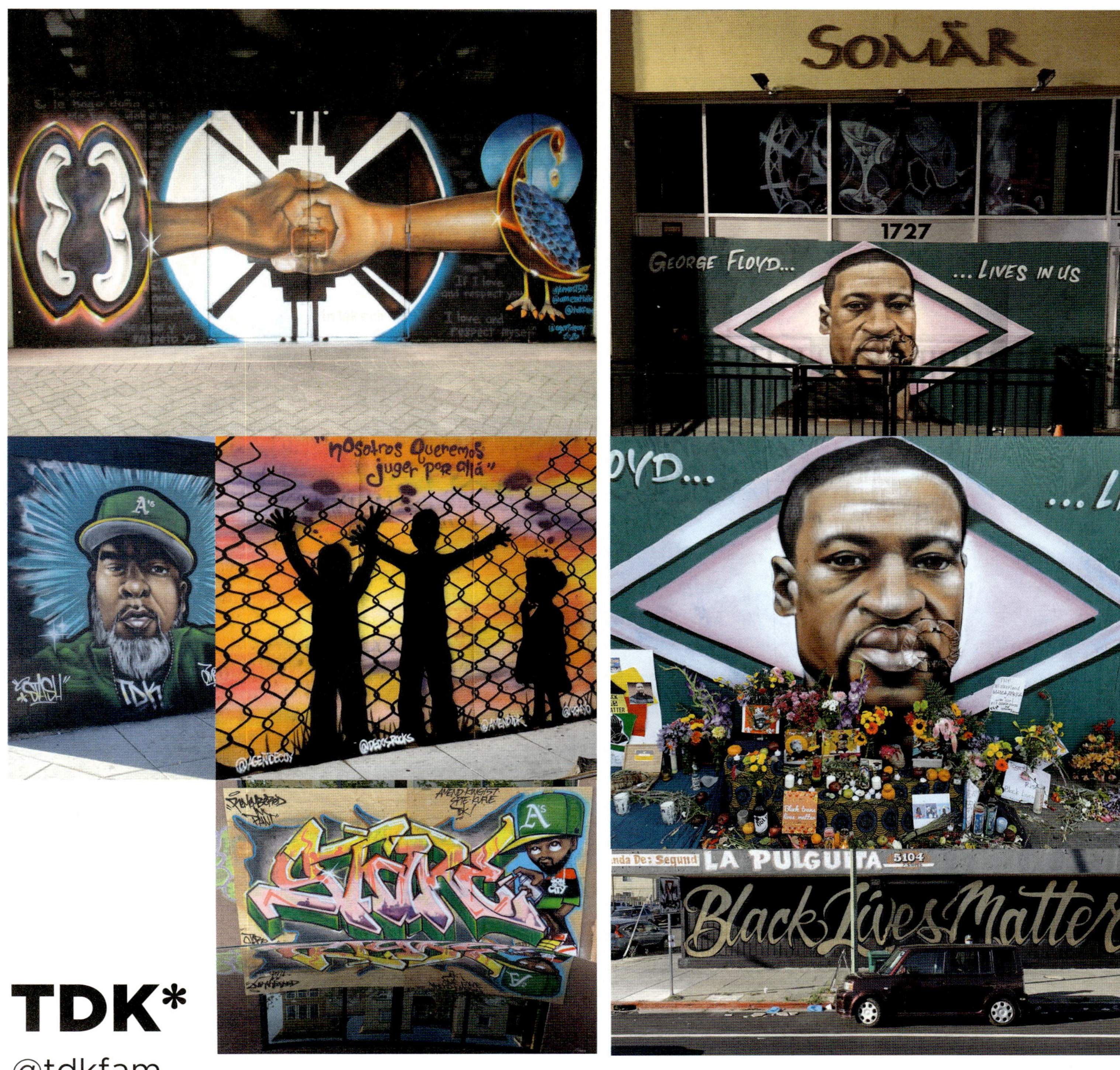


# TDK*

@tdkfam

***Those Damn Kids (collective), a collaboration between :** Spie, Kufue (@kemest510), King 157, and Amend (@amendtdk)

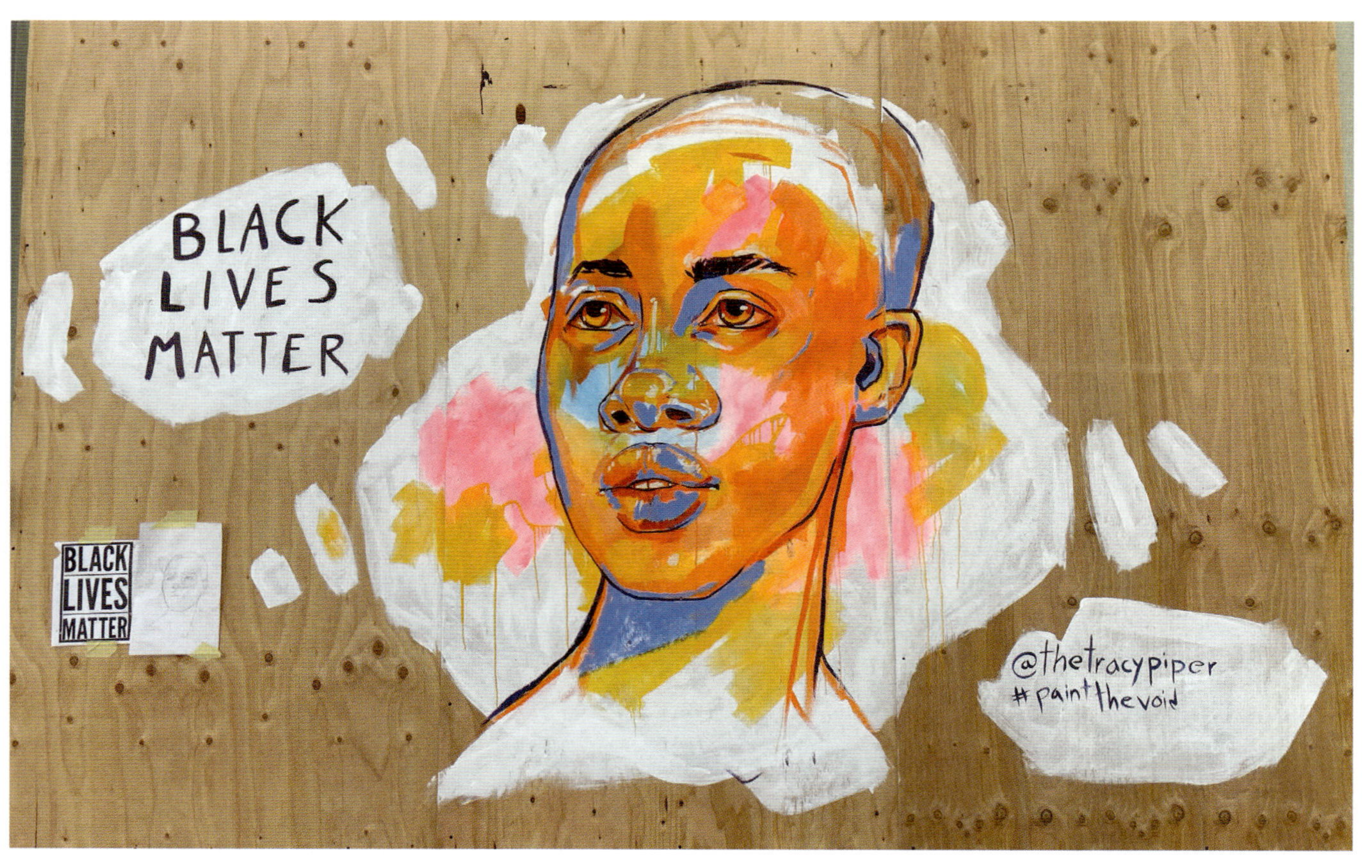


**Old Oakland**

# The Tracy Piper

@thetracypiper

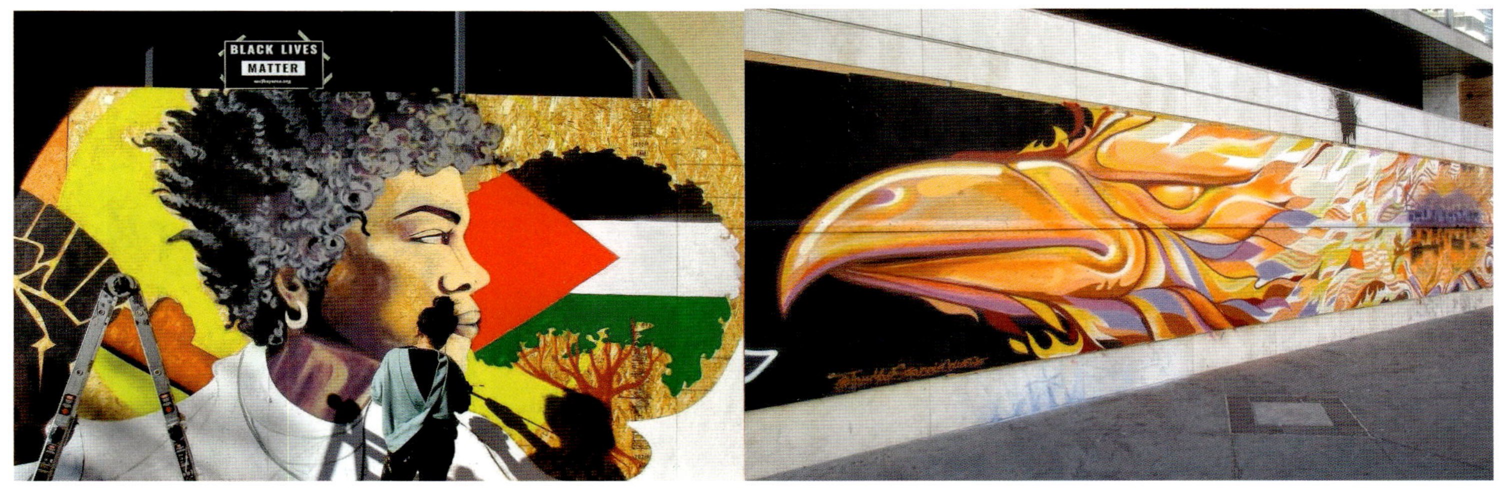

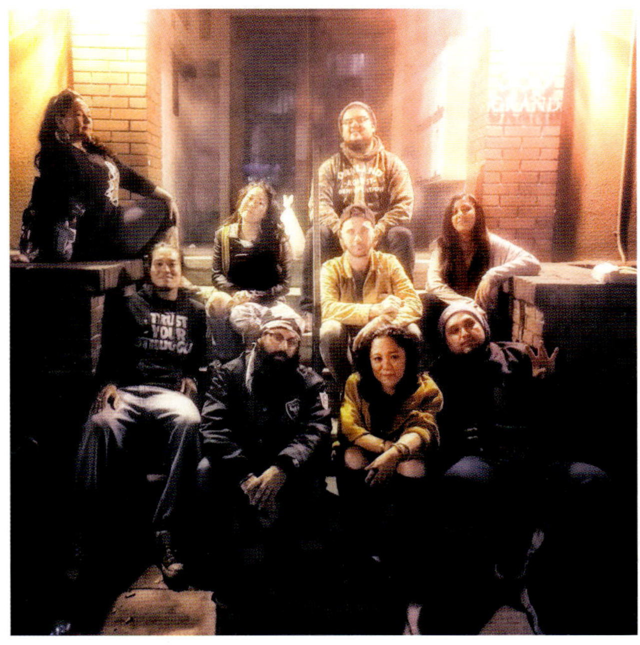

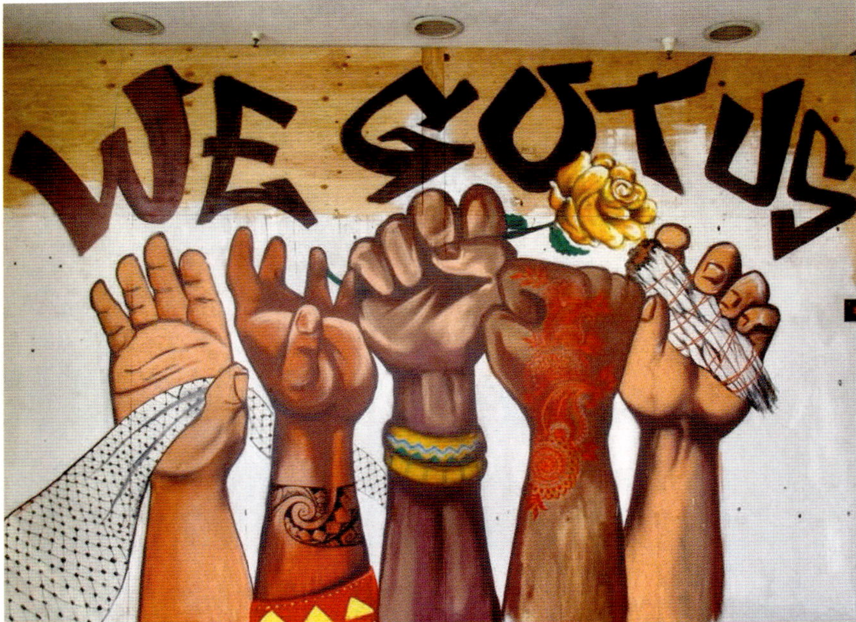


# Trust Your Struggle*

@trustyourstruggle



***a collective collaboration between:** Robert Trujillo (@robert_tres), Miguel "Bounce" Perez (@misterbouncer),
Cece Carpio (@cececarpio), Nisha K. Sethi, THITIWAT "T" PHROMRATANAPONGSE,
and Priya K Handa (@priya.k.handa)

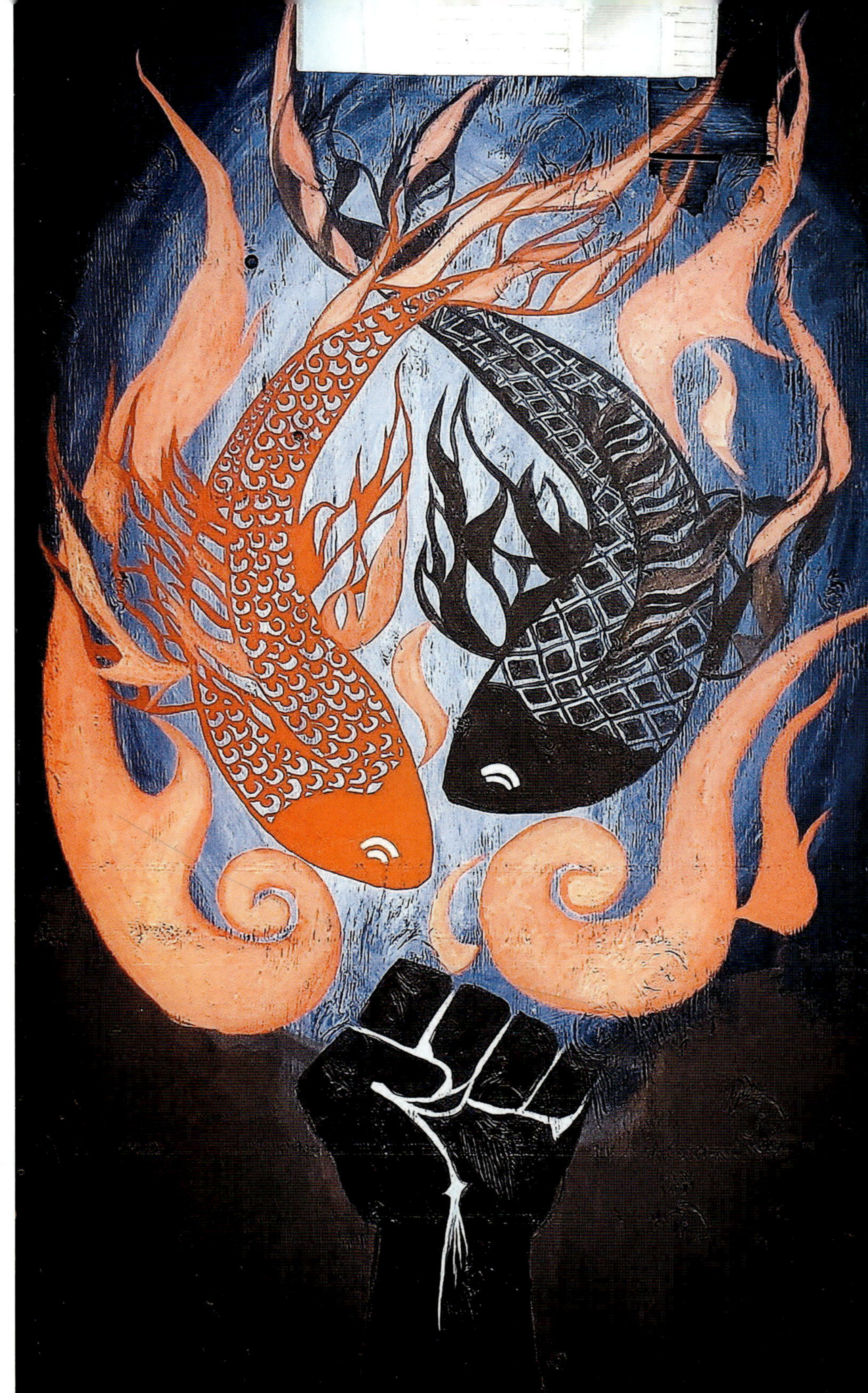

# Wanli Wang

@wanli.ww

**Old Oakland**
Urban Eclectics
735 Washington Street

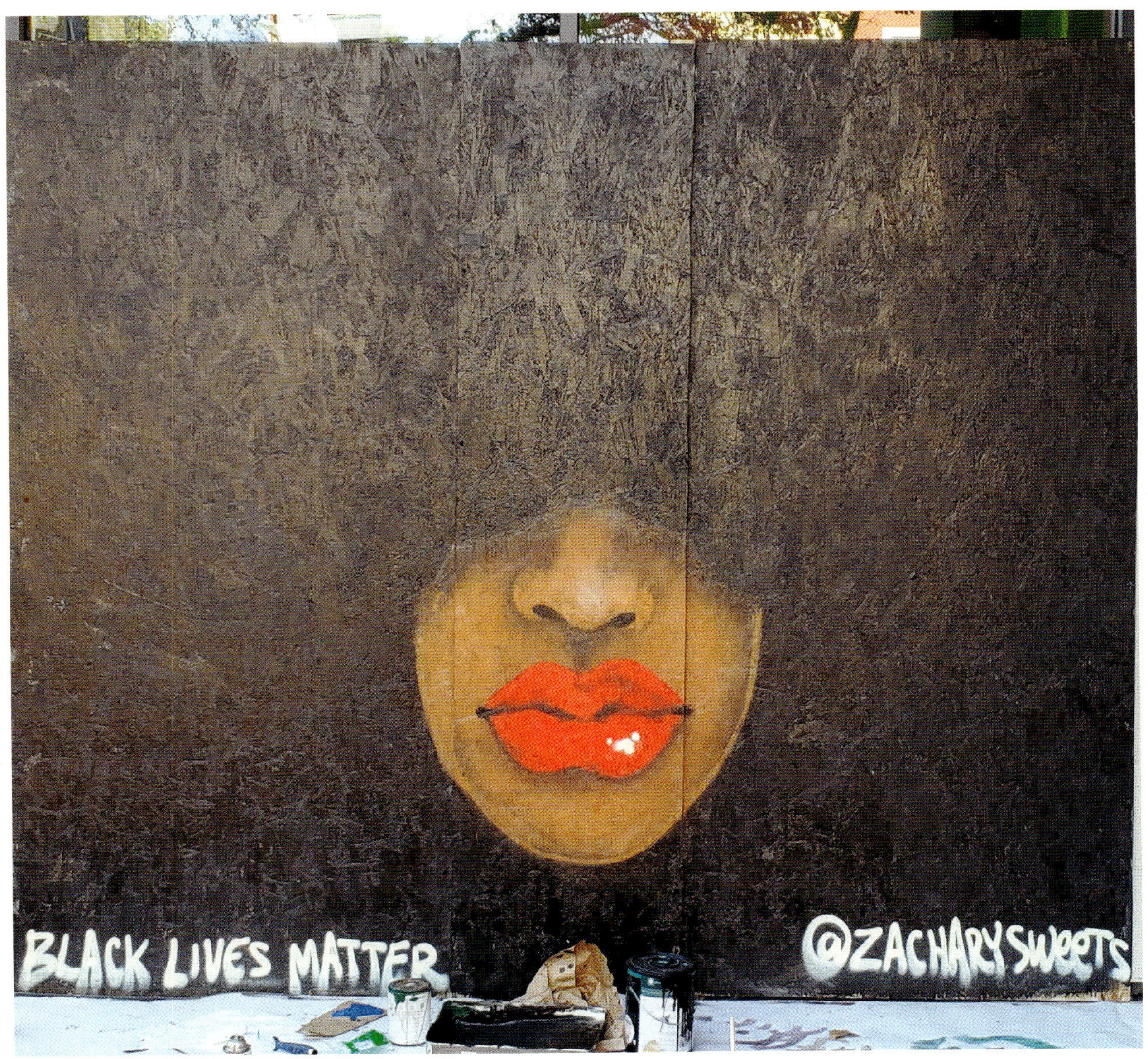


# Zachary Sweet

@zacharysweets

**Fruitvale**
Fruitvale BART
Station Plaza

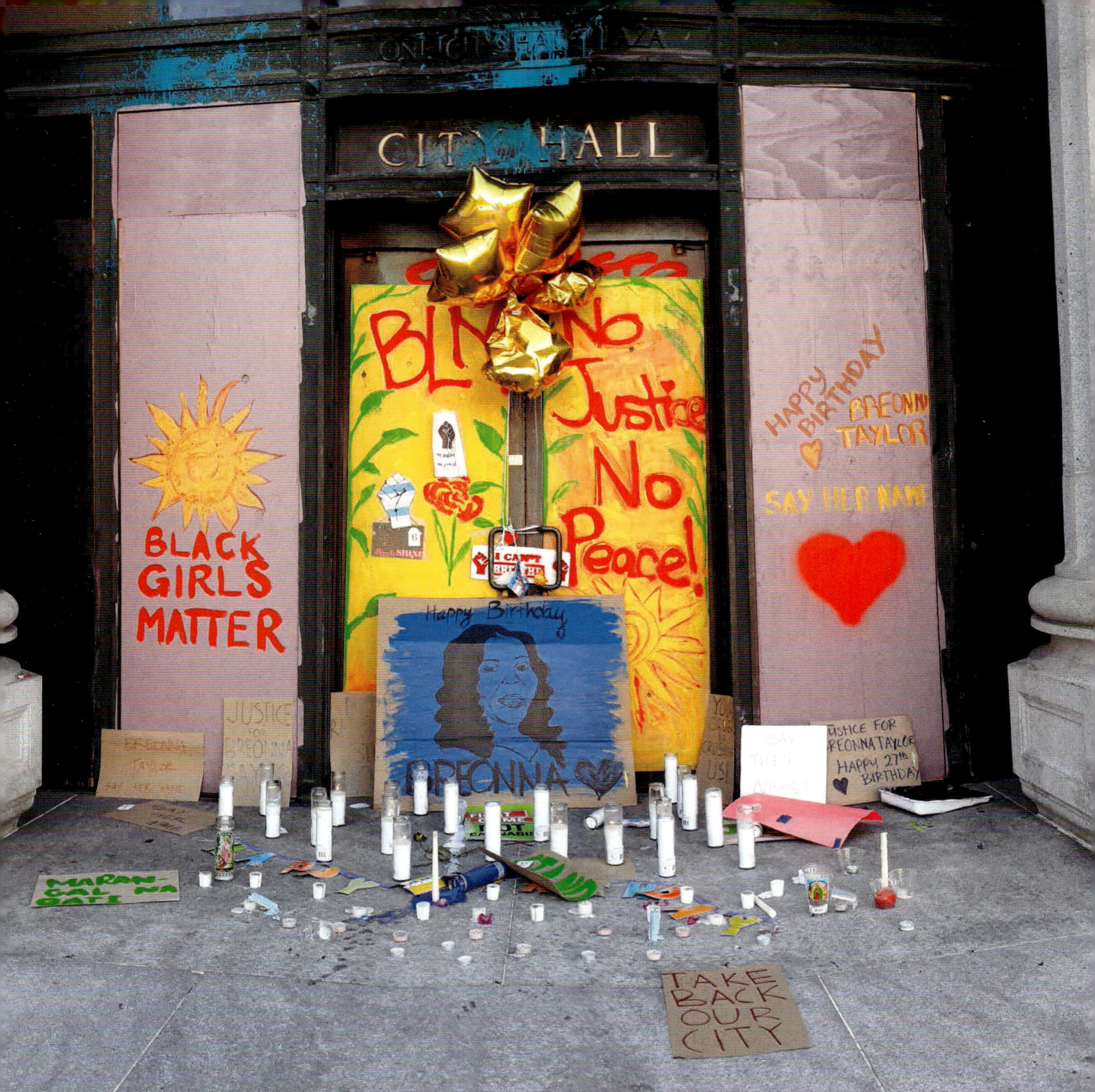
ONE CITY HALL PLAZA
CITY HALL
BLM NO Justice No Peace!
BLACK GIRLS MATTER
I CAN'T BREATHE
Happy Birthday
BREONNA
HAPPY BIRTHDAY BREONNA TAYLOR
SAY HER NAME
JUSTICE FOR BREONNA
JUSTICE FOR BREONNA TAYLOR HAPPY 27th BIRTHDAY
SAY THEIR NAMES
TAKE BACK OUR CITY

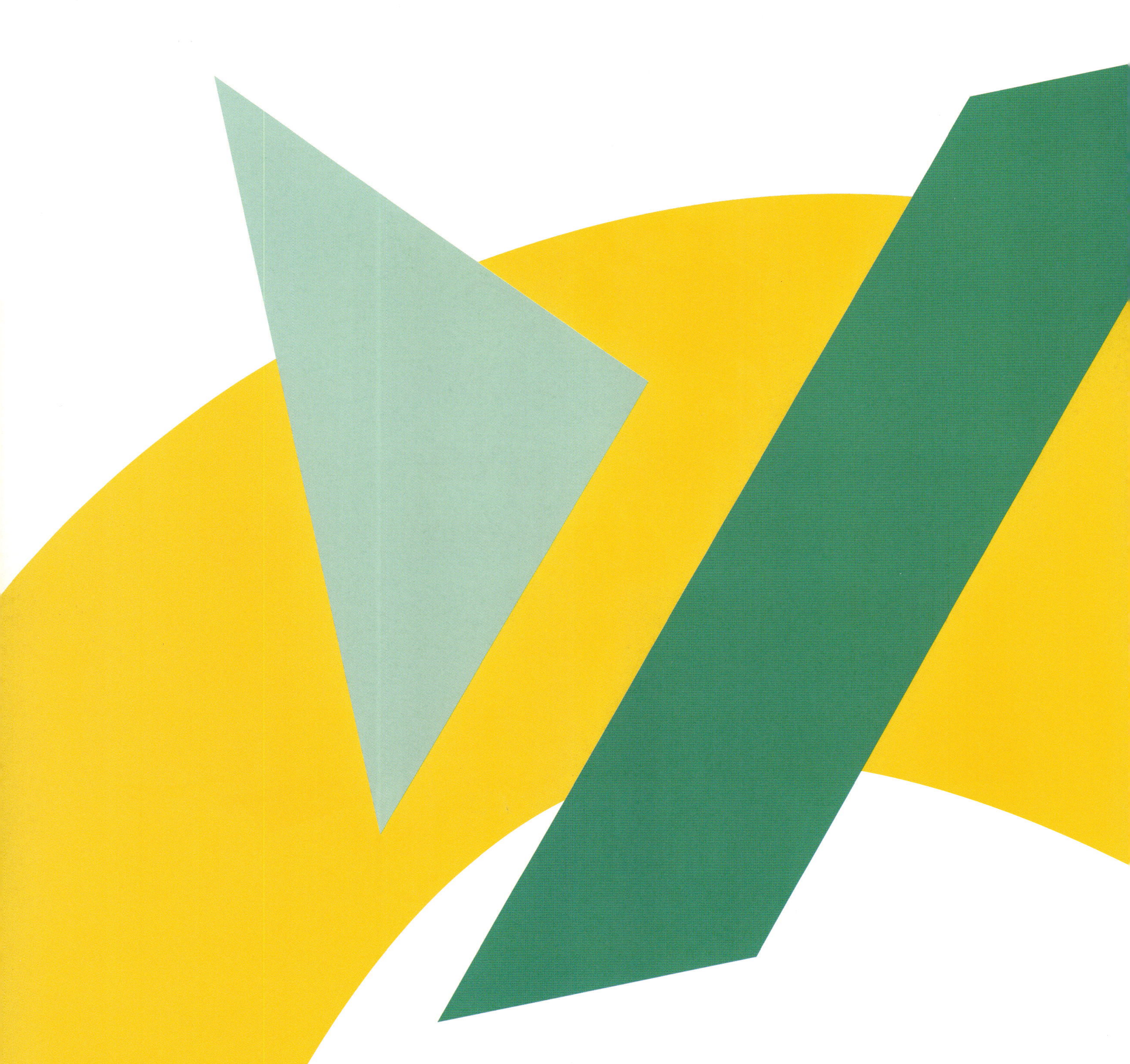

# 5 ESSAYS

# The Ugliest Beautiful
## Cat Brooks

For eight minutes and forty-six seconds Derrick Chauvin bore his knee into the neck of George Floyd, who repeatedly called for his dead mama to help. To pull back the veil—help him journey home.

### Breathing While Black.

Breonna Taylor was executed in her home. In her bed. Next to her love.

### Sleeping While Black.

Black America was rocked. Again. The brutality of it all.

### Dying While Black.

White allies were rocked too. Murder by cop. Because he was Black. Everyone agrees with that part. Even the ones who don't have a problem with genocide.

### Hunted While Black.

Months spent screaming the names of Breonna Taylor and George Floyd as if ... as if we can resurrect the dead.

### Wailing While Black.

Oakland rocked too. Until the curfew was announced with a barrage of rubber bullets, tear gas and flashbangs on children. Our children. Black children.

### Growing Up Black.

Two pandemics. COVID and the Cops. Both deadly. We broke it. The curfew. 8,000 strong. Masked up. Socially Distanced. (Kind of) Closer than we'd been in months.

### Raging While Black.

This ugly, beautiful, radical, rational moment is not "the beginning." Another stop on a looooooooooong continuum of Black resistance.

At least in Oakland, anyone speaking on resistance to police terror, should "begin" with the Black Panther Party. Thank Lil' Bobby. Minister Huey. Sister Tarika.

But if we have to use that paradigm ... this "beginning," then this phase began with the murder—and the resistance to the murder of—Oscar Grant.

## *Resisting While Black.*

### A Man Is Murdered: A Movement is Born

In the early hours of New Year's, 2009, BART police officer Johannes Mehserle executed Oscar Grant on the Fruitvale Platform. "Bitch. Ass. Nigger." They called him. Before the bullet.

## *Oh yes, honey, 21ˢᵗ Century lynchings are a thing …*

The protracted struggle for justice for Oscar would be the catalyst for a seismic shift in the movement. None of us saw it coming. The tear gas was blinding.

### Repercussions and Consequences

Oakland exploded. While the graffiti-stained walls carried Oscar's name, they also bore the weight of an out-of-control police department's legacy of hate, racism, brutality, and violence.

## *Run boy, run fast, they are the hunters—you are the prey … Run boy, run fast … OPD gonna catch a nigga today ….*

Johannes Mehserle became the first cop in all of California's sunny, progressive, beach lined history to be tried and convicted for killing someone in the line of duty. Despite California being the deadliest state in the union for officer-involved shootings … then and now.

## *Ezell Ford, Alan Blueford, Yuvette Henderson, Angel Ramos, Stephon Clark, Gregario Mack, Erik Salgado, Dante Parker, Mario Woods, Jessica Williams, Willie McCoy, Ronnell Foster, Brian Macias, Linda Carol Clark, Steven Washington, Oscar Morales, Nathan Manning, Chinedu Okobi, Rakeem Rucks, Angel Ramos.*

Mehserle was convicted only of involuntary manslaughter and served meager months in jail. We shuck and jive around the contradiction that the path to "justice" lies within the carceral state we desperately desire to dismantle.

## *Contradicting and Black.*

Amazing and beautiful and sacred and hard and ugly and exhausting … organizing … the people organized. Argued over strategy and tactics. About the role of white folks, race vs. class, reform vs. revolution, anarchy vs. nationalism vs. socialism.

## *Not All Of Us Were Black.*

### Windows Don't Die

They only wanted to talk about windows. The electeds and the suits. Problem was. Nothing was off-limits for some folks. Including immigrant businesses, Black-owned businesses, youth-group orgs … nothing. Some of us became targets of the state for acts we did not commit. No one cared about Chase. But leave them moms' and pops' biz alone, son. AND. If you want people to stop

breaking windows—Stop. Fucking. Killing. Us.

### *Some of Them Were Black.*

### What The Fuck Are We Doing This For?

For over a year, people organized, marched, traveled to and from Los Angeles, made art, attended meetings, were tear gassed, arrested and brutalized. Mehserle was found guilty of involuntary manslaughter.

Bullshit verdict. Bullshit sentence.

### *You remember you a nigger now .... niggaaaaaa???*

Five days after Mehserle's sentencing, OPD shot and killed a barber from East Oakland named Derrick Jones. He was unarmed. No protests. No rebellions. No weeping windows. Life had moved on.

### *Business as Usual While Black.*

Movement fatigue. Nigga fatigue. We have to turn off some of our nigga just to make it through the daily reality of being Black. Immobile with grief. Homicidal with rage. Both appropriate. Neither sustainable. Turn off. Tune out. Survive.

### Black people make up 28% of the almost 1,000 killed by police in 2020 despite being only 13% of the population

### Anti Police-Terror—What?

A core group of Black organizers came together during that year of struggle. Me, Turha, Tha Ghetto Prophet, Asantewaa, Carroll Fife, Che ... others who flowed through. But this was the squad. Formative years. Laying the foundation. Feeding the people, political education, cultural cultivation ... The state kept killing us.

### *Hunted and Black.*

So we kept protesting. Murders here. Murders there. The whole damn system. Thousands in the streets. Broken windows. Burdened freeways. Agitated America.

### *Alan Blueford, Maurice Shavers, Jose Mengia, Antonio Mestas, Jose Navarro, Rekia Boyd, Tamir Rice, Jeffrey Ragland, Miriam Carey, Natasha McKenna, Aiyanna Stanley Jones, Michael Brown, Eric Garner, Richard Perkings, Demouriah Hogg, Yonas Alegheni.*

I know folks who don't march. Say it's wasted time. Say we been doing that shit for decades and the only thing changed is the nooses to guns and Klansmen to cops. Our death is the only constant. Nigga Porn.

## Dying While Black.

Protest keeps the names of our beloveds in the air. When the ancestors are called. The ancestors move.

## Conjuring While Black.

The time came for shifting. Killing us was egregious. But. Occupying armies. Profiling. Incarceration. Rape. Beatings. Psychological warfare. Every. Day. Where was the offense?

APTP danced our way into our community with the first Reclaiming Kings Radical Legacy March of 2015. 10,000 strong. Blasting "Fuck The Police." Blissful rebellion.

## Black and Disturbing.

We got to work. Models for first response to state violence, models of family care, pushing radical reforms in a system not broken - nothing to "fix." Something had to stem the blood flow. Radical reform. Chip away at this system. Piece. By. Bloody. Piece.

## Compromising While Black.

### Murder, Rape and A National Tour

In 2015, Oakland Mayor Libby Schaaf and then Oakland Police Chief Sean Whent went on a national tour. Tap dancing to sounds of Black bodies dropping, they sang songs of a department reformed and a model for other law enforcement agencies to follow. "Hella" off key. OPD killed nine Black men in 2015.

Jerry Means: 2/7/15. Gunshot. ***Mental Health Crisis While Black.*** Corey Pollard: 2/13/15. Gunshot. ***Suicidal While Black.*** Demouria Hogg: 6/6/2015. Gunshot. ***Sleeping While Black.*** Richard Linyard: 7/9/2015: Asphyxiated while hiding between buildings. ***Dodging PoPo While Black.*** Antonio Clements: 8/3/15. Gunshot. ***Apparently one of those crazy negroes who***

***shot at a cop while Black.*** Nathaniel Wilks: 8/12/2015. Gunshot. ***Running While Black.*** Yonas Alehegne. Gunshot. ***Homeless While Black.*** Richard Perkins: Gunshot. Honest While Black. Jason Alexander Brown. Gunshot. ***Suicidal While Black.***

And one Black woman. Yuvette Henderson. Murdered by the Emeryville Police Department in broad daylight with an AR-15. Covered up by OPD. February 3, 2015. ***Shoplifting While Black.***

### Can We Stop Paying These Fools?! Defund OPD

Laughed out of rooms. Screaming defund. The audacity of us. Black folks with demands. So-called "Crime" is the result of conditions created by the state to maintain the status quo of race-based capitalism in Amerikkka. Police are violence responders ... not violence interrupters. Safety is: Whole communities. Economic opportunities. Quality education. Mental health and trauma support. Substance abuse prevention and treatment. Stable families. Economically equitable societies. ***Getting to the gun before the bullet flies***

*instead of standing with the mother as she puts her child in the ground.*

## Ha! Strategizing While Black.

### A Luta Continua

So many young people don't know his name. Oscar. There have been too many bodies. They don't remember the tanks. Snipers on top of government buildings, Arab activists with "I Am Oscar Grant" signs in their hands during Arab Spring, the Nation storming the DA's office, Brothas without a penny to their name trekking back and forth to LA for the trial, Turha pulling people out of tear gas, nationwide conference calls, wee-hour meetings, Tasers and tough guys with badges determined not to lose. The youth don't remember the then because they are too overwhelmed living the now.

The fight for Oscar changed the world. Say his name in your prayers and thank him for his sacrifice.

No one knows what abolition NOW looks like and if they say they do. Lies. I don't know: but I dream of: complete and total transformation. Tearing down prisons. Dismantling police. It all has to go. Capitalism. Whte Supremacy. Patriarchy.

Capture pieces of freedom now. Disentangle. Build. Community security teams, Community Care not Cops for Community Crisis. Collectively dream and visualize. Decarcerate now. Heal the survivors and nurture perpetrators of violence. Honor our trauma. Acknowledge our wounding. Exorcise the demons of patriarchy.

BLACK organizers rock. Time for extraction. Charge cops. Update policies. Elect our people. Ride the continuum.

Don't do it like the generations before us. Don't grind till you drop. Love the people and yourselves. Cherish your family. Protect your soul.

Revolution is a labor of love. Martyrs are not required.

Sustain. There is a long way to go. But we are winning.

Winning.

Winning.

## Winning While Black.

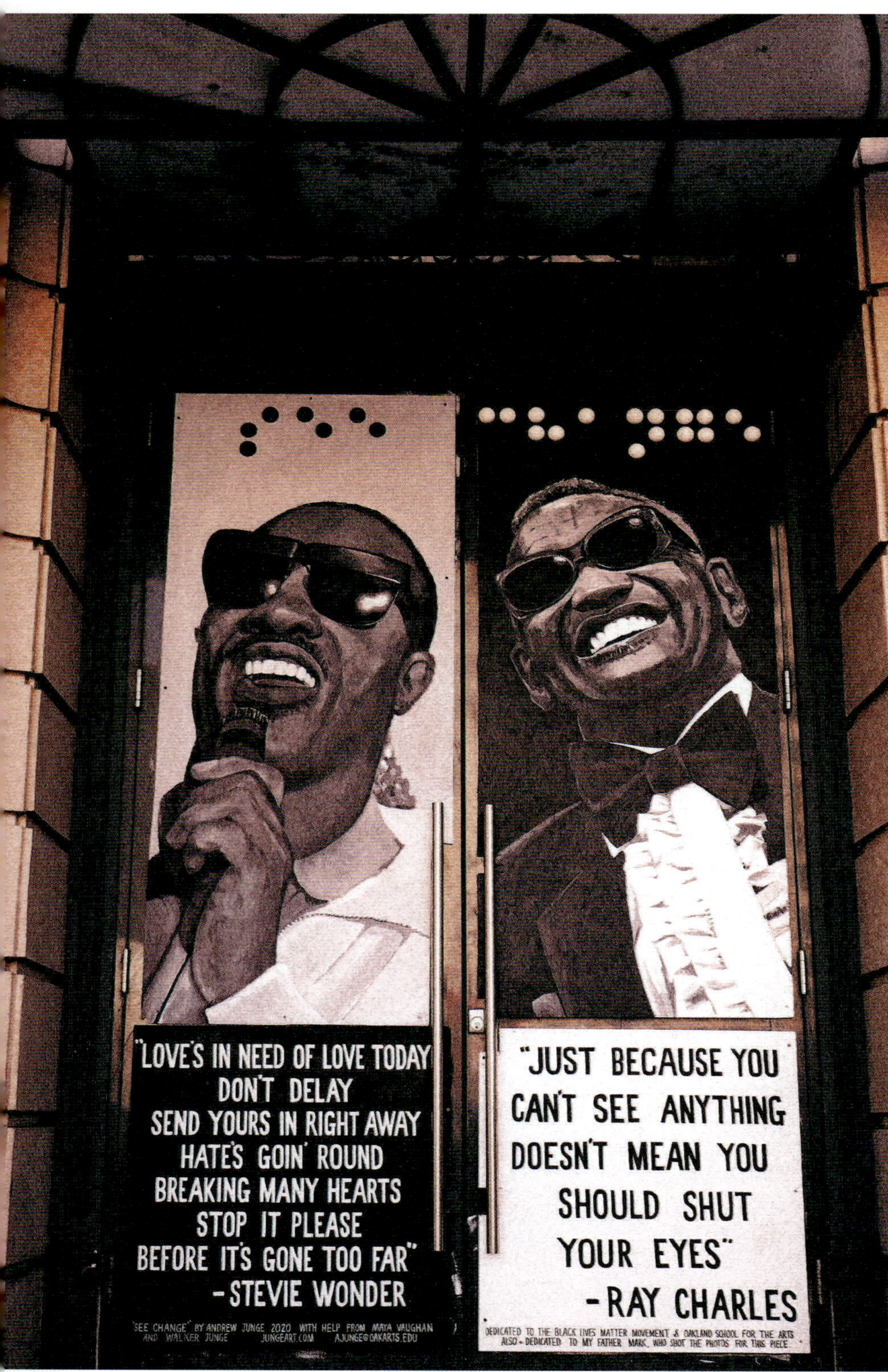


photo by Rohan DaCosta

# What This Revolution Takes: Transformation at All Levels!

Mizan Alkebulan-Abakah, MPH &
Sizwe Andrews-Abakah of Spearitwurx

I see the Systems of Oppression
Legacy of slavery, this' never a question
Joy Degruy dropped an interesting perspective
You should check her book, this is only a suggestion
Okay, we smash the institutions, tell me what we left with?
A lot of mess if we romanticizing next steps
You heal that s*** up with your brother yet?
You on speaking terms with your mother yet?
No attempts made? Ain't trying to hear none of it!
And I get it, yo this s*** is really tough to get
But to me, this is where the revolution sits
And where my contribution fits
It's both-and really
For security, we know we need artillery
No debates here
Just want to make clear
That bullets ain't all it's going to take here

**Spear or the Nation AKA Sizwe Andrews-Abakah**

As we march, make art, post hashtags, and vote, what is the revolution going to take? How do we smash these systems of oppression that are deeply embedded in the fabric of Amerikkka? Beyond armed warfare in the streets, beyond slogans that make our lives matter, how do we treat each other? How do we feel looking in the mirror? Spearitwurx suggests that this is the deeper part of the revolution that we must make as clear as the writing on the wall.

We believe the revolution requires a transformation at all levels: Internal, Interpersonal, Institutional, and Ideological. It's these layers that address change in ourselves, our relationships, and in these institutions that perpetuate injustice, pain, and trauma. Our liberation is in this work, and it's not easy.

As revolutions address root causes, the transformation begins at the Internal layer. The work at this level focuses on who we are and the values and beliefs that we hold true. Do we believe we are worthy of justice, peace, equity, and respect? Let us create a safe space to delve deep into the root of our being, uncover our insecurities

and pain, bringing forth the power that is the very best of ourselves to organize, mobilize, and lead.

If our revolution is truly "guided by the deepest sense of love," then let's change our Interpersonal relationships. It's the heart-to-heart, eye-to-eye kind of connection and reflection that shifts from the transactional relationships—what we can produce, purchase, or pimp—to the transformative relationships that elevate our human experience beyond the confines of capitalism and patriarchy. Our relationships and the social interactions we have with other humans determine the kind of person we are and the world we are making. Do we cause harm to others with our thoughts, words, or actions? Do we speak our truth in a way that inspires, not devours, another's spirit? Do we treat each other with the same dignity, respect, and honor that we demand the police do for us? These interpersonal reflections can change the institutions that impact our lives.

From our schools and the media to the police and court systems, we require a change at this Institutional level to sustain justice. This institutional transformation shifts the policies and practices that perpetuate oppression and injustice. Yet, we know that these systems and their policies and practices are made by people, by human beings who have thoughts, ideas, and feelings. We can transform the Ideologies, dismantling white supremacy, patriarchy, and capitalism, committing our lives to align with and honor life. So this work includes changing the hearts and minds of the People, to heal the hurt that fuels the rage, and transform the very essence of our human experience. We each have the power to make this change in every space we occupy.

Spearitwurx understands that Revolution is a process. We are committed to being the change we want to see. Let's do the work to live in our highest selves, to look out for those who suffer, and build a culture of love, truth, and wellness that blankets our world in this righteous art of living. The signs are clear, the time is now for transformation at all levels. All power to the People!

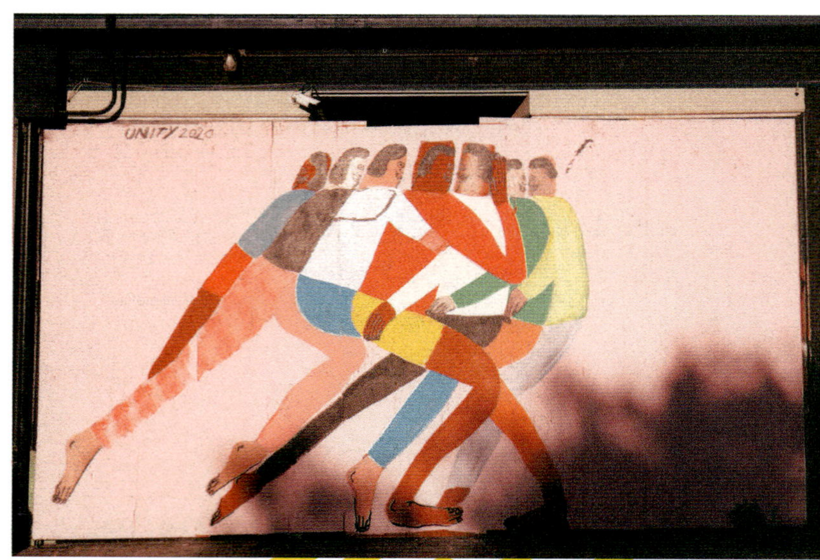


photo by Rohan DaCosta

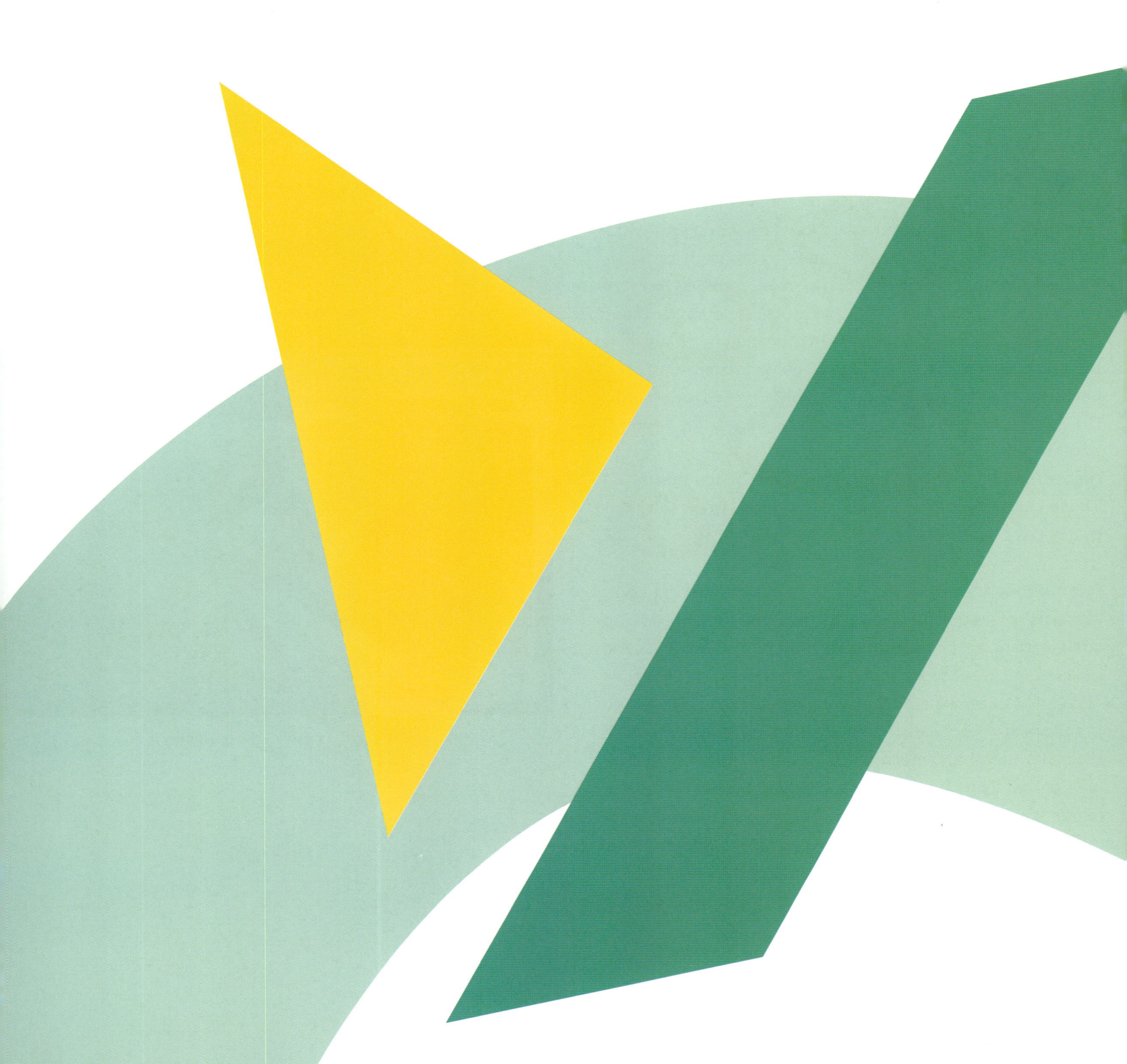

# POETRY

6

# Poem

## Sonia Sanchez

What I have seen in the twentieth century is the release of Nelson Mandela from 27 years of imprisonment, fist raised in victory, South African spirit still soaring high;

What I have seen in the twentieth century is Malcolm, hurricane man, shaking us free of our wounds, moving us into the fire that cleanses;

What I have seen in the twentieth century is Fannie Lou Hamer, bathing her flesh in freedom, arresting the old South with her vision for a new South;

What I have seen in the twentieth century is Martin, a nonviolent man silenced by violence, sequestering our eyes on mountaintops;

What I have seen in the twentieth century is the wilderness of African-American women, years trembling like butterflies, traversing the limits of pavements and pain, praising our hands in kitchens and corporations in schools and factories in courtrooms and bedrooms, probing for the peace and beauty and power that are ours;

And today.  Walking toward the twenty-first century, with our yesterdays feasting on its past, I move as an African woman, disposed to dreams and truth, disposed to cutting through stone while shaping our laughter like rubies.

Today.  My simple passion is to write our names in history and walk in the light that is woman.

from *Sonia Sanchez Collected Poems,* 2021 Beacon Press
Originally from *Wounded in the House of a Friend*

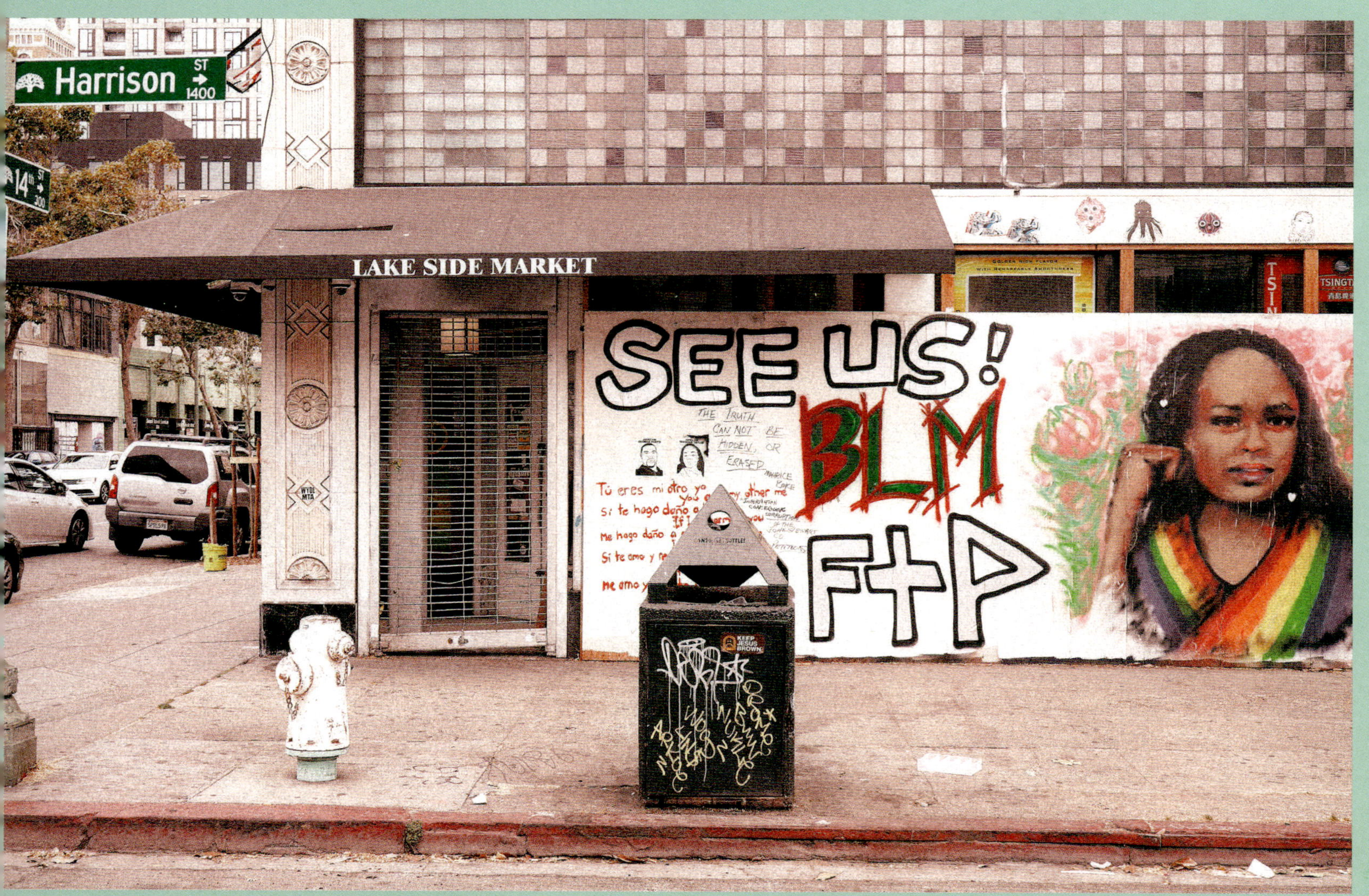


photo by Rohan DaCosta

# The Revolutionary Predicament

Arnoldo García

What a predicament

No revolution in sight

What is revolution you'd probably ask.

Yea what is revolution

Revolution is you being home

Revolution is you being free

Revolution is you having a job

Revolution is you not being harassed by police or men with guns

Revolution is you living to be a 100.

Revolution is you talking to me about your dreams

Revolution is you raising your son and daughter

Revolution is you becoming a grandfather, a great-grandfather, a great-great-grandfather…

Revolution is you never having to go to prison

Revolution is family dinner every Sunday or Monday, Tuesday, Wednesday, Thursday, Friday, or Saturday

Prison is where dreams are free, where revolutions are sleeping off the depression of humans

What is a prison you will ask

A prison is a wall around our laughter

A prisoner is the muffled joy of the revolution to come

A prison is the place where capitalists will wither away, evaporate, turn into dust

A prison is a womb of suffering to give birth to freedom that will make men fly away into the sky

A prison is a conspiracy against horizons and her artists

When will you come home?

When will prisons become obsolete?

When will you walk freely, safely, down the street?

When will we tear down the prison walls?

When will you dream so that prison doesn't matter?

When will I dream freely, unafraid of prisons?

When will you become my guide, my north star, the ehecatl wind?

When will the fires burn down the prisons and turn our suffering into ashes?

When will we be free together?

When will my neighbors visit you, visit their own prisons?

We are all prisoners.

Prisons are poverty, the viral wound of capitalism.

You cannot imprison all of us, you cannot have prisoners and be free, you cannot.

Each prisoner each jail cell are families in anguish

No toys, no sale, no generosity will erase this wound from their face.

Right now police are lauded

Some of them shoot our sons and daughters dead and get away with killing

Some of our sons and daughters shoot other's sons and daughters and get sent away forever

Prison is a tomb for the living dead.

Prison is a steel-encased grave where the flower of my heart breaths in spite of being crushed

Everyone he says sleeps all day long, sleeping off the criminal system, dreaming it away.

Everyone is asleep and steps into a world without walls and shrieking men.

Prisoners all.

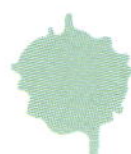

Do you know how free you are?

You are free inside and outside the prison

You and I are equally free inside or outside

The walls unite us our tears unite us our sadness unites us separate but equal

Prison is the imagination of the unfree of the exploiters plus police, bosses, landlords and their cronies to punch us in the face or force us to read their books.

Prison extracts profits and prophets from our bodies

When we are no longer worth anything their prisons
become the streets of our homelessness
become our robbing other prophets of their day's wages
The prisoners prey on the unprisoned
The profits prey on the prophets
Our freedom becomes our silence our quietude
Drowning out the barking prison guards and wardens.

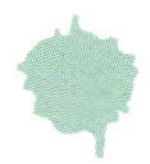

To their revolution of prisons and hate
Our counter-revolution of freedom and love
To their revolution of wars and militarism
Our counter-revolution of solidarity and peace
To their revolution of privatization, gentrification and expulsion
Our counter-revolution of community, sharing and intimacy
To their revolution of pesticides, dispossessions and land grabbing
Our counter-revolution of soil with soul, communal laughter and dusty ancestors
To their revolution in 5G, banking without limits and national security
Our counter-revolution of ink and talking around the kitchen table sipping coffee
and acting human with each other
To their revolution of jailing black and brown
Our counter-revolution of a rainbow blade skinning whiteness off the face of the earth
To their revolution of distrust and shadows
Our counter-revolution of dialogue and suns
To their revolution of Christopher Columbus
Our counter-revolution of the sixth sun that swallows all the 1492s,
reversing time once and for all, returning us to the source

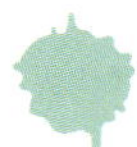

Quetzalcóatl the color of sun
Quetzalcóatl the color of the obsidian moon

Quetzalcóatl the color of the veins of liquid light

Quetzalcóatl the color of the autumn heart

Quetzalcóatl is in prison and the sun cannot be jailed

Quetzalcóatl is my great-great-great-great-great-great-great-great-great-great-great-great-great-great-great-great-great-great-great-great...grandfather

And now Quetzalcóatl is my grandson self-gestating incarcerated

An Albino offering to the suffocating imperial night

Black-feathered-serpent-man-child to raise the ancestors from their sleep

Red chanting prayer-song to find our place in the natural world

Amber wind to soften our hands and heal our wounds

The north star mother that will seize the light and ingest our sons and daughters

The clandestine movement of tenderness and secret languages of liberations

The sun that slices the horizon morn and eve flesh offering, the lunar menstruation

The yellow-hearted sister wintering in the shadow of our mourning

We surround each other with the four directions of our desire and lands

You perish slowly in a cell

I perish slowly in a house

Quetzalcóatl is white black red yellow, dirt and sky, howling and meditations

Quetzalcóatl kneels in prison to take a video-call

Transmitting sorrow, transmitting loneliness, transmitting forgiveness,

Transmitting rage and embrace, transmitting conflagrations yet to come

No walls can stop this

No walls can separate us

The walls unite us

The prisoners must come out new

or they will come out to make us wail again and again

a human wounding a shaming to make us prisoners again and again

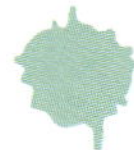

When you were being born

Your father was in a prison for minors

Shirley went to get him on her word to bring you to the hospital to meet you

Then Shirley drove him back, delivered him to his tormentors

Your birth freed your father but he decided to go back to never appear again.

I would hold you on my shoulder as I sat on a rocking chair

Your knees curled up beneath your stomach

You gasped for air

I would hold you up like this to help you breathe,

a wheezing song that kept you up through the night

Now you are a prisoner and your daughter and son are waiting for you

They can free you

Will you decide to return to the house of life

Or forever doubt your life and love

and find yourself committed to the house of corrections?


Your father showed up

at your one-year-old birthday party

with another one-year-old baby in a car seat

He came as far as the steps and never came in

He bought you shoes when you were still a toddler

And then he would disappear again and again

into the bowels of the streets and prison

In the end, he almost came in and started showing up

Your mom took you to the hospital once

After he had been shot seven or nine times and survived

But he wasn't a cat, never gave up his ways

and his life ended on a street drive-by

When we went to his funeral

You comforted his family, they didn't console you

Tonight from afar I give you my condolences

Your loss, a father even though he wasn't present when needed to be

You have your own life to live and no one else's

Which path will you take?

Which life will you live or not live?

Who will you show up for?

[I will live free
just like you
Anger is grief turned against yourself.]

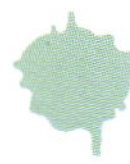

Everywhere
there are prisons
laying an ambush
You are the howl of our ancestors
That no wall can mute
That no prison will keep
Our talisman is the sun
that fits inside the fists of our rage
The walls that unite us
must also crumble.

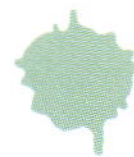

I met your father
He was with your mom and aunt
He was a teenager
Jaw jutting
Scowl on his lips and dark shades over his eyes
Wouldn't even say hello
Sat there staring into the living room space.

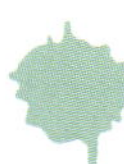

Can you sing your song
Can you dream your dream
in prison

And be happy?

How do you see yourself?

Who do you see?

What happened to the capoeira-whirling child

What happened to the skateboarding daredevil

What happened to the spray-can artist

What happened to the green-hair-goop boy

Doo-rag-don't-mess-with-the-Black-man's-hair child?

Man-child,

are you condemned

are you a prisoner

Are you a free man readying for self-emancipation?

The prison is made for self-destruction or for self-determination

Destroy the sun that got you there

Create the sun so that you can emerge different, free, unafraid

The sun of your skin...

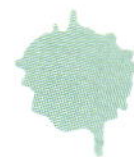

Do not eat your own flesh

Do not devour your family

Do not blame the night for the darkness

Do not blame the day for your sadness

Do not blame the prison for our separation

We all have a part in what has happened to you, to us

I am using all the power of my words

To rise again to the old ways

Where there were no prisons

and families, love and old age were guaranteed by each other

Will you make it back

into the house

where you belong

where we are waiting for you?

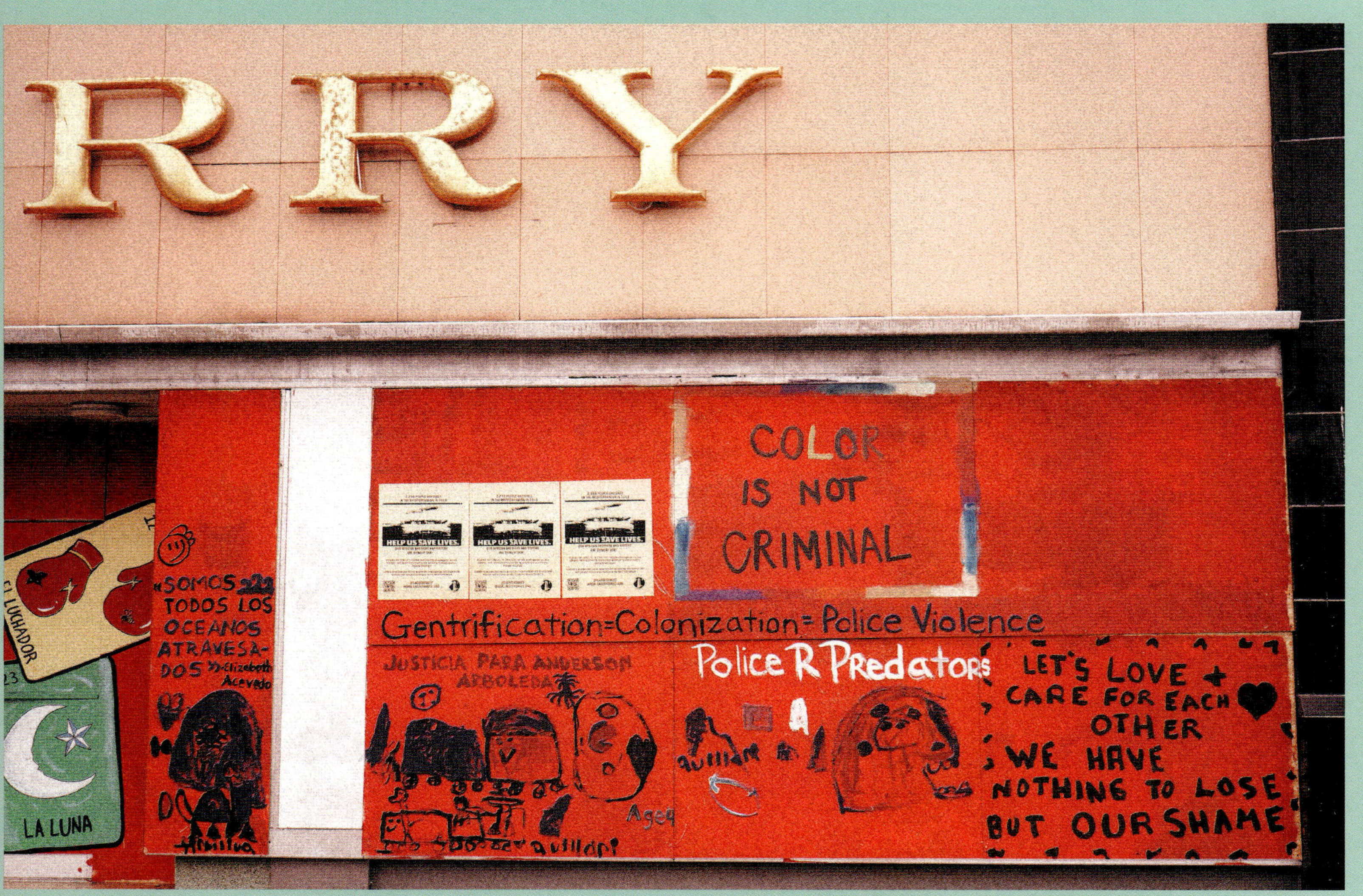


photo by Rohan DaCosta

# town biz

Ayodele Nzinga

oakland
ohlone land
the town
drums
welcome
full of spirit(s)
orisha speak ebonics
doors open
tribe of the white t
where shades of garvey
walked
daddy grace danced
in his footsteps
huey newton slept here
fed children
gathered struggle
seed dressed them
black leather immaculate
& wrote history
told us
serve the people
there is no higher calling
blood on these streets
dreams dared
seales for mayor
li'l bobby hutton died here
confronted on all fronts
known for stunting

quick to go left
to get you right
home of the scraper bike
open all night
watch us swang
watch us swang
bougie gate keepers
have danced
for crumbs here
washed down with
poor people's tears
statues erected to some
dumb hyphy going
done gone dumb

we keep the fire lit
loaded lyrics
hard beats
& st. politicks
we police
the police
we home in the streets
descendants of legacy
underground heavies
sharp machetes
retired slaves
sideshow unruly
nappy heretics
rewriting scripts
fist in the air
freedom on lips
liberated narratives
raised on african funk
poured from southern trunks

flatbed protest

celebrate malcom x

brigades' comrades

fruit of islam

sunday morning gospel

black in all its shades

jimbes by the lake

burdens rested

souls soothed

sunshine & black smiles

we ride

with unresolved heartache

making life between breaks

smell of bar b que

red beans on dinner plates

fried chicken in

the corner stores

& memories of what

ain't no more

I know some places

police won't go alone

& cats who can

recite the 500 names

of god off the dome

wild wild west baby

legends of lumpen

stolen & returned

uncaged

oral testimony

keeps thoughts

of free at last

from being lonely

new cowboys

appeared here

like a new frontier

skinny jeans & no fear

downpressors catch

reckonings here

liberations an imperative

we stay clear

pressing forward

remembering

we have re-membered

many things

beyond checkers &

chess deep water game

hail mary

tupac

& the ghost of

claude mckay

pressed

against the

wall fighting back

rebel warrior black

we multiply

across divides

it's a soul thang

even removed

the stain remains

# Flames of Genesis

## James Cagney

every night i am murdered in my sleep
only to awaken radiant and naked beneath dawn's monsoon of blood

this white genesis occupied
by the proudly illiterate
after labelling the tree of knowledge a controlled substance

every night the bushes open its jaws of switches
and my shift begins anew

my task in the garden of perennial thistles
      i am forced to sharecrop:

name the bite style of each fresh animal
rushing from the double-gated house above me

describe the complex flavors in poisoned
saliva:   pepper citrus        rust

tag ivory monuments in bubble lettering
new words for being spat out and eaten again

determine the fine tasting notes between
      mauling for recreation
or slaughter triggered by fear

i am made in the image of illegally moving targets

my ribs open nightly

blossom of beef mushrooms
its aroma singing to the sky

night opens its drooling jaws
in praise of me

# hang
Maisha Quint

as in opposite of crawl:

hands dragging knees

that bleed but instead

legs dangle

after head.

as in limp

from a rope

that swings

back and forth.

as in strung up

like lights

blaze brilliant

in the night.

as in opposite of crawl:

hands dragging knees

that bleed

but alive.

to get the hang

of something

to become

capable

first find the tree

preferably one

sturdy enough

for two

maybe three

bark able to burn

if need be

trunk wide

but branches

high enough

for two

maybe three

preferably one

on open field

large enough

for thousands to see

the two

maybe three

sway free


as in proud display

like trophies

or plaques


*a group of children*

*snapped the teeth*

*out of his head*

*to sell*

*as souvenirs*

as in pin up

on the wall

writing scrawled

along postcard edges:

*Bill, this was some raw bunch*

to learn the method

or

arrangement of

to become accustomed to

*over 10,000 spectators*

*including city officials and police*

*gathered to watch*

*hang*

on the corner

in twos

maybe threes

shrugged backs in dark sweatshirts

hands stuffed in jeans

black boys watch

cops circle

two

maybe three

as in

helicopter in sky

waiting

see black boys

fly

from street corner

run

mad dog wild



as in


(black boy)


                limp


    like


                slack rope

tape off

the perimeter


isolate

the body


calm the officer

offer coffee

or water


crowds will gather

*hang*

as in opposite of crawl:

hands dragging knees

that bleed

but instead

crowds will gather.

# Catching My Breath

## Mizan Alkebulan-Abakah, MPH

Here it comes again
That tightness, that pain.
Feeling the weight of oppression constricting my breath.
Sirens, gunshots, dogs barking.
Tightness—like a noose on necks
Squeezing Liberty, squeezed to death.

I wheeze on my inhale, struggling to grasp the nourishment of oxygenated air.
Tightness. Pulse pounding ribs. Eyes bloodshot.
Each breathe a subtle whistle as my lungs are pressured to fill up, turning blue to purple.
Each breath a moment of suffocation from power imbalances.
Purple to red.
Racism is stifling. Capitalism inhibits vibrancy. Male supremacy, a sick perversion of the essence of life.

I inhale and it burns. Red to fire
Like the knee to the neck of my 3 sons, my husband, my brother—
Tight chest. Heart wrenched deep with the grief of a mother's loss
Then tossed into a hashtag and swag—fit for rallies and marches—a nation on fire.
The charge...is to breathe.
To break the yoke that chokes unprovoked.

Enough is enough!
I cough, ejecting fear as phlegm, thick and sticky.
I cough, expelling doubt with explosive conviction that there is another way.

I. Must. Inhale.
Inhale sage. Lavender.
Inhale Peppermint. Eucalyptus.

Inhale deep to re-member. To bring me back to my body.
Ancestral memory absorbed.
Reminded of  the power of the wind, Oya.
Poised to make each inhale more meaningful, more nourishing, more like freedom in the flesh.
"Breathe," she says, wind on my lips.
Blowing Fire. Phoenix rising from the inside.
Catching my breath.

Breathe in and trust that there is power in my breath.
Power in my life.
Each inhale now a coat of armor for my airways of love and courage and tiny tenacity that
teaches us to tango with time.

I breath, in my time, my rhythm, my rhyme.
I release my fear and inhale
I release the pain in my body—exhale.
Shoulders drop, spine aligned, easeful and alert. Exhale.
My breath an act of resistance,
my breath an art of resilience.

Inhale, and exhale and it all becomes the now.
The present moment when justice is the process of self reflection and mass movement.
Inhale and exhale as a paired package of people power in the present.
Deep as the flow of lava, strengthened to the core, igniting flames that fuel freedom.
Breath birthing life eternally.
Ancestors walking with me—orange and gold—Serengeti strong.
Shining light through my lungs like liberation on my tongue.
I breathe for those who couldn't. Reciprocity.

*Re-generational energy*
*Inhale and exhale in this present moment*
*In this now*
*where I am safe. I am protected. I am here and I am well.*
*I can breathe.*

# Say Her Name
## Nia McAllister

They locked up *History* today
Barred the doors | threw away the key
and called her truth *False*

Four walls between her and her children
Said | *hush* | *these walls not for talking, only homewrecking*
Here we learn grievance cannot be rehearsed

*Justice* only got catcalled once today
(not bad for a missing woman)
If she's invisible in the first place, who's to say she was ever here?

Sis got taken too—now we take to the streets saying
No *Justice*
No *Peace!*

We yell our Sisters' names against the chorus of
    *What'd she have on?*
To which we cry Defiance
    *So, she was asking for it?*
To which we remind them

Nobody's got time to look inviting when there are revolutions growing beneath our tongues
    *What's that? Couldn't hear over all the white noise*
Here we learn: Fragility doesn't listen anyways

So, as *History* tells us, we must repeat ourselves:

No Justice
No Peace.

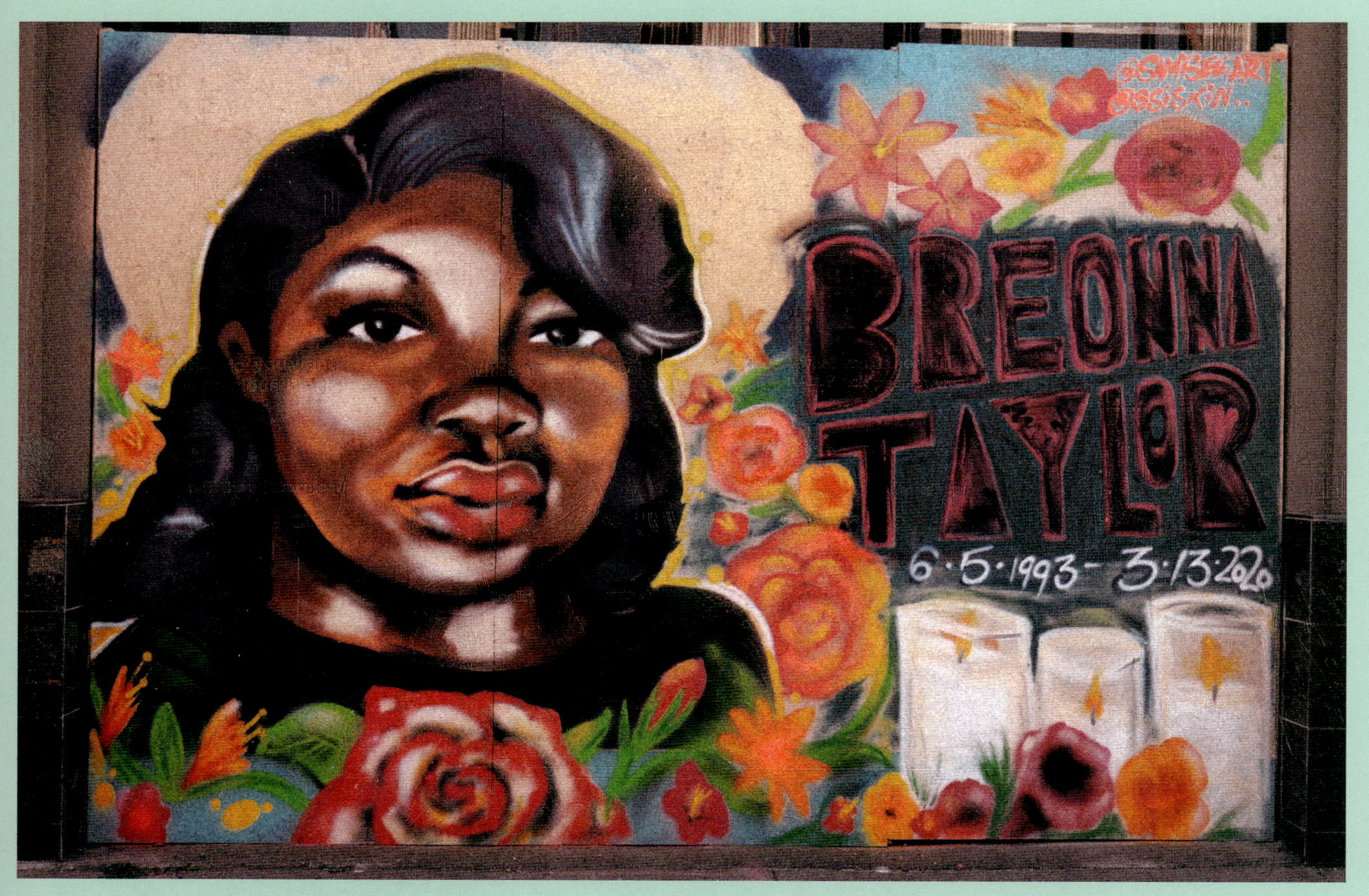


photo by Rohan DaCosta

# I Do Not Know the Spelling of Money

Tongo Eisen-Martin

I go to the railroad tracks
And follow them to the station of my enemies

A cobalt-toothed man pitches pennies at my mugshot negative

All over the united states, there are
                              toddlers in the rock

I see why everyone out here got in the big cosmic basket
And why blood agreements mean a lot
And why I get shot back at

I understand the psycho-spiritual refusal to write white history or take the glass freeway

                              White skin tattooed on my right forearm
                              Ricochet sewage near where I collapsed
                                        into a rat-infested manhood

My new existence as living graffiti

                                        In the kitchen with
                              a lot of gun cylinders to hack up
                                        House of God in part
                                        No cops in part

                              My body brings down the Christmas

The new bullets pray over blankets made from old bullets

Pray over the 28th hour's next beauty mark

Extrajudicial confederate statue restoration
The waist band before the next protest poster

By the way,
Time is not an illusion, your honor
I will save your desk for last
You are witty, your honor
You're moving money again, your honor

It is only raining one thing: non-white cops

       And prison guard shadows
         Reminding me of
         Spoiled milk floating on an oil spill

         A neighborhood making a lot of fuss over its
     demise

         A new lake for a Black Panther Party

Malcom X's ballroom jacket slung over my son's shoulders
             Pharmacy doors mid-slide
              The figment of village
            A noon noose to a new white preacher
            Wiretaps in the discount kitchen tile
               All in an abstract painting of a
             president

Bought slavers some time, didn't it?

The tantric screeches of military bolts and Election-Tuesday cars

A cold-blooded study in leg irons
Leg irons in tornado shelters
Leg irons inside your body

Proof that some white people have actually fondled nooses
        That sundown couples
        made their vows of love over
                opaque peach plastic
                and bolt action audiences

Man, the Medgar Evers-second is definitely my favorite law of science

Fondled news clippings and primitive Methodists

My arm changes imperialisms
Simple policing vs. Structural frenzies
Elementary school script vs. Even whiter white spectrums

Artless bleeding and
The challenge of watching civilians think

            "Terrible rituals they have around the corner. They let their elders beg for public
                                    mercy…beg for settler polity"

    "I am going to go ahead and sharpen these kids' heads into arrows myself and see how
                                    much gravy spills out of family crests."

Modern fans of war
        What with their t-shirt poems
        And t-shirt guilt

And me, having on the cheapest pair of shoes on the bus,
I have no choice but to read the city walls for signs of my life

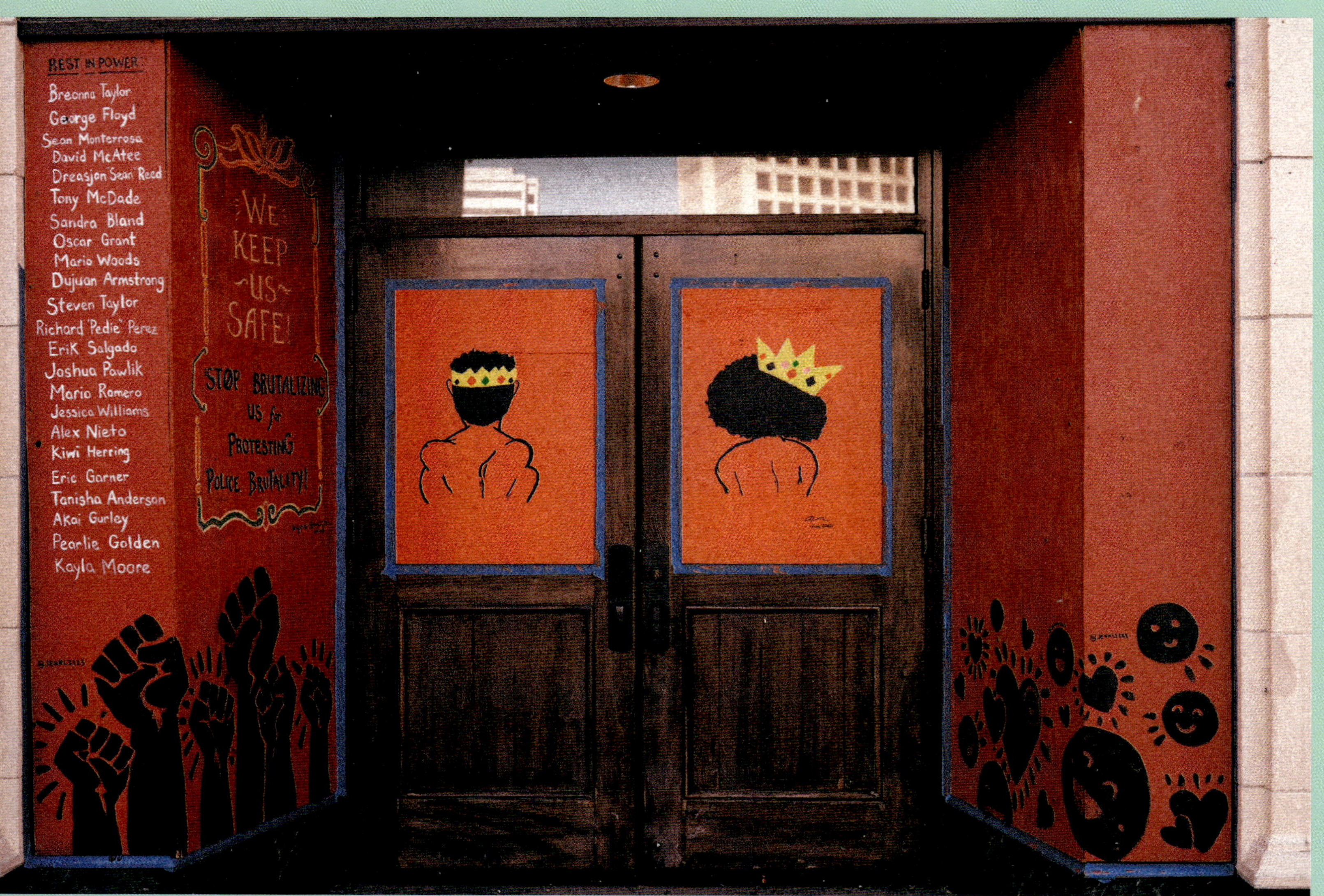


photo by Rohan DaCosta

# The Arc of Protest

Tureeda Mikell

Devil in the details derail
Liberation
Rolls up on a big wheel
Revelation…
Paul reveres this Epiphany!
Somebody's Manifest Destiny theory
Waits to be real
Compared to what?
Whose liberty do we trust?

Don't care what the law is
Who be the Judge?
The adjudicator?
The mediator?
The referee between
The father's son and his ghost fantasy?

Didn't hear a woman mentioned in this trilogy?
Is she Ghost?

Heard freedom ring at Joe-Joe's house the other day
Singing with Mickey's Monkey
    Dum de la la la la

Derailing emancipation
Crippling human consideration
Negotiating Peace?
    Which piece?

Who'll be the umpire to decide
Which side of the bread slice is buttered?
Got money for wars but not for the poor?

> *In our language there are thirty words for wealth*
> *And only one of them relates to money*

English derails details truths
Argues well against what constitutes
The manufacturing of consent rules
Serves up hegemony's milk toast
Bathed in sheep shit shallow water
Want us to try it
Tell us we'll like it
Like Mikey, he ate everything

How Hollowood views alternative facts
Sold on t.v. news racks
Track nouns verbs conjured words
Coining acronyms for dollars
The 1% minority authors the good decision!

Sprinkling powdered sugar on fresh cow patties
Exceeding olfactory's threshold
Socializing PTSD wormholes

> *Masked breath drops scope*
> *Strung out on fairytale dope*

Jack falls down breaks his crown
Jill comes running after, yellin'

> *You been clowned FOOL but I got you!*
> *Don't worry bout your future*

Pharma got drugs to numb son!

Details derail sense
Generations hooked like fish on
Illusion of inclusion sub-limb dish
You too can be a human crucifix

Wanna be like jesus?
Jesus for sale
Jesus in jail
Jesus on the corner
Jesus needs bail
Jesus executed
Pass the plate please
Derails sunflowers, bees
Arc's covenant with sun biology

Sadistic seats favor A.I. viral 5 technology
Deckin' necks with boughs of folly
F'in with thoracic melody
Freezin' hearts in lyri-cidal symphonies
Traffickin' mind body soul
Two seconds from frostbite control
Sticking tongues to a flagpole
Pledging allegiance
Dependents tag
    One nation under dog
    With liberty and justice for some

Sit, heel, stay, obey
Unconditionally?
No responsibility?
Love your enemy
Judge not!

Say what???

Some said
They'd name names in protest
Of those try'na break their sex
Wreck their nest

Others said
Chill be still
Hear see and speak no evil

Details metaphysical tones
Met the physical bone thought sin
If hyper vigilance is shown

And
The people bifurcated in fear
of C9 funk affliction
Failed judgment of suicide hunger
Police gang violence homelessness and addiction
Witnessing an increase under totalitarian disease
Clearly the oligarch's narcissistic piece
Praised decrease of critical think

Troubled waters resist asking
        WHY dear lord do you say
        Physician, heal thyself?
        How can we heal
        If we can't judge
        The cards you deal?

            Can you play leapfrog?
            Water getting hotter now
            Where you gonna jump?


Which Art got your Covenant?

# Trapped . . .

## Umar Bin Hassan

The children on the corners ... in the jails ... in the Wind ... What spider is this who spins a web of baubles and bangles. Are we trapped? Will we forever stay entwined? Throwing benjamins up into the air when you should be on the ground searching for gold. Finding comfort and sanctuary in Master charge, Visa, Debt and illusion. One last cheer for the almighty dollar. Dark clouds on the horizon. Understanding is being dashed against the rocks. The ripples of the sea bring forth blood. Common decency and respect have settled in for the winter. Playing with one another in the kiddie corner. Laughing and giggling at each adolescent touch. Unknown poets seek our ears. Calling out to us from deep and unmarked graves. When will we stop and wonder why? Have we all become mannequins standing limp in the face of truth. Big City lights loosing us amongst the asphalt lies and candy cotton swirl of carnival minds. Whew ... Whew ... Even the Wind is trying to tell us to seek higher ground. The Children on the corners ... in the jails ... in the Wind ... Why are there so many reflections of loneliness when there are supposed to be people around me. Their tears are out of control. They are flooding my vision of tomorrow. Bombs dropping constantly in other countries. Unborn babies dying in carefully planned cremations. Time and time again we are being harassed by spastic heroes. Heroes who speak maggots for words. Heroes who vomit in the eyes of sabbath. Heroes who unleash killer locusts upon our dignity. Run ... Run ... The ocean is going to sail without us. The stars have no sympathy for our allegiance with darkness. The birds are

not singing. They are not winging ... And we can't fly. Grounded with the sinister burden of free enterprise ... and the bling bling and suvs and soaring gas prices and high crime areas and low esteem and mass murder and insults upon our intelligence and mtv cribs and political corruption and ... the children on the corners ... in the Wind ... What spider is this who spins a web of baubles and bangles. Are we trapped. Will we forever stay entwined.

# R U Ready
## (from *Bleeding Between the Bars*)
### DonJuan Carter-Woodard

Sacrifice and the days of humiliation
We created a maze of contradictions

Strange fruit use to be hanging

Now they just store it away
In prison cells wasting time and
spoiling away

Cover the heart with a look of unconcern
Used to wait in line
Waiting to get our
turn

For equality, stability, respect and
reparation
But glory is not ever given
Glory is for the taking

Separation was a tool to leave us
helpless

Needing to come together like the
beads on a necklace
Younger generations got the power
and the platform

Elders got all the knowledge
Man, what else can we ask for

History is made just by taking action
Sometimes ain't no talking needed to
really get it cracking

Long as we all agree what we are
fighting for
All these comrades dying showing us what we are
fighting for

Kids in the street watching time just pass
O.G.'s scared to leave the past in an hourglass

"It's nation time"
That's what they was yelling
Our teachers are dying
But are we keeping the lessons

These hands right here they do for self
We handle our business not begging for help

A leader was born and I'm preparing myself
But my elders taught me first I can't do it myself

Can't solve our problems with the same thinking we use to create them
Our old habits didn't work so it's time to replace them

I live as a soldier
But I'll die as a legend

Now who's coming with me?
That's the question

# I'm Not Fooled

## Amiri Baraka

*compliments of Amina Baraka*

This is still Slavery
Not fooled at all
This is still slavery
Even with OBAMA.  I'M STILL NOT FOOLED
THIS IS STILL SLAVERY.  NOT FOOLED AT ALL
IF IT WASN'T SLAVERY OBAMA COULD FIGHT BACK
HE'S DONE THINGS.  GOOD THINGS, BUT
I'M STILL NOT FOOLED, THIS IS STILL SLAVERY
So what you gonna act like Miles, tellin me "So What?"
Out yr brains closed mouth, and on the open streets
Not only so what but bump me, chump me, chump us all, you say
Actin like Miles but you ain't Miles, you the dressed up slave
    master ghost
Just as you always was. I ain't fooled. It's still slavery still is still
    is. I ain't fooled
Excuse me
The fone ringing.

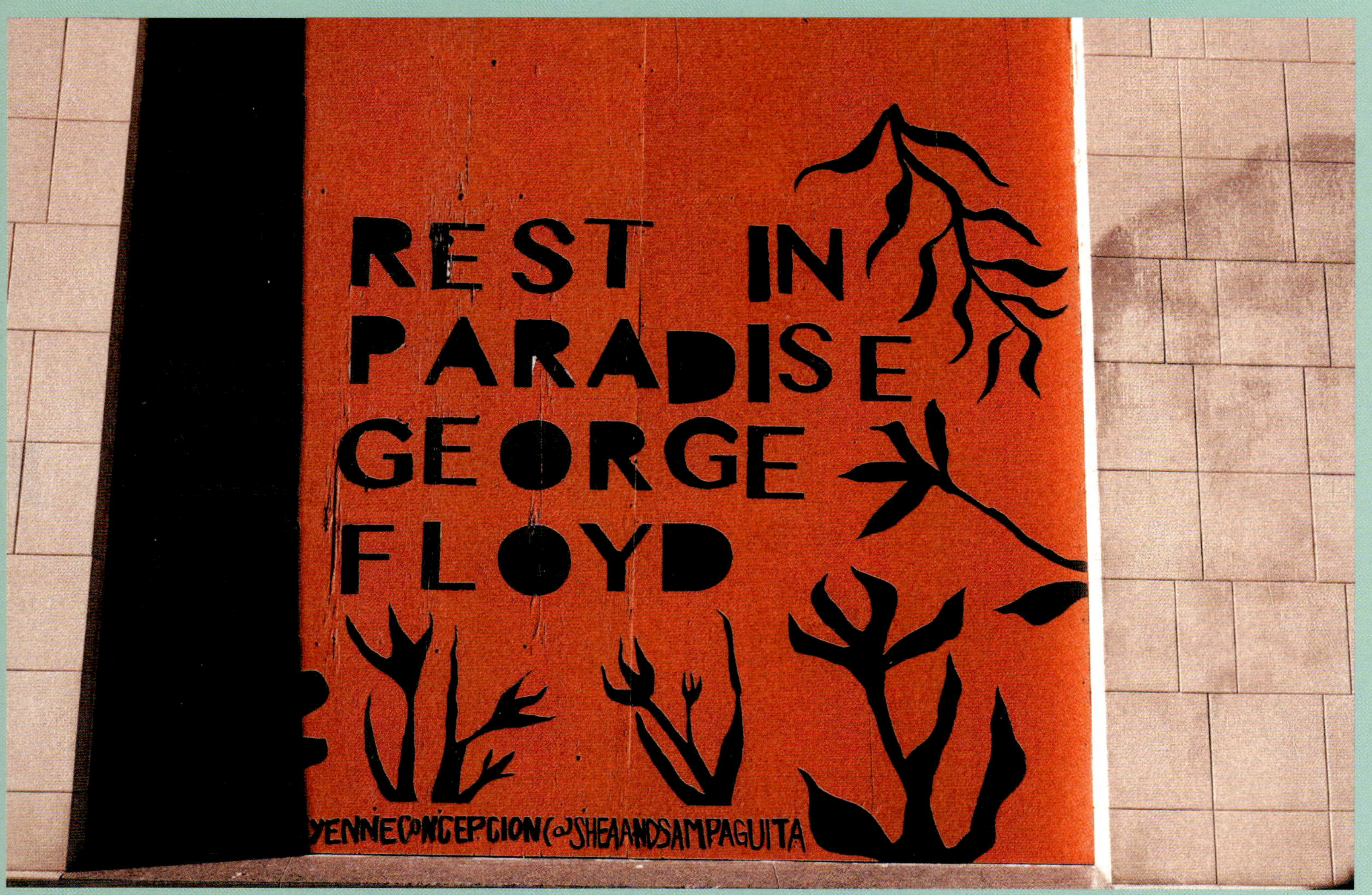


photo by Rohan DaCosta

# Bios

**Alex Sodari (Venmo: @Alex-Sodari)** is a Mexican American artist living in Oakland, California. Graduating in Illustration from the California College of the Arts, he is a member of DIY Arts Nonprofit Rock Paper Scissors Collective, and cofounder of the Mission Art and Comic Expo. His work is inspired by comics and literature, ecology, community, psychedelia, social justice, and the natural world.

**Amiri Baraka** The political activist and accomplished writer Amiri Baraka devoted his life to defend the rights of African Americans through his poems, essays, and dramas. Most of his writing pieces were subjected on racism and detailed the culture and literature of the Black community. Some of the prominent ones include, *Funk Lore: New Poems*, *The Music: Reflections of Jazz and Blues and New Music, New Poetry*. Also his work as a Jazz critic is commendable. amiribaraka.com

**Andre Jones (Venmo: @bampart)** a.k.a. Natty Rebel's professional career started in 1998 while he was a student at Virginia Commonwealth University. He obtained a Bachelor's degree in Fine Arts while still working as a designer and silk screener for a T-shirt company. Through this position, he gained the necessary experience to become the company's lead graphic designer. Within a few months, he started his own T-shirt printing business, Natty Rebel Unlimited, and moved to New York shortly after graduating. After receiving recognition in New York for his design work and T-shirts, he realized his true passion was in painting murals. The next couple of years would see him traveling back and forth between New York and Pennsylvania where he produced several murals with the Mural Arts Program in Philadelphia. Andre currently lives in Richmond, California, where he founded a non-profit organization, Bay Area Mural Program Inc. His vision for the future is to continually facilitate community-based public art that engages the community it serves.

**Angelica Lopez** Using multiple mediums such as acrylic paints, inks, and aerosol, angelica helps shed light to empower and uplift communities of color such as her own. Growing up, angelica was influenced by her two older sisters who quickly introduced her to the world of community organizing, art, and ancient mexica traditions. At the age of 15, angelica was already involved in organizing, where she helped mobilize school walkouts and marches. Angelica's goal is to continue to bring beauty, creativity, knowledge, and power back to her community and build strong connections along the way. To this day, she can be found at eastside arts alliance cultural center, where she continues to co-teach a visual element art program; empowering youth one art piece at a time.

**Arnoldo Garcia** is a community organizer, poet, and musician living between Oakland and the borders. He co-founded Creative Change Collaborative, which trains community activists and educators to support intergenerational, multi-racial leadership for restorative justice. His work has been published online on La Bloga, Art of the Commune and Poets Responding @PoetryofResistance, and in the San Francisco Revolutionary Poets Brigade anthologies. Arnoldo has been a featured poet at in-person and online gatherings with the Chiapas Support Committee's "CompArte" Zapatista festivals, the Aunt Lute Press series "Home in the Bay," and the Richmond Art Center's art-show "Gathering in the Spirit of Gwarth-ee-lass."

**Ayodele Nzinga** is an independent North American African artist; creating on unceded Lisjan Ohlone territory in The Town, a.k.a. Oakland, California. Nzinga considers herself a Cultural Architect; she creates structures that enable culture-making. She is a storyteller who uses various mediums to bring narratives to life. She is referred to as a renaissance woman and considers herself to be a Race Woman. She holds an MA & an MFA in Writing and Consciousness and a Ph.D. in Transformative Education & Change. She is a member of the Alameda County Women's Hall of Fame, a YBCA fellow, a Map fellow, and the founder of BAMBD CDC. Nzinga is the founder and producer of BAMBDFEST International, an annual month-long art and culture festival. She is the founder and Artistic Director of the Lower Bottom Playaz, Oakland's premiere North American African theater company, the only troupe to produce August Wilson's American Century Cycle in chronological order. She is the author of *A Narrative Inquiry into Performance Pedagogy*, *The Horse Eaters*, *SorrowLand Oracle*, and *Incandescent*. Her work can be found in *Tarot in Pandemic & Revolution*, *The Patrice Lumumba Anthology*, *Denial*, *Black Bird Press*, and numerous other anthologies. She is the inaugural Poet Laureate of Oakland, California.

**Binta Oyafemi** shapes new urban forms and urban materials, evoking power, Black space, and the senses. Inspired by the Black Panthers, Black Shakers, Ayofemi's works infuse an Afrofuturist narrative with objects and experiences gathered, honed, milled and performed. Ayofemi's artwork GROUND, a series of sites and buildings beginning in Oakland, generates new narratives around urban voids, economy, displacement, freedom, duration, and radical imagination. Ayofemi explores movement, making, manufacturing, and authorship of public and private space. Ayofemi's activation of vacant sites, from an urban meadow to a reimagined corner store, suggests a state of mutability and transformation. Ayofemi's work has been featured by Untitled, Kadist Foundation, SFMOMA, the Carpenter Center, the Wattis Institute, the Asian Art Museum, the New Museum, dOCUMENTA, the British Arts Council, Rebuild Foundation, the AIA, the City of Oakland, and as a community partner of Black Cultural Zone.

**Carolyn Johnson** joined the East Oakland Black Cultural Zone Collaborative in 2019 as its first Executive Director and is the founding CEO of the Black Cultural Zone Community Development Corporation, which was formed in 2020 by the Collaborative. She has more than thirty years of experience in entrepreneurship and business management, non-profit operations, finance and commercial real estate including development, financing, and brokerage. She is a native of Oakland-born and raised—and a proud graduate of Castlemont High School. For more, visit blackculturalzone.org.

**Cat Brooks** is KPFA co-host of UpFront and a long-time performer, organizer, and activist. She played a central role in the struggle for justice for Oscar Grant, and spent the last decade working with impacted communities and families to rapidly respond to police violence and radically transform the ways our communities are policed and incarcerated. She is the co-founder of the Anti Police-Terror Project (APTP) and the Executive Director of The Justice Teams Network. Cat was also the runner-up in Oakland's 2018 mayoral election, facing incumbent Libby Schaaf.

**Cece Carpio** Using acrylic, ink, aerosol, and installations, Cece Carpio tell stories of immigration, ancestry, resistance, and resilience. She documents evolving traditions through combining folkloric forms, bold portraits and natural elements with urban art techniques. Her work is influenced by people she have met and places she've been. Cece paints everyday

people who have been invincible in order to share their thriving presence, to show the dignity and power of their existence. Cece has produced and exhibited work in the Philippines, Fiji Islands, Cuba, Mexico, Guatemala, Nicaragua, Italy, Norway, Ireland, United Kingdom, India, Guam, and throughout the United States. She has been awarded the Rockwood Institute Fellowship for leaders engaged in the Arts as critical agent of change. She also received New York Foundation of the Art Immigrant Artist Fellowship, a teaching residency at Café R.E.D and La Botica Espacio Cultural at Xela, Guatemala, and artist residency with KulArts at SOMA San Francisco. The City of Oakland, Yerba Buena Center for the Arts, UC Berkeley, and Oakland Museum of CA, have commissioned her work. She is currently working as the Galleries Manager for the San Francisco Arts Commission, and is a Public Art Advisor for the City of Oakland. She can often be found collaborating with her collective, Trust Your Struggle, teaching, and traveling around the world in pursuit of the perfect wall.

**Chris Granillo (Venmo: @chrisgranilloart)** Born (1982) and raised in California, Chris Granillo found early artistic and creative inspiration through his barrio Community with Chicano / Mexican roots to north and southern Mexico. Granillo's work and style/subjects of preference are, abstract, Figurative, cubism ,surrealism, landscapes, and folk. Granillo is currently working in the San Francisco Bay Area. Using mix media on paper and canvas, dabbeling into the wider pallette of artistic mediums such as printmaking, sculpture, and murals. Instagram/ Facebook: @chrisgranilloart

**Corbrae Smith (Venmo: @corbrae-smith)** I am a local artist /art teacher here in Oakland, California. I studied art at the Academy of Art University, San Francisco, where I eventually received my degree in traditional illustration. My whole life I have identified as an artist and wanted to create the most impact I could using my art as the vehicle. I am dedicated to my community and passionate about what I create for them. My goal is to beautify walls, help kids find their voice through their own creativity, and to make a change.

**Derrick "Rtystk" Shavers (Venmo: @kmbafunds)** lives and works in Oakland, California, where his signature "Kiss My Black Arts" message has quickly become iconic. Rtystk established the Kiss My Black Arts Collective in 2012 which serves as a platform for artists to organize community building and economic development projects. The "Kiss My Black Arts" slogan offers an open-ended proclamation for the viewer to decipher it as either a demand or an appreciation. Both inviting and enticing the public through the use of a double entendre, the motto presents an experience for the individuals to converse through perception. Rtystk works prolifically and spontaneously with patterns, motifs, and images of friends and family. The canvases, many self-stretched, are approached with vibrant, upbeat colors imbued with African cultural references which he calls "creative discourse." The conversation conveys a system of dialogue through lines, shapes, and colors while showing the artistic process. By borrowing and incorporating elements of protest art, Rtystk bridges the gap between visual art and constructive communication between familiar strangers and those alike.

**DeVante Brooks** also known as Aeos One (pronounced A-Yos), is a calligrapher, sign painter, and muralist. Aeos has a background in street art and graffiti that spans over a decade and is a proud member of the international art collective, Aerosoul. His affinity for psychology and philosophy are utilized in the visual arts as a means to empower and serve his community of West Oakland.

**DonJuan Carter-Woodard** Father, son, artist, teacher, activist

and all around student of life. Has been doing Poetry (Spoken Word) and Hip-Hop since the '90s. Youth Coordinator and Poetry facilitator at Eastside Arts Alliance. Author of *Bleeding Between the Bars*. Constantly learning new ways to express myself and bring a dose of reality from the ground floor.

**Elena Serrano** Program Director and founding member of the EastSide Arts Alliance Collective. Serrano is a cultural strategist and community organizer. As Program Director for EastSide Arts Alliance she coordinates community and cultural events and the annual Malcolm X JazzArts Festival (currently in its 22nd year!). She also coordinates EastSide Arts Alliance's fundraising efforts. Serrano has over 30 years working in all aspects of non-profit arts management including work at La Peña Cultural Center in Berkeley and the Malonga Casquelourd Center for the Arts in downtown Oakland. Currently, she is helping to lift up Oakland's cultural hubs, serving communities of color, as sites for power building and community self-determination.

**Eric Liang Norberg** has been a practicing Hip Hop aerosol writer/artist and calligrapher for over 38 years. He is a visual artist/painter/muralist as well as an arts educator at the high school level and assists young people in harnessing and utilizing their radical imaginations through the visual arts/photography and community justice activism. The chromatic palette and intricate designs of his art are ways that he highlights international struggles for liberation and calls for recognition of our ancestors' resilience. Collaborations with artists and communities around the San Francisco Bay Area and internationally continue to be many. Partnering with Greg Morozumi (TallerSinFronteras: EastSide Arts Alliance) and Mike "DREAM" Francisco (1969–2000) during the 1990s produced many panel discussions and presentations at schools/universities on the role of art and political activism. Gallery installations, "No Justice No Peace—Word from the Underground" (Graff writers' response to the '92 LA uprising) and "Amerikan Terrorism—Shadows on the Global Street" (addressing 50 years since the atomic bombing of Hiroshima and Nagasaki, toxic degradation of indigenous lands, and patriarchal violence) were monumental events for the community.

**G. Jung Morozumi** Program/Outreach Director for EastSide Arts Alliance, Greg Morozumi, is a visual artist and founding member of Taller Sin Fronteras, a screen-printing collective. He has been involved in community and cultural organizing for more than 40 years. Morozumi currently coordinates community forums and art exhibitions and special projects (including the Community Archive and Resource Project) for the EastSide Arts Alliance. Morozumi served as the community outreach coordinator and programs assistant at La Peña Cultural Center in Berkeley, while curating visual arts exhibitions on that site. Morozumi has hosted, moderated, and served as a panelist for numerous cultural programs and public forums.

**Inbal Rubin (Venmo: @inbal-rubin)** is a SWANA woman, educator, muralist, and artist based in Oakland, California. For nearly two decades, the city she calls home has had a profound influence on her art, teaching, and very being on this Earth. Whether she is in the classroom or in the streets, Bali uses her art as a mechanism for critical dialogue about community struggle and collective liberation. Early on in her life she recognized the transformative power of the intersections of art, political action, identity, and humanization, which has led to her continuous commitment to personal growth, community care, and art. For the last 18 years as an arts educator, she has developed her craft and drive to empower her own voice while activating and supporting young people

to develop their craft and voice as artists, as well. Inbal is someone who is clear about the importance of authenticity and honesty as she navigates this world and understands the role and responsibility of art as a vehicle to reimagine, transform and redefine beauty and justice as we know it.

**Irene Takahashi-Coker** (Venmo: @ @ireneshiori) is a Bay Area native from Hayward, California. Following in her mother's artistic footsteps as a young child, Irene started drawing, painting and doing small arts and crafts at a young age. During her high school years she was drawn towards black and grey pencil realism and portraits- particularly portraits of women. Irene honed some of her portrait skills through drawing classes at Chabot Community College and years of tattooing and finally got the chance to use spray paint mediums for portraits. During the uprising of protests for Black Lives Matter, she found making portraits of Black folks, particularly Black Women, was one of the small ways she could contribute in solidarity and representation—focusing on the life, strength, and beauty of each individual in their portrait.

**Illuminaries** The Illuminaries are Steve Ha and Tim Hon and Romali Licudan and Eric Nodora. They are Bay Area and San Diego professional street art muralists and graphic artists specializing in high impact, energizing decor. Their passion is improving indoor and outdoor spaces with the creative use of traditional or digital mediums.

**James Cagney** is the author of *Black Steel Magnolias In The Hour Of Chaos Theory*, winner of the 2019 PEN Oakland Josephine Miles Award. His second book, *Martian: The Saint of Loneliness* won the 2021 Academy of American Poets James Laughlin Award. It is due to be released by Nomadic Press in 2022. For more information, please visit jamescagneypoet.com

**Kalani Ware** (Venmo: @kalani-ware) Kalani is a visual artist from Oakland, California, with roots in Hawai'i. He creates, experiments, and explores his creativity in color. He strives to create works that will inspire others. The variation of colors, shapes, and textures he uses not only represents the diverse and multicultural society we live in, but our connection to society and each other. His current body of work focuses on these same ideas, sometimes incorporating people. What he loves most about abstract art is that it is subjective. Kalani hopes that people can engage, ask questions, and find happiness in his work. Although primarily focused on abstract works, a large majority of Kalani's work over the years is widely diverse, from painting landscapes to celebrity figures.

**Keena Azania Romano** exercises her creative mind through the exploration of diverse artistic mediums as a way to engage and understand individual and collective purpose. Romano received her BFA from Pomona College then returned to her native Bay Area to pursue a career in the Arts. Her Murals can be spotted from Sacramento, California, to Oaxaca, Mexico. Inspired by cultural rituals and practices, Romano combines spirituality with urban experience to produce work that draws upon the quest for a greater understanding of intersectional beauty in this world. She fuses traditional native arts with contemporary inner-city techniques to reflect a new language that encourages the healing and empowerment process between community members and their environments. Her style is described as "vibrant and insightful." She aspires to travel and create a colorful trail of art by exploring the modern Diaspora based on her multi-ethnic experience.

**Kiara "Ignacia" Hardy** (Venmo: @invertedperceptions) Dedicating her life to seeing the world from many perspectives, Ignacia loves using different mediums of creative expression. Along with using her hands to draw and paint, she also loves photography, graphic design, hair braiding, and DJing!

Ignacia strongly believes in "happy accidents" and that there is beauty in everything, if you invert your perception.

**Kufue** For over two decades Kufue has been providing Hip Hop culture to young people from California to the East Coast. He moved from the east coast in junior high and grew up painting in Oakland and the larger Bay Area. Since graduating from San Francisco State University with a degree in Behavioral Sciences in 2000, Kufue's professional trajectory has been consistently focused on inner city youth, from the ages of 12–21 years of age—providing youth development services and facilitating Hip Hop workshops and Ethnic Studies and Africana Studies classes in community and school settings, reaching the most disengaged youth. Kufue's straight forward youth development approach, meeting the young people and their families where they are, and his engaging educational strategies makes him an effective practitioner, with many examples of transformation among the students he touches—reengaging them in the class room and redirecting their life journeys toward positive and healthy choices. All of this is done through using spray can art and culture to create visual discourse for voices that have been silenced by systemic oppression.

**Leslie "Dime" Lopez (Venmo: @artbydime)** was born and raised in East Oakland, California, and began her artistic path as a pre-teen organizing, painting murals, and tagging graffiti. Well known for her style-writing letters, bright paintings, and community led murals, her self taught work bridges the Graffiti and Fine Art worlds Inspired by nature's four elements. Her noticeable handstyles are left love letters and messages in the barrio and her murals flourish beyond the walls. Dime is a natural storyteller that has a passion for using art to heal, liberate, and empower communities of color. Her work is rooted in the fight for social justice, and bringing joy and hope to underserved communities. For 20 years and spray can in hand, Dime has dedicated her life to providing healthy outlets for young people, led visual art projects, workshops, and taught classes throughout her city and beyond. She has internationally exhibited her work in galleries, museums, apparel, print, and fashion. Many of her powerful collaborations are painted with youth and joined in by an intergenerational audience. Dime is a part of BSK graffiti crew, core member of the EastSide Arts Alliance, and founding member of worldwide graffiti women crew Few and Far Women. She works in Deep East Oakland at Elmhurst Middle School engaging and supporting families with resources, and is a Cultural Arts Ambassador for the Fruitvale District. Dime is a mother and remains active in the neighborhood she was raised in. With her husband and two boys, she organizes large art projects, cars shows, and free events where she brings art, resources, and her big heart to uplift the block.

**Maisha Quint** Born in Oakland and raised in Berkeley, maisha quint has been a staunch anti-prison organizer since high school. She has organized with the Committee to Free the San Francisco 8, Friends of Marilyn Buck, Committee for the Defense of Human Rights, Stop the Gang Injunctions Coalition, and several other grassroots organizations and campaigns.

**Mario Alexander Navasero (Venmo: @mantis75)** is an Oakland, California, native and is a resident artist at Faultline Artspace in East Oakland. He is primarily an abstract painter with use of a wide range of mediums. Mario is self-taught and after many years of practice, he has consistently shown artwork mostly within the immediate Bay Area. He also guest curates for various galleries, installs shows, and is very active within the Bay Area art community.

**Miguel "Bounce" Perez** is a multidisciplinary artist making a living as a tattooer and muralist. His artwork has been seen everywhere from publications to motion pictures. Aside from being the cofounder of the legendary Pueblo Nuevo Gallery, he is also an important member of the world-renowned artist

collective, Trust Your Struggle. Miguel's work has given him the opportunity to paint and build with communities worldwide. For more, please visit miguelbounceperez.com

**Mizan Alkebulan-Abakah, MPH** has worked for over 20 years as a community organizer and youth development professional. Her commitment to social justice has fueled her work as a crisis intervention specialist, health educator, curriculum writer, multi-modal workshop facilitator, community researcher, staff wellness coach, and School-Based Health Center Supervisor. Mizan is a certified Radical Healing Trainer and has a Masters Degree in Public Health. Mizan is also an installation artist, and has exhibited work throughout the Bay Area, including  the "Black Woman is God" exhibit and The Black Panthers—50-Year Anniversary. She is the lead artist and curator of the Experience Sankofa Project. As an artist and Certified Therapeutic Yoga instructor with a background in public health, Mizan incorporates creative expression and dynamic mindfulness into her facilitation and programmatic design for the collective good.

**Nia McAllister** is a Bay Area-born poet, writer, and environmental justice advocate working at the intersection of art, activism, and public engagement. She received a B.A. in Environmental Analysis: Race, Class, Gender, and the Environment from Pomona College. Through her work, she creates participatory spaces for creative expression and literary dialogue and is committed to amplifying the work of Black artists on a global scale. Her writing and poetry have been featured on the Poets of Color Podcast and published in *Radicle* magazine, *Meridians* journal, *The Black Liberation Blueprint*, and other forthcoming publications.

**Nisha K. Sethi** Born and raised in Berkeley, California, Nisha K. Sethi is a multi-disciplinary artist whose passion lies in using art and design as tools for social change. She started her creative journey as a street artist and eventually evolved into a seasoned Graphic Designer and Sign Painter. Her skills in typography and design have been strengthened through education, experience, and constant experimentation. Nisha currently rides with Trust Your Struggle mural collective and works in Los Angeles and San Francisco as a freelance Visual Designer and professional Sign Painter specializing in hand-lettering.

**Nyia Luna** is 21-years young and was born and raised in Milwaukee's Southside. She is currently based out of Oakland, California, where she is a partner of three non-profits: Bay Area Mural Program, Graffiti Camp for Girls, Hip Hop for Change. She is currently leading a class at various elementary and high schools. This semester, Nyia and her students are painting a mural on their school van!

**Oree Originol** is a visual artist born on September 11, 1984, in Glendale, California. As a child, he discovered his talent in making art at school and has since developed his skills on his own. Growing up in Los Angeles, he was inspired by street culture which became his outlet to graffiti. He used OREE as his "tagger" name deriving from an inside joke with childhood friends poking fun of his big ears. In 2009, he moved to the Bay Area in pursuit of a career as an artist and social activist. He began painting colorful abstract compositions of various shapes which became his identifying style of work. Eventually, he expanded his skills into digital art which moved up the forefront of his creative output, especially in 2014, when he took a whole new focus and launched "Justice For Our Lives," a digital portrait series of people killed by US law enforcement. For the following seven years, he created a total of 100 black and white portraits that would become the visual backdrop to numerous Black Lives Matter protests in the Bay Area and beyond. His portraits have been reproduced and shared worldwide in public demonstrations, classrooms, museums, and online. In 2016, his project exhibited at the Yerba Buena Center for the Arts, San Francisco, California, and in 2020 at

Ohio, and continues to troubadour the world with them as well as performing spoken word. In mid-1993, he released his first solo album, *Be Bop or Be Dead*, produced by Bill Laswell. Hassan combined rap, house, and jazz elements on the record. He later went on to record *To the Last,* which was also produced by Bill Laswell. In early 1999, Umar performed spoken-work at the legendary Snaps-N-Taps in Columbus, Ohio, and met Carl Zero, local area reggae promoter and owner of Roots Records. The two worked together with several musicians and released the *Life is Good* CD on Stay Focused Recordings. A second release from Umar and Leon Mobley, of Innocent Criminal fame, is due out any day on Stay Focused.

**Wanli Wang** is a multidisciplinary artist currently in San Francisco Bay Area, California, working as a software engineer at LinkedIn. Her artistic specialties include photography, illustration, and graphic design. In the wake of many recent tragedies, from George Floyd to Breonna Taylor, Wanli created this BLM mural to show that solidarity among minorities is critical to advancing racial justice. Wanli painted the mural in Oakland, California. It contains elements from African American and Asian cultures, symbolizing solidarity, prosperity, and strength. The raised fist is the handle of a torch, representing liberty and hope for the Black Lives Matter movement. The koi fish is associated with perseverance, courage, and character strength in Asia. Alternating colors on the koi's dorsal fins represent Asian support for African Americans and vice versa. Two fishes swimming together in the same direction stand for both races' unified efforts to achieve racial equality. Wanli has explored various ways to support underrepresented groups. She volunteers as an event photographer for Oakland First Fridays, a monthly festival to support local entrepreneurs and artists of all backgrounds. Through artistic activism, Wanli will continue to promote social equality and reform.

**Yazmin "Shi Shi" Madriz** was raised in Bazuklas (Berkeley)

California. They had a humble beginning, growing up without many material riches. However, they had two wonderful parents that worked like machines every day of their lives to provide their children with basic necessities. Not having much allowed them to see the beauty and gold that we, struggling people, hold in our hearts and communities. We may struggle with incarceration, unhealthy livelihoods, and family dynamics within our communities yet, they aim to create art that voices our pain, love, and the faith that enables us to move forward. Their intention is to educate and depict pride and dignity through art illustrating the revolutionary stories and culture of my community.

**Zoe Boston** (Venmo: @Zoe-Boston-1) HER NAME IS ZOË BOSTON. Zoë is an artist in almost every sense of the word. She has been drawing for as long as she can remember but did not begin painting until she returned to the West Coast. Born in Los Angeles and raised in Upstate NY, she now resides in the Oakland Bay Area. Zoë's inspirations come from God, life, love, music, food, and everything in between. She is dedicated to being true to herself, which in-turn, transforms her work into passion on walls and canvas.

**Terrion "Shido" Smith (Venmo: @Shogun-Shido)** is a mixed media creator currently residing in Oakland, California, with a primary focus in visual arts. Terrion's vision lies within their passion for ancestral arts, abstract expressionism, and storytelling. Throughout their life experience, they've faced a series of trials relating to fear, worry, and doubt. After having spent a period of time focusing on knowledge of self and projections of experience, they've realized they can use their creative platform to transmute that energy to promote love, power, wisdom. In doing so, they hope to create a spark of inspiration, promote positive living, and influence those who visually digest their creations to reflect these qualities onto themselves and others.

**The Tracy Piper (Venmo: @Tracy-Piper)** (b. Oakland, California, 1987) is a female-identifying, contemporary painter and art activist. Best known for her vibrant portraits and figurative acrylic paintings, Piper's illustrative work tackles social constructs in an abstract-realist style.

**Trust Your Struggle Collective** is an artist collective of visual artists, educators, and cultural workers dedicated to social justice, environmental sustainability, and community organizing through the medium of public art and activism. Our work includes, but is not limited to: graphic design, printmaking, photography, illustration, graffiti, multimedia installations and mural painting. For more information, visit trustyourstruggle.org.

**Timothy B. (Venmo: @Timothyb_art)** is a groundbreaking multimedia artist who is recognized internationally for pushing boundaries with vibrant murals and afro-indigenous illustrations. He's shaping the future of Oakland with work inspired by his afro-futuristic perception of reality along with his African ancestral background. His work creates an immersive experience empowering communities of color to embrace messages of peace and positivity that inspire change. The motivational words that guide him are that "anything is possible when love, faith, focus, and urgency is the foundation."

**Tongo Eisen-Martin** Originally from San Francisco, Tongo Eisen-Martin is a poet, movement worker, and educator. His latest curriculum on extrajudicial killing of Black people, We Charge Genocide Again, has been used as an educational and organizing tool throughout the country. His book titled, *Someone's Dead Already* was nominated for a California Book Award. His book *Heaven Is All Goodbyes* was published by the City Lights Pocket Poets series, was shortlisted for the Griffins Poetry Prize and won a California Book Award and an American Book Award. His latest book *Blood On The Fog* was released this fall in the City Lights Pocket Poets series. In 2020, he co-founded Black Freighter Press to publish revolutionary works. He is San Francisco's eighth Poet Laureate.

**Tureeda Mikell** is a story medicine woman, award-winning poet, mental health advocate, lyricist, Qigong therapist, and U. C. BAWP Fellow. As a survivor of child abuse, her passion for youth's voices to be heard caused her to publish over seventy at-risk student anthologies from five Bay Area counties via California Poets in the Schools. She has Zoomed or traveled nationally and internationally across five continents, from China, Europe, UK, to Africa. Tureeda was featured in Octavia Butler's 70th birthday, The Black Panther's 55th Anniversary, Afrofuturism, and the de Young Museum's "Soul of a Nation." Her full-length book, *Synchronicity, The Oracle of Sun Medicine* (Nomadic Press, 2020) was nominated for a California Book Award. She is coauthor and curator with Elena Serrano of EastSide Arts Alliance of the *Patrice Lumumba Anthology,* released in January 2021 by Nomadic Press.

**Umar Bin Hassan** In the early '70s, Umar Bin Hassan was a member of the civil rights era Last Poets. He joined the group in 1969 after seeing the Last Poets perform in his native Akron,

a husband, father, small business owner, artist, muralist… He's a maker. He likes making stuff. He thinks that it would be amazing if he could make a difference. One day at a time. One kind interaction at a time. Give all you can to this life—it's the only one you get.

**Sizwe Andrews-Abakah of Spearitwurx** is an Educator, Radical Healer, and Mentor and has worked throughout the Bay Area. He has supported African American Wellness through the National Campaign for Black Male Achievement, Oakland Freedom School, Flourish Agenda's Camp Akili, Oakland Unified School District's Manhood Development Program, and Determination Black Men's Group at United Roots to name a few. He approaches the work with passion and insight. Sizwe believes that contentedness is our currency and building authentic intimacy is key in our relationships. The practice of being vulnerable with each other can helps us get to a place of transformation and liberation. Sizwe utilizes his skills as performer to build awareness, connection, and open doors to self-mastery. Sizwe, also known as Spear of the Nation, is an MC and producer. Spear has released 2 joint albums with Lunar Heights, 3 solo projects and has been featured on a host of songs over the past 20 years of his career. Sizwe is the lead actor in two films produced by 393 films: *Tent City*, which highlights the impact of unprocessed grief on mental health in America, the toll that gentrification has taken on the city of Oakland and ignites a call to action to reclaim our humanity in the midst of our ever-changing world; and *So Beautiful*, a docudrama that was shot in South Africa, in the land of Sizwe (Eastern Cape).

**Sonia Sanchez**—poet, activist, scholar—was the Laura Carnell Professor of English and Women's Studies at Temple University. She is the recipient of both the Robert Frost Medal for distinguished lifetime service to American poetry and the Langston Hughes Poetry Award. One of the most important writers of the Black Arts Movement, Sanchez is the author of sixteen books. In 2021, Sonia won the Dorothy and Lillian Gish Prize Lifetime Achievement award.

**Taylor Apple (Venmo: @Taylorapple1)** (b.1994) is a queer Latinx interdisciplinary artist originally from NYC. Growing up within a family of immigrants has afforded her a unique and humbling outlook on the world. Her work draws influence from culture while maintaining a regal immediacy when making. It's important that the work evokes experiences & moments in time that are essential to self and humanity.

**TDK (a.k.a. Those Damn Kids)** The beginning of our crew was like belonging to a family. Before writing graffiti, several boys in Alameda started riding the Hip-Hop wave by struttin' and break dancing at Encinal High School with the Rock On Creation Krew in 1982. Graffiti writing aligned with Bboying and the boys started FBI (Fresh Bombers Incorporated). Like all other metropolitan cities across the USA, the integration of Djs, MCs, Bboys, and graffiti writer crowd was essential to the social development of Oakland youth with Hip-Hop back in the mid '80s to early '90s. The FBI crew name evolved to be TDA (The Devastating Artists) and this original group consisted of Dream, Gyro, Dyl, Break, Done, and Jammin' Jay in 1984. The name changed to TDK for "The Devastating Kings" and evolved to be the popular "Those Damn Kids" in 1986.

**Thitiwat "T" Phromratanapongse** is a Thai American artist native to the Los Angeles area and operates out of the Bay Area. He received his Bachelor of Arts in Asian American Studies from UCLA, which led him to work for the Estria Foundation, a non-profit organization centered around social issues and environmental awareness through mural art. Since then, he has continued to engage in community driven projects with artist Brett Cook and Bay Area Trust Your Struggle Collective. His work features high attention to detail with brushstrokes rooted in calligraphy to build his imagery.

the Smithsonian American Art Museum, Washington D.C., who also own digital copies for their permanent collection. Oree continues to grow in his creative development and have an impact on his community.

**Rachel Wolfe-Goldsmith** (Venmo: @wolfe-pack) Born January 13, 1991, is a fine art painter and muralist based in Oakland, California. Her education came from being immersed in life. She spent her early twenties traveling the United States and the world, building relationships with artists and mentors while painting everywhere along the way. Rachel is a mixed-race, Jewish, queer woman who perceives the world through a broad range, her work reflects her diverse heritage. She is always rooting for the underdog and is interested in communicating a sense of freedom and empowerment through her work

**Randolph Belle** is an Oakland-based artist, entrepreneur, and activator of community-based initiatives.  His career in the creative sector spans over 30 years. He is the owner of RBA Creative, a design, communications, and public affairs firm, the co-founder of Creative Development Partners, a boutique real estate development and consulting company, founder of Support Oakland Artists, a non-profit arts marketing and management organization, and a founding organizational partner of the East Oakland Black Cultural Zone Collaborative. Randolph operates out of an East Oakland co-working space for creative professionals, also called RBA Creative, which he runs with his wife Erica.

**Robin D. G. Kelley**  is an American historian and academic, who is the Gary B. Nash Professor of American History at UCLA. From 2006 to 2011, he was Professor of American Studies and Ethnicity at the University of Southern California (USC), and from 2003 to 2006 he was the William B. Ransford Professor of Cultural and Historical Studies at Columbia University. From 1994 to 2003, he was a professor of history and Africana Studies at New York University (NYU) as well the chair of NYU's history department from 2002 to 2003. Kelley has also served as a Hess Scholar-in-Residence at Brooklyn College. In the summer of 2000, he was honored as a Montgomery Fellow at Dartmouth College, where he taught and mentored a class of sophomores, as well as wrote the majority of the book Freedom Dreams. During the academic year 2009–10, Kelley served as Harold Vyvyan Harmsworth Professor of American History at Oxford University, the first African-American historian to do so since the chair was established in 1922. He was awarded the Guggenheim Fellowship in 2014. He is also the author of a biography of Thelonious Monk.

**Robert Liu-Trujillo** is a life-long Bay Area resident. Born in Oakland, California, he's the child of student activists who watched lots of science fiction and took him to many demonstrations. Always drawing, Rob grew up to be an artist falling in love with graffiti, fine art, illustration, murals, and children's books—in that order, sort of. Through storytelling, he's been able to scratch the surface of so many untold stories. Rob is the author and illustrator of *Furqan's First Flat Top* and he's illustrated numerous other children's books. He's a dad of a teenage boy and a little girl. He loves ice cream and his wife who laughs big and corrects his grammar every chance she gets. Down with the system and soggy french fries! Rob is a co-founder of The Trust Your Struggle Collective, a contributor to The Social Justice Childrens Bk Holiday Fair, *Tone Magazine*, The Bullhorn Blog, and the founder of Come Bien Books.

**Shawn Gibson** (Venmo: @Shawn-Gibson-10) was born in Stockton and grew up in Salinas. He has been into art his whole life and moved to San Francisco in 2012 to go to Delancey Street, a two-year residential program to help people like me learn how to be productive members of society. He stayed there for four years to get all that he could, while giving as much as he could back to the community. August 15th 2022 will be the 10-year marker from his previous life. He is now

# OTHER WAYS TO SUPPORT NOMADIC PRESS WRITERS

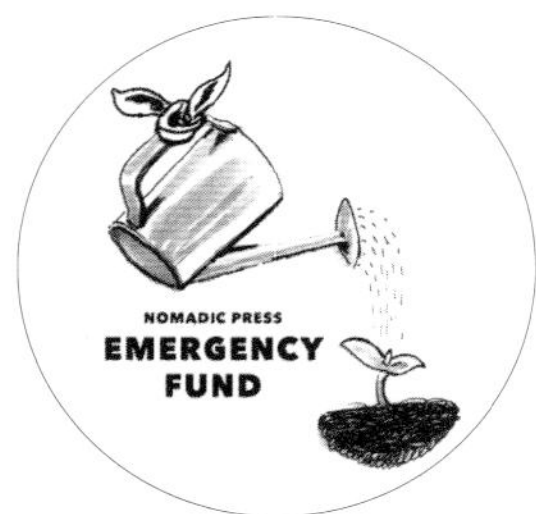

**Nomadic Press Emergency Fund**

**Nomadic Press Black Writers Fund**

Right before Labor Day 2020 (and in response to the effects of COVID), Nomadic Press launched its Emergency Fund, a forever fund meant to support Nomadic Press-published writers who have no income, are unemployed, don't qualify for unemployment, have no healthcare, or are just generally in need of covering unexpected or impactful expenses.

Funds are first come, first serve, and are available as long as there is money in the account, and there is a dignity centered internal application that interested folks submit. Disbursements are made for any amount up to $300.

All donations made to this fund are kept in a separate account. The Nomadic Press Emergency Fund (NPEF) account and associated processes (like the application) are overseen by Nomadic Press authors and the group meets every month.

On Juneteenth (June 19) 2020, Nomadic Press launched the Nomadic Press Black Writers Fund (NPBWF), a forever fund that will be directly built into the fabric of our organization for as long as Nomadic Press exists and puts additional monies directly into the pockets of our Black writers at the end of each year.

Here is how it works:

$1 of each book sale goes into the fund.

At the end of each year, all Nomadic Press authors have the opportunity to voluntarily donate none, part, or all of their royalties to the fund.

Anyone from our larger communities can donate to the fund. This is where you come in!

At the end of the year, whatever monies are in the fund will be evenly distributed to all Black Nomadic Press authors that have been published by the date of disbursement (mid-to-late December).

The fund (and associated, separate bank account) has an oversight team comprised of four authors (Ayodele Nzinga, Daniel B. Summerhill, Dazié Grego-Sykes, and Odelia Younge) + Nomadic Press Executive Director J. K. Fowler.

**Please consider supporting these funds. You can also more generally support Nomadic Press by donating to our general fund via nomadicpress.org/donate and by continuing to buy our books. As always, thank you for your support!**

**Scan the QR code for more information and/or to donate. You can also donate at nomadicpress.org/store.**

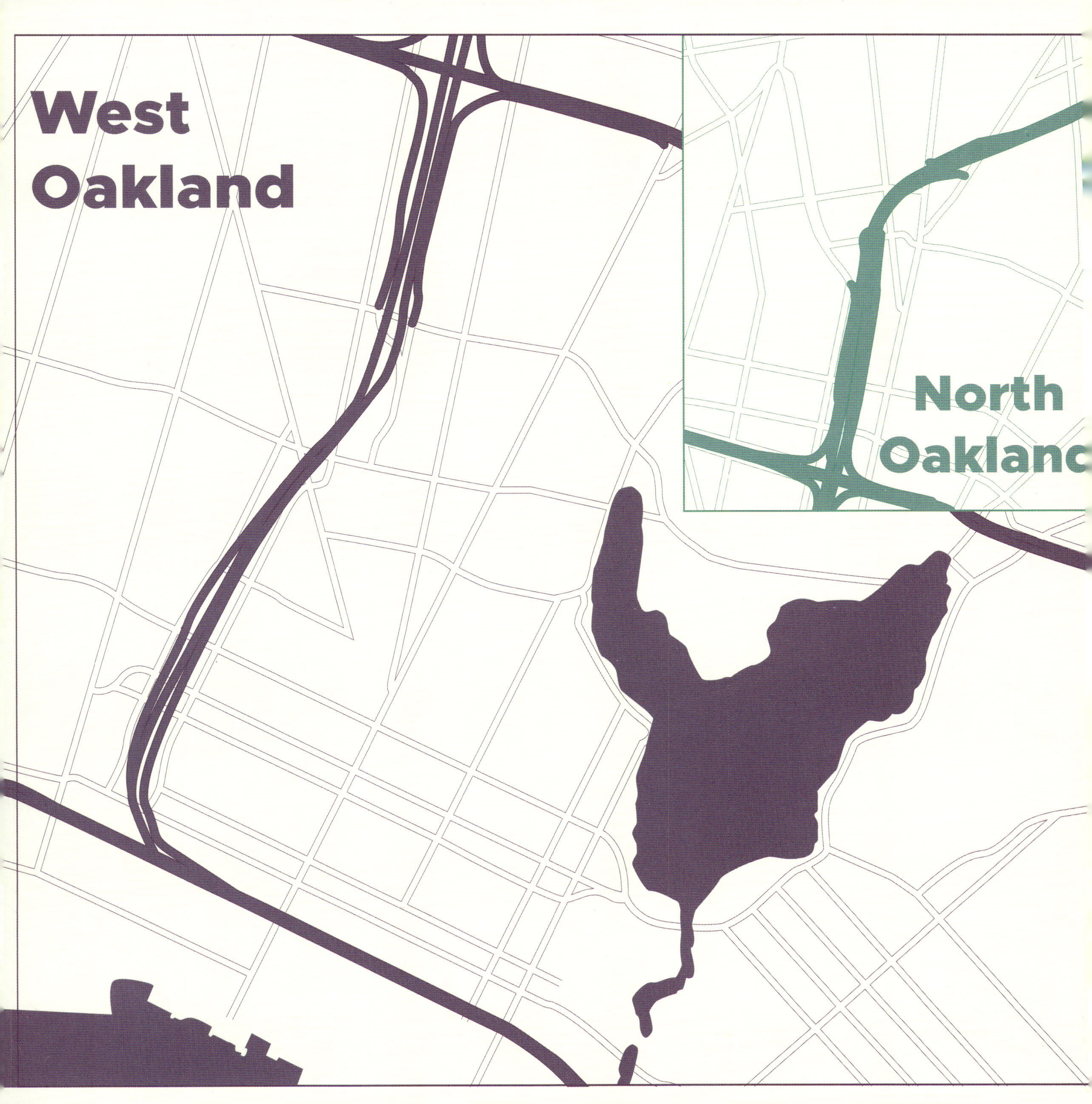
West
Oakland
North
Oakland

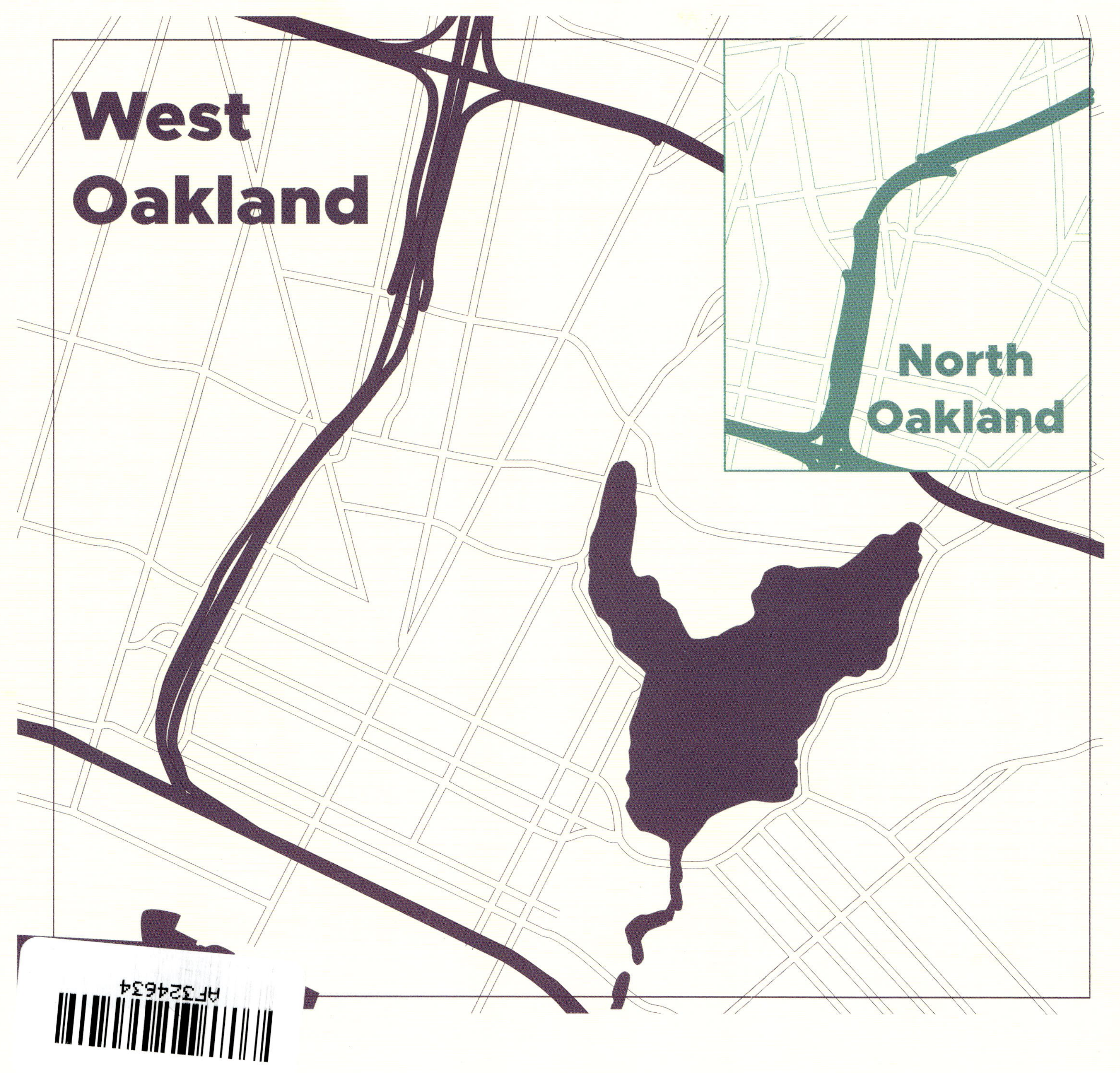
West
Oakland
North
Oakland